THE COMPLETE BOOK OF TURKISH COOKING

AYLA ESEN ALGAR

KEGAN PAUL INTERNATIONAL
London and New York

First published in 1985 by Kegan Paul International
First paperback edition 1988

This edition published in 1995 by
Kegan Paul International
UK: P.O. Box 256, London WC1B 3SW, England
Tel: (0171) 580 5511 Fax: (0171) 436 0899
E-mail: books@keganpau.demon.co.uk
Internet: http://www.demon.co.uk/keganpaul/
USA: 562 West 113th Street, New York, NY 10025, USA
Tel: (212) 666 1000 Fax: (212) 316 3100

Distributed by
John Wiley & Sons Ltd
Southern Cross Trading Estate
1 Oldlands Way, Bognor Regis
West Sussex, PO22 9SA, England
Tel: (01243) 779 777 Fax: (01243) 820 250

Columbia University Press
562 West 113th Street
New York, NY 10025, USA
Tel: (212) 666 1000 Fax: (212) 316 3100

© Ayla Esen Algar 1985, 1995

Cover illustration by Su Huntley

Printed in Great Britain

ISBN 0–7103–0524–9

British Library Cataloguing in Publication Data
Complete Book of Turkish Cooking – New ed
I. Title
641.59561

ISBN 0–7103–0524–9

Library of Congress Cataloging-in-Publication Data
Algar, Ayla Esen.
    The complete book of Turkish cooking / Ayla Esen Algar.
    344 p. cm.
    Originally published: London : New York : Kegan Paul
International, 1988.
    Includes bibliographical references and index.
    ISBN 0–7103–0524–9
    1. Cookery, Turkish. I. Title.
TX725.T8A44 1995
641.59561—dc20   95–4555
                                        CIP

Contents

Acknowledgements

My chief debt is to my grandmother, from whom as a little girl I unconsciously acquired a sense of pleasure in offering food as an expression of love. Then I remember with gratitude my mother, my aunts, and all the other members of my family and my friends in Turkey, thanks to whom love, laughter, friendship and company have for me always been intermingled with the smell, color and taste of food. As for my sons — Dennis, James, Larry and Selim — to them go my thanks for the appreciation — subtle and not so subtle — they have lavished on my food. My husband, whose comprehensive enthusiasm for Turkish cuisine extends even to the drinking of pickle juice at Çemberlitaş, has encouraged and helped me in numerous ways.

Above all, my heartfelt thanks go to Moinuddin Shaikh who not only gave the first impetus to the project but continued, under trying circumstances and at great expense, to support my efforts for its completion.

Finally, many thanks to Hilary Turner, my link with London, for seeing the book through the press.

Ayla Esen Algar
Berkeley, California
July, 1985

Anneannemin aziz hatırasına
ve sevgili anneme

Introduction

"Eat of the good things We have provided for you as sustenance."

Qur'an 2:58

The main claim to interest of any cuisine is, of course, the stimulation it gives to the appetite and the satisfaction it provides to the palate. But food, properly considered, is not a simple matter of preparation and consumption, which are often complex undertakings in themselves; it also touches upon religious prescriptions and customs, aesthetic tastes, geographic and climatic conditions, social stratification and prosperity. The study of food, then, is a proper although generally neglected concern of the historian, and the cuisine of a people may be regarded, in the words of the hero of a nineteenth-century Turkish novel, as a "complete civilization in itself."[1]

The integration of food with social, religious, and cultural life was certainly very marked with the Ottoman Turks, and even though the state and civilization they created have crumbled, much of their gastronomical legacy survives in present-day Turkey. To place the delicacies of Turkish cuisine in historical perspective, and to enable the users of this book to supplement the delights of the palate with the pleasures of historical reminiscence, we invite them to peruse this survey of food in Turkish history, or—looked at somewhat differently—Turkish history in food.

Little is known of the culinary habits of the largely nomadic pre-Islamic Turks who inhabited the eastern and northeastern reaches of Central Asia. It is probable that their diet consisted largely of milk products and meat, and that they did not challenge the rule that elaborate cuisine is a by-product of the settled life. One of the earliest Turkish states, that of the Uyghurs who settled in what is now known as Sinkiang in the eighth century of the Christian era, was heavily influenced by the neighboring civilization of China, and this influence may have extended to matters of food. The name of one Turkish dish, *mantı* (a kind of dumpling; see p. 253), is actually derived from Chinese, and the borrowing presumably took place during this period of close contact with China.[2] On the other hand, the Uyghurs distinguished themselves from the Chinese by eating at low tables, a custom that was later transported westward in the great waves of Turkish migration and that persists today in Anatolia.[3]

The recorded history of Turkish cuisine begins in about the tenth century, when the Turks came into contact with the Irano-Islamic culture of West Asia and definitively entered the orbit of Islamic religion and civilization. Like other aspects of that civilization, its cuisine was the joint creation of different ethnic elements who borrowed from each other in an uninhibited interchange. Nonetheless, it is possible to assign a definite origin to certain dishes on the basis of etymological or other evidence. *Pilav,* for example, is originally an Iranian dish (the Turkish word being derived from Persian *pulau*), although the Turks came to evolve many distinctive rice dishes not found among the Iranians. Other dishes, by contrast, are originally Turkish, and the words designating them in Persian (and sometimes Arabic) are Turkish. Bulgur (cracked wheat; see p. 219), for example, is a Turkish contribution to the culinary stock of the Near Eastern peoples.[4]

Another contribution of the Turks, one much less familiar to us, is *tutmaç.* An early Turkish lexicon described it as "a well-known Turkish dish";[5] now all but forgotten, it appears to have been a thick soup made with noodles, lentils, and sometimes yogurt.[6] It attained such popularity that a thirteenth-century Persian poet, Shams ad-Din Shastkulah, described it as "caliph of the world of appetite" and claimed that "from the limits of Iraq all the way to Khorasan, you can find no one who will deny its deliciousness."[7]

The name *tutmaç* has virtually disappeared from Turkish cuisine, although dishes similar to it are still prepared.[8] *Börek,* another dish (or, more correctly, a group of dishes) that can be traced to the early centuries of Turkish association with Islam, remains today a mainstay of the Turkish culinary system. The etymology of the word *börek* is uncertain. Although it occurs in Persian as *burak,* the word is clearly of Turkish origin.[9] It may be derived from the root *bur-,* meaning "wrap" or "twist"; this is plausible, since the filling of the *börek* is wrapped or twisted in the dough that encloses it.[10] One account links the invention of *börek* specifically to Bugra Khan (d. 994), a ruler of Eastern Turkistan, from whose realm it gradually spread westward to Khorasan.[11] In any event, the appearance of *börek* is known to antedate the arrival of the Turks in Anatolia. In fact, *börek* came to occupy such a high place in the Turko-Iranian cuisine of Western Asia that it was even considered a rival to *pilav,* the otherwise unchallenged king of the banquet. The rise of *börek* is reflected in a curious poem by the Persian poet Bushaq-i At'ima, describing an imaginary battle between *börek* and *pilav,* which are personified as two rival monarchs.[12]

Another part of the pre-Anatolian legacy of Turkish cuisine is the *güveç,* a kind of vegetable stew cooked in an earthenware pot. The original form of the word appears to be *kömeç* or *gömmeç,* meaning "buried"; that is, the pot would be buried in hot ashes to cook its contents, a method still used for baking bread in both Central Asia and Anatolia.[13]

One branch of the Turkish peoples settled in Anatolia from the eleventh century onward, and a new and significant period in Turkish history began. Having emerged from the landlocked confines of Central Asia, the Turks were now in a position to have a decisive effect upon the destinies of the Balkans, the Arab world, and much of the Mediterranean basin. Political prominence went hand-in-hand with cultural splendor, so that the Ottoman centuries came to mark the apogee of Turkish history.

It is not surprising, then, that Turkish cuisine attained new heights of elaboration and complexity in the Ottoman period. It came to overshadow fully the cuisine of Central Asia the Western Turks had left behind, a cuisine that was in any event greatly impoverished by the agricultural decay and economic stagnation that resulted from the ravages of the Mongols and their successors.[14] In Anatolia and the Balkans, the Turks gained access to new types of food: fruits and vegetables generally unavailable in Central Asia, olive oil in abundance, and seafood. The dishes concocted using these were combined with fare of Central Asian origin—*böreks, kebabs, pilavs,* and so on—to produce one of the most complex, delicate, and elaborate culinary systems in the world.

The chief predecessors of the Ottomans in the Turkicization and Islamicization of Anatolia were the Seljuqs, a dynasty that ruled much of the eastern Islamic world before being reduced to its Anatolian domains. Fragmentary information about food in Seljuq-ruled Anatolia can be derived from a variety of texts. For example, a description of a feast given by the Seljuq Sultan 'Ala ad-Din Kayqubad in 1237 mentions that a variety of kebabs were served (including duck and chicken broiled on spits), together with pepper-seasoned *pilav* and *zerde* (a saffron-flavored rice pudding, eaten cold; see p. 288).[15] In addition, the poetry of the celebrated Sufi and founder of the Mevlevi order, Mevlana Jalal ad-Din Rumi, is, perhaps surprisingly, an important source for the culinary history of the period. Numerous dishes and foodstuffs— wheat soup, *tutmaç,* kebabs, eggplant, spinach, bulgur, pickles, halva, and *kadayıf* (a dessert; see p. 301)—figure in the rich and imaginative imagery one encounters throughout his work.[16] From still other sources, we know that meatless vegetable dishes had already made their appearance in the Seljuq period. For example, dishes known as *kalyeler* and consisting of lightly boiled eggplant or squash covered with melted butter and ground walnuts were much favored. Also in evidence in Seljuq times were leafy vegetables, particularly spinach, served without meat and covered with garlic-yogurt.[17]

It has been suggested that, during this formative period of Turkish-Islamic culture in Anatolia, there were substantial borrowings from the social and material culture of the Greeks residing there, borrowings that were decisive in the area of cuisine. The occurrence in Anatolian Turkish of Greek loanwords relating to food has been cited as evidence.[18] The large number of Greek loanwords in Turkish designating varieties of fish proves incontestably that the Turks learned about seafood from the Greeks. The more general claim, however, that the Turks were the apprentices of the Greeks in all things culinary is unwarranted. Not only are most of the typical features of Turkish cuisine of pre-Anatolian origin, as we have seen, but the balance of the etymological evidence points to an exactly opposite conclusion: a transmission of culinary influence from Turks to Greeks. For the words of Turkish origin relating to food found in Greek far outnumber such Greek words found in Turkish. Even today, the traveler in Greece who knows Turkish will have little difficulty in making out the menu. So whatever borrowings may have taken place from the Greek milieu, they were limited, and in any event subsumed into a synthesis that was powerfully Turkish and Islamic in nature.

The fullest and most elaborate development of Turkish cuisine in the Ottoman period took place, not surprisingly, in the palaces of the sultans. In fact the progress of the Ottoman dynasty can almost be traced through the growing complexity and opulence of its culinary arrangements. The early sultans ate relatively simply, often in the company of men of religion and ministers of state. After the conquest of Istanbul in 1453—the key event in the transformation of the Ottomans into a world power—it became customary for them to eat in splendid isolation. Sultan Mehmed the Conqueror once stated, "It is not my practice to have anyone eat in the company of my noble person, unless it be one of my family. My revered ancestors used to eat with their ministers, but I have abolished the custom."[19] When vassal rulers like the Khan of the Crimea were invited to feast with the sultan, physical separation between suzerain and subordinate was always maintained, with the food of the sultan served to him separately on a raised dais.

As the feeding of the sultan took on a ceremonial aspect, symbolic of his lofty power, the staff of the palace kitchen grew both in number and in complexity of organization. At the end of the sixteenth century, there were two hundred servants at most employed in preparing food for the palace; only fifty years later, the palace kitchen staff had swollen to 1,370.[20] In keeping with the genius for administrative hierarchy that pervaded Ottoman state and society, these employees were organized into a pyramid headed by the *matbah emini*, the trustee or supervisor of the royal kitchens. He was responsible for overseeing the entire operation, including the purchase and acquisition of foodstuffs, their preparation, cooking, and serving. His chief assistants were the *matbah kahyası*, who kept a close eye on expenditures and the food entering and leaving the kitchen, and the *kilercibaşı*, whose job it was to see that the palace pantry was adequately stocked at all times and also to preside over the actual business of cooking the food.[21]

Under these three operated a whole series of cooks, who in turn had apprentices and assistants at their command. Their functions were differentiated according to two criteria: the class of consumer for whom their wares were ultimately destined and the particular variety of dish they prepared. The cooks working in the *aşağı matbah* (lower kitchen) prepared food for all the inhabitants of the palace with the exception of the sultan and his immediate family, as well as for any petitioners who might have business at the palace. The total of those fed from this kitchen each day might reach five or ten thousand, according to different estimates.[22] The food of the sultan himself, together with that of his offspring, wives, and mother, was prepared in a special kitchen, known for some reason as the *kuşhane* (birdhouse). Twelve chief cooks toiled there, in the hope of pleasing the royal palate, under the supervision of a cook known as the *serçini*.[23]

What is truly remarkable about the kitchens of the Ottoman palace is the high degree of specialization that prevailed among the different cooks and their subordinates, a specialization that mirrored the whole complex variety of Turkish cuisine. The preparation of soups, kebabs, *pilavs*, vegetable dishes, fish, different kinds of bread (including the distinctive *fodla*, baked only in the palace), various bakery products, such as *simit* and *kurabiye*, assorted varieties of candy and *helva*, syrup and jam, as well as drinks like *hoşaf* (a kind of fruit punch) and *boza*—each of these was a separate art to be learned while a man served as an apprentice and then cultivated and refined through a lifetime of toil.[24] Indeed, so thoroughgoing was the specialization practiced in the palace kitchens that by the mid-eighteenth century the preparation of each of six varieties of *helva* had been entrusted to a separate master chef, assisted by a hundred apprentices.[25]

The lavish organization and production of the Ottoman palace kitchens were not merely for the sake of conspicuous consumption or the self-aggrandizement of the ruler. For the distribution of food from the royal kitchen was a means of establishing a material and at the same time symbolic link. Food would go to individuals as a mark of honor, either regularly or occasionally, and one day each year, the tenth of Muharram, the dish known as *aşure* (see p.290) would be prepared in the palace kitchens for distribution to all who gathered at the palace gates.[26] Then, too, it was a tradition from the time of Süleyman the Lawgiver onward that, on the fifteenth day of Ramadan, specially cooked trays of *baklava* would be given to the army. The military elite known as the janissaries used to collect their *baklava* from the palace and then take it to their barracks in a riotous parade that occasionally entailed the sacking of the shops they passed.[27]

The place of food in the life of the janissary corps was not restricted to the annual *baklava* allotment. The commander of each of its three divisions was designated *çorbacı* (soupman), and other ranks were known as *aşçıbaşı* (chief cook), *karakullukçu* (scullion), *çörekçi* (baker of round loaves of bread), and *gözlemici* (pancake-maker). In their application to the janissaries, these terms came to lose all connection with the actual preparation of food, although presumably they had once borne their literal meaning. Nonetheless, the focus and most treasured possession of each janissary division remained at all times its *kazgan*, the huge cauldron *pilav* was cooked in; whenever the janissaries decided to revolt—which was often—they would symbolically overturn their *kazgans*.[28]

The elaborate and varied food prepared and consumed in the palace was not the exclusive preserve of the sultan's family and the rest of the Ottoman elite. Almost every dish and category of food cooked in the palace kitchens was known to the citizenry at large. Of course this does not mean that everyone ate on the same grand scale as the residents of the palace. People in the countryside had a less complex diet, although not necessarily a less nourishing one. In addition, there have always been regional variations in Turkish cuisine, determined in part by the availability or unavailability of certain vegetables, herbs, or spices in a given area. But the inhabitants of most of the great Ottoman cities were generally able to enjoy the full range of Turkish cuisine.

This was particularly true of Istanbul, the Ottoman capital, which acted as an entrepôt where all the varied agricultural produce of the vast Ottoman realm, from Wallachia in the north to the Yemen in the south, was readily available. The preparation and sale of food in the markets of Istanbul were in the hands of a series of guilds (esnaf), which were as highly specialized and diversified as the master chefs at the palace. Each guild stood under the spiritual patronage of a prophet or a companion of the Prophet Muhammad, by virtue of some legendary association between the patron and the commodity in which the guild traded. (The patron of the cheesemakers was, for example, the Prophet Abraham, who was believed to have invented cheese). Evliya Çelebi, the celebrated Turkish traveler of the seventeenth century, has left a detailed and vivid account of the food-related guilds of Istanbul. He lists no fewer than forty-three such guilds, including bakers and butchers, cheesemakers and yogurt-merchants, pastry chefs and börek-makers, traders in pickles, and sausage-merchants.[29] Together with the other trade guilds, all of these would participate in the great parades that formed such a distinctive feature of Istanbul life; mounted on floats pulled by oxen, they displayed their skills and distributed free samples of their wares among the spectators.[30]

These parades were organized by the state, which also took a close supervisory interest in the functioning of the guilds, especially those dealing in food. Regulations were promulgated with the aim of controlling not only prices but also quality. A set of regulations issued in 1680 by Mehmed IV specified, for example, that böreks calling for the use of meat should be filled only with mutton, no other meat, and also that lokma (see p. 278) should be made with either rose jam or honey.[31]

Turkish poetry in the Ottoman period is generally characterized by a seriousness of subject and tone; there is no known Turkish counterpart to Bushaq-i At'ima, the Persian, whose entire poetic career was dedicated to the celebration of food. Yet such was the place held by food in the life of the Ottoman Turks that gastronomic themes are occasionally encountered in their poetry. The sixteenth-century poet Revani, who began his career as matbah emini to Sultan Selim I, wrote a narrative poem entitled İşretname (The Book of Pleasure), devoted primarily to singing the praises of wine, but also including a dish-by-dish description of a banquet that preceded the wine-bibbing.[32] Still more remarkable is the work of Kaygusuz Abdal, a poet of the fifteenth century who belonged to an antinomian Sufi order, the Bektashis. His poetry contains frequent references to various dishes and even prayers to God for huge quantities of food:

> What this Kaygusuz really needs
> Is a big cauldron of duck pilav,
> Then a hundred and fifty loaves of greasy bread—
> I'd like them soft, if you don't mind![33]

By no means did all Bektashis, and still less the members of Sufi orders that observed Islamic law, share the enormous appetites of Kaygusuz Abdal. But the preparation and consumption of food held an important place in the life of Turkish Sufis: these were acts replete with moral and even quasi-ritual significance, a means of both observing and reinforcing spiritual decorum and discipline.

There were also a number of ritual dishes prepared, of which the chief was *aşure*. According to tradition, a number of significant events happened on the tenth day of Muharram: Adam's encounter with Eve, Abraham's deliverance from the fire, Joseph's reunion with Jacob. Of particular relevance, however, was the fact that it was on that day that the waters of the great flood subsided, permitting Noah and his family to leave the ark. Before doing so, they brought together all the foodstuffs remaining on board—chickpeas, beans, wheat, rice, raisins, nuts, dried fruit, and so on—and made them into a kind of sweet soup. In memory of this last meal taken on the ark, a similar mixture has traditionally been cooked in Turkey on the tenth of Muharram and called *aşure*. The overwhelming significance of the day for Muslims, however, is that it witnessed the martyrdom of Imam Husayn, the grandson of the Prophet. As a result, the cooking and eating of *aşure* has in effect become a way of commemorating that event, and its legendary association with Noah has been obscured.

The ritual preparation of *aşure* was particularly important among the Bektashis, who included a formal reverence for the Twelve Imams in their syncretic scheme of religious belief. On the evening of the tenth of Muharram, the inhabitants of each Bektashi hospice would gather in the kitchen for the cooking of *aşure* in a great cauldron kept exclusively for that purpose. Everyone took a turn at the sacred task of stirring the mixture, while the *baba* (elder of the hospice) led them in a recitation of poems recounting the martyrdom of Imam Husayn. In the morning, the cauldron was taken down from the fire to the accompaniment of a prayer recited by the *baba*.[34] Similar but less complex ceremonies took place among some Mevlevis who had come under Bektashi influence; the dish they prepared was identical with *aşure*, but their name for it was *aş*.[35]

For both Bektashis and Mevlevis, the kitchen played a central role in the life of the order; it was a place imbued with ritual significance and it served as a place of training and initiation. The hearth where food was cooked (*ocak*) was a sacred place for the Bektashis, and the dervish supervising the kitchen stood second only to the *baba*.[36]

Among the Mevlevis, a complex hierarchy of kitchen-related ranks existed. After absolving a preliminary retreat of forty days, the initiate would be assigned to the kitchen to serve there for a thousand and one days. He would be trained in any one of fifteen functions by a triumvirate consisting of the *kazancı dede* (cauldron elder), the *aşçı dede* (also known as *ser tabbah*, chief cook), and the *bulaşıkçı dede* [supervisor of dishwashing).[37]

If this hierarchical organization of the Mevlevi kitchen seems reminiscent of the arrangements existing in the palace, let it be pointed out that in the Mevlevi kitchen a symbolic as well as a practical purpose was at work. The cooking of food was seen as analogous to the "cooking,"—i.e., the maturing of man's soul.[38] Both processes involved the extraction of hidden essences. The outer work, defined by quasi-ritual norms, served as both a reflection of and a support for the inner work.

This exalted view of the kitchen and all that went on there was virtually confined to the Bektashi and Mevlevi orders. But food did have some quasi-ritual significance among other Sufis. A long-standing tradition among almost all Sufi orders was the charitable provision of food (generally soup) to the poor and to wayfarers; this custom was observed with particular tenacity by the İshaki dervishes, who had a chain of hospices extending across Anatolia.[39] Other orders, notably the Naqshbandis, would often eat some kind of candy or *helva* after completing their exercises of *dhikr* (the invocation of the divine name), in order, they said, to complement the inner sweetness of the *dhikr* with the sweetness of the palate.[40]

The religious associations and uses of food were by no means confined to the Sufi orders, widespread though their influence was in Turkish society. A number of occasions in the religious calendar called for special culinary arrangements or the cooking of particular dishes.

Paradoxically, the most important among these was the fasting month of Ramadan, in Turkey as elsewhere the main season for gastronomic ingenuity and indulgence. The approach of Ramadan was heralded by—among other things—stocking the pantries to overflowing with different kinds of jams, syrups, cheeses, pickles, (see p. 202) *sucuk* (see p. 145), *pastırma*, and *güllaç*. At sundown, as soon as the time for *iftar* (breaking the fast) was proclaimed—by the firing of a cannon in big cities and the beating of a drum in smaller places—a feast would begin that amply compensated for the rigors of the day's fast. First came a spread of small dishes filled with such items as dates (preferably brought from Medina), olives, cheese, pickles, and pieces of *sucuk* and *pastırma*. Then came soup—generally rice, noodle, or tripe—as the first course of the meal proper. The meal continued with a meat dish, two varieties of vegetables, *pilav*, *börek*, and—in contrast with the evening meal during the rest of the year—a dessert.[41] Naturally such a full, indeed filling, meal was not within everyone's means, but most people participated in the gastronomic abundance of

Ramadan nights. It was always possible to visit the houses of the rich, where the doors were flung open to feed all who chanced by. Indeed, for civil servants—always a large class during the Ottoman period—it was considered a duty to call on each of their superiors' homes for *iftar* at least once during Ramadan.[42] Nor did matters end with *iftar* and the evening meal. In Istanbul, after performing *teravih* (the special Ramadan prayers) at the mosque, one would commonly go on a kind of eating expedition to a quarter of the city famous for a particular item: Ayasofya for round loaves of bread, Hocapaşa for *simit*, Hasanpaşa for *poğaca* and *pide*, Eyüp for kebabs, Karaköy for *lokma* and *börek*, Beykoz for *paça*, *kaymak*, and yogurt, Yedikule for sheep's heads, and so on.[43]

As for the festival of breaking the fast that brings the month of Ramadan to an end, it has always been popularly known in Turkey as Şeker Bayramı (the Festival of Sweet Things), a name that speaks for itself. In addition to candy and sweet pastries, special varieties of *börek*, *cörek*, and *simit* are prepared for the occasion.[44]

The other great festival in the religious calendar, Kurban Bayramı, involves, of course, the sacrifice of an animal, which has generally been a sheep in Turkey, both for consumption by one's own family, and for distribution among one's neighbors and the needy, but there are no particular dishes or culinary arrangements associated with this festival.

In addition to these two main festivals, Turkish Muslims have always celebrated four nights known as Kandil Geceleri, that is, nights on which the mosques are illuminated. These are the nights of Rabi' al-Awwal 12, the birthday of the Prophet; the first Friday in Rajab, known as Regaib Gecesi (the Night of Wishes); Rajab 27, the night on which the Prophet ascended to the heavens; and Sha'ban 15, Berat Gecesi, the night men's destinies for the following year are determined. These nights are primarily occasions for special prayer and devotion, but their coming used to be marked, and to some degree still is, by the cooking of *lokma* and the baking of a special round loaf.[45]

It goes without saying that feasts have always accompanied happy events like circumcisions and weddings. In general, there has been no fixed menu for these occasions or particular dishes associated with them, but in some places, notably Bursa, it was traditional for such feasts to consist of what were called the four basics (*usul-u erba'a*): soup, a meat dish, some kind of *helva*, and *pilav* or *zerde*.[46]

Another traditional type of meal, now almost completely defunct, was the *helva sohbeti* (the helva gathering) encountered mostly in Istanbul. In order to while away the long winter nights, particularly during the period known as *erba'in* (the forty coldest days of winter, lasting from December 22 to January 30), friends would invite each other to their homes to enjoy not only *helva* but a whole variety of other foods, mostly heavy meat dishes and pastries. Storytellers would also be summoned to amuse the guests. Gatherings like these were not always restricted to the winter. The prosperous inhabitants of a given locality might invite each other in rotation every Thursday evening, and the main dish for the next week's feast might be chosen by lot.[47]

In countless ways, then, the rich and varied cuisine evolved by the Ottoman Turks was interwoven with their political, religious, social, and cultural life; its elaborateness mirrored the complexity of Ottoman civilization itself.

Almost equally important, from a historical point of view, was the effect that it left on the cuisine of almost all neighboring lands. Wherever the Ottomans went, they bequeathed a legacy of culinary refinement. The cuisine of Syria and, to a lesser extent, Iraq is even now heavily marked by Turkish influence. Throughout the Arab world, it was a mark of distinction, until recent times, to eat Turkish dishes, much as a liking for Persian food had earlier been a sign of refinement and good taste.[48] The culinary vocabularies of all the Balkan languages contain many Turkish loanwords, and the traveler who approaches Turkey overland through Europe realizes by Belgrade at the latest that he has entered the Turkish culinary zone. Turkish cuisine has left its mark as far north as Russia: the Russian word *pirog*, meaning pie (more familiar to the West in the plural of its diminutive form, *pirozhki*) is almost certainly derived from the Turkish *börek*.

As for Western Europe, it is true that Turkish food remained relatively unknown there until quite recently. But to Turkish influence are owed the origins of the major social amenities of modern Europe—coffee drinking and the café. Soon after it entered general use in Turkey, coffee passed along the Mediterranean to Western Europe. In 1644, a merchant by the name of Sieur de la Roque returned to Marseilles after a prolonged residence in the Ottoman lands, where he had acquired the coffee habit. He began serving coffee to his friends, who then popularized it throughout the city. A quarter of a century later, a Turkish envoy, Süleyman Ağa Müteferrika, came to the court of Louis XIV. He served coffee to all who came to visit him, and the drinking of coffee became first a fashion and then a fixture of Parisian society.[49] Long since past are the days of the glory and prosperity of the Ottomans, but fastidious dedication to quality in food still persists and food continues to fulfill a significant social function in Turkey. It still is very much an instrument of human contact and a prime ingredient of that charm, hospitality, and warmth foreign visitors so fondly recall.

Despite all the changes brought about in the Turkish family by the modern age, the family remains a strong unit. Its cohesiveness is regularly expressed at the dinner table, where the most important issues that affect the family are discussed. One simple rule regulating family life is that the members of the family sit down and eat together. In the mornings, they do not simply jump out of bed and grab a bowl of cereal to eat alone while they frantically attend to other kinds of business. Brief though the time spent together may be, everyone sits down to a breakfast prepared by one member of the family and eats together. And in the evening, a mother can almost always count on her children—of whatever age—to be present for the evening meal. The evening meal is an important occasion; it is inexcusable for a teenager to be elsewhere except for a very good reason. Indeed, people actually look forward to this time of day, not least of all the young. They come to the table with a certain excitement and eagerness to share in a meal that they know has been prepared for them with effort and care, and to discuss with each other the happenings of the day. It is the knowledge that her efforts will be appreciated that makes the mother or grandmother who prepares the meal willing to devote long hours to it.

The evening meal is always consumed in a leisurely fashion, to the accompaniment of conversation. Mothers find out from their children what they have done during the day, and since school is quite demanding and taken seriously, the events of the day are still very much present in the minds of the children and carefully listened to by the parents. In short, the taking of a meal is far more than the consumption of food.

If a close friend happens to drop by during dinner, he will be automatically expected to join the family at the table. Such an unexpected arrival is not considered an imposition; on the contrary, an attitude of "the more, the merrier" prevails in the household. To drop in on a Turkish family is a very special experience; one is immediately enveloped in warm waves of welcome. Everyone turns to the newcomer and listens to his news with genuine interest.

Not only how but where meals are eaten is of significance. No visitor to Istanbul can fail to remember that city's colorful outdoor or seaside cafés or the wide range of restaurants, extending all the way from the humble fish restaurants under the Galata Bridge, at the mouth of the Golden Horn, to the sophisticated establishments that line the shores of the Bosporus. It may even be claimed that the outdoor café commonly associated with Paris had its origins in Turkey, whence it traveled to France and Vienna in the seventeenth century.

People like to take their meals outdoors, particularly on breezy summer evenings. Even in the shabbiest homes of old Istanbul, families manage to find a worn-out wooden table and set it up on whatever patch of soil they call their backyard. Hanging a naked light bulb from the branches of a wizened fruit tree, they then enjoy their modest meal, followed by many glasses of tea shared with friends, and sit talking softly into the late hours of the night.

Similarly, if one passes through the well-to-do residential sections of Istanbul —or even more, Izmir—one hears the soft murmurs of people conversing and the gentle clinking of silverware and china coming from large balconies overlooking the sea.

No matter whether the neighborhood be poor or prosperous, there is an ever-present and inescapable aroma of food: lamb or fish being grilled, stuffed bell peppers simmering in their juices, the distinctive smell of garlic and yogurt intermingled, eggplant and long green peppers being fried, sweet melons and fresh bread with their inviting aromas—all these distinct and unmistakable smells give a special life to the neighborhood.

But food may be even more than sociability and the shared conviviality of a neighborhood; an offering of food can often be an offering of love. One of my own fondest memories is of my beloved grandmother supplying the right food or drink as a remedy for all sorts of discomfort. A sore throat called for *sahlep*, and a rough cough for freshly brewed camomile tea kept stored in a jar. The lassitude and sleepiness brought on by long hours of study would be swiftly dispelled by a tray full of *böreks*, slices of bread, tea, and homemade jam, which would appear at just the right moment. When I was sick in bed, there would always be some special soup to comfort me, accompanied by softly spoken terms of endearment, the light touch of loving hands patting my hair, and invariably smiling eyes looking into my own . . .

The loving gift of food was by no means restricted to relatives. Anyone coming to the door of the house on a bleak, stormy winter's day, even the postman, would be offered a cup of hot tea to drink before going on his way. Friends who did not mind spending two, three, or even four hours traveling from one end of Istanbul to the other by ferries and buses to visit my grandmother would arrive at her door —sweaty and hot during the summer, cold and shivering during the winter—and immediately be offered what was known as *yorgunluk kahvesi*, coffee to relieve their tiredness. Then in mid-afternoon, the table would be laid for tea. All sorts of nice things would appear: warm *böreks*, slices of good bread, fresh butter, little cakes, different kinds of homemade jam, and freshly brewed tea.

Even without guests, midafternoon tea still has an almost ritual quality in the Turkish home, and for this reason it is unthinkable that it should be taken alone. It generally coincides with the children's coming home from school, and it is one of the many occasions when they interact with their parents and other adults. The children do not simply fill up a tray and withdraw to their rooms, nor do they have to be coerced into sitting with the adults. On the contrary, they are pleased to sit with them for a little while and answer their questions about schoolwork and other concerns. From an early age, the Turkish child is used to seeing many adults, both relatives and friends, visiting the home, so his adult environment does not consist only of his father and mother. One of the beneficial effects of this is that when children reach adolescence, no break of communication occurs between them and adults: adults continue to be as much a part of their life as their peers. It is not at all unusual for the visitor to a Turkish home to be greeted by a teenage son or daughter of the household, who will be only too happy to sit down and engage in conversation. It is also not unusual to see an adult friend of the family sharing his problems with the young people of the house. In short, sharp distinctions between the generations do not exist, and mealtimes are one occasion when this becomes especially apparent.

When I was a little girl, my grandmother's home always had a certain magic about it. During the day, most activity centered around her large kitchen. But once my aunts returned from school, I used to move to the salon where my aunts and their friends played the piano and listened to French love ballads and Italian operas on the gramophone. (The reader will note that the household, although very traditional in some ways, was less so in other ways!) And then in the evening a whole host of guests would arrive to dine at my grandmother's table.

She had learned to cook at a relatively late age, certainly after she had passed thirty. After the changes wrought by the First World War had compelled my grandparents to leave Damascus and return to Istanbul, she found herself without cooks and servants for the first time. So she began to cook, and what a marvelous cook she became. She persisted in her extravagance, cooking lavishly and always sharing her food with the numerous guests she and my grandfather were accustomed to entertaining. Sometimes one or two destitute friends of an uncle or aunt became semipermanent houseguests and were taken care of in every way for a year or even longer.

In her later years, prosperity and abundance became no more than a memory. She lost her husband at an unexpectedly early age, and this blow was followed by the successive and tragic loss of her two sons. But when I used to visit her, living within her modest means in a tiny flat in Ankara, there were almost always friends gathered around her table. Gone were the grand house, the music, and the extravagance, but the old qualities of generosity and hospitality, the spirit of giving and sharing, the desire for the presence of friends—all these were very much evident. Even when she was in her seventies, I watched her spending hours in the kitchen, and relying on her good health and tremendous energy, she would give her best to the preparing of food. Her efforts were rewarded when her guests would say, "Why is it this dish tastes so different when you make it, Saime Hanım?" She would acknowledge the compliment with a contented smile.

When I went back to Istanbul at a troubled time in my life with three little boys of my own, she insisted on coming to take care of us, although she was now in her eighties. I agreed, and although there were others to help, she took on all of the cooking without ever complaining or showing a trace of tiredness. All she would say, once in a while, was, "Dear Ayla, please tell the greengrocer to be more careful in selecting the vegetables he sends us. The last batch of eggplants were not all they should have been," or, "You should order the butter from someone else; the last butter we got could have been fresher."

It will be apparent by now that it was from this grand lady that I gained my inspiration to cook. Like her, my serious interest in cooking began relatively late, when I was in my early thirties, and as I look back, it seems to me now that part of my devotion to cooking has sprung from the desire to create an unseen bond between us. What is certain is that I owe to her not only my sense of taste and whatever mastery of technique I may possess but, more importantly, an appreciative desire for company and the ability to express that desire with offerings of food. So in many ways, both hidden and apparent, this book is my tribute to her memory.

Notes to the Introduction

1 Abdülhak Şinasi Hisar, *Çamlıcadaki Eniştemiz* (Istanbul, 1967), p. 85.

2 Gerhard Doerfer, *Die mongolischen und türkischen Elemente im Neupersischen* (Wiesbaden, 1965), IV:1, p. 23. From Turkish, the word *mantı* also passed into Persian (see Muhammad Mu'in, *Farhang-i Farsi* [Tehran, 134 Sh./196], IV, p. 4381) and Tajiki (see M. V. Rahimi and L. V. Uspenskaya, *Tadzhiksko-Russkii Slovar'* [Moscow, 1954], p. 215).

3 Annemarie von Gabain, *Das Leben im uigurischen Königreich* (Wiesbaden, 1973), pp. 91, 94.

4 Maxime Rodinson, "Recherches sur les documents arabes relatifs à la cuisine," *Revue des Etudes Islamiques*, 1949, p. 151.

5 Mahmud Kasghari, *Diwan Lughat at-Turk*, Istanbul, 1335/1915, I, p. 452.

6 See commentary by R.A. Nicholson on the *Mathnawi of Jalal ad-Din Rumi*, E. J. W. Gibb Memorial Series (London, 1937), IV: 7, p. 249.

7 Quoted in Zabihullah Safa, *Tarikh-i Adabiyat dar Iran* (Tehran, 1339 Sh./1961), II, pp. 852-856.

8 See H. Z. Koşay and A. Ülkücan, *Anadolu Yemekleri ve Türk Mutfağı* (Ankara, 1961), p. 116.

9 See Doerfer, *Die mongolischen und türkischen Elemente*, IV:2, p. 331, and 'Ali Akbar Dikhuda, *Lughatnama*, art. *burak*.

10 W. Radloff, *Versuch eines Wörterbuches der Türk-Dialecte* (St. Petersburg, 1911), IV, p. 1698.

11 See Abdulghani Mirzoev, *Abu Ishaq va Fa'aliyat-i Adabi-yi U* (Dushanbe, 1971), pp. 131-132.

12 Ibid., pp. 31, 118-121.

13 Radloff, *Versuch*, II, p. 1651; Hüseyin Kazım Kadri, *Büyük Türk Lugatı* (Istanbul, 1943), IV, p. 190; Sir Gerard Clauson, *An Etymological Dictionary of Pre-Thirteenth Century Turkish* (Oxford, 1972), p. 722.

14 From the nineteenth century onward, the cuisine of the Turkic peoples of Central Asia was further modified by growing Russian influence. See K. Makhmudov, *Uzbekskie Blyuda* (Tashkent, 1963), pp. 5-6.

15 See Zeki Oral, "Selçuk Devri Yemekleri ve Ekmekleri: i,"*Türk Etnografya Dergisi*, I:2 (1956), p. 73.

16 See Annemarie Schimmel, *The Triumphal Sun: A Study of the Works of Jalaloddin Rumi* (London and the Hague, 1978), pp. 138-148.

17 Zeki Oral, "Selçuk Devri Yemekleri ve Ekmekleri: ii," *Türk Etnografya Dergisi*, 1:3 (1957), p. 30.

18 Speros Vryonis, *The Decline of Mediaeval Hellenism in Asia Minor* (Los Angeles and Berkeley, 1971), pp. 482-483. Vryonis' attribution of a Greek etymology to the Turkish word *pastırma* (cured pressed meat) is unwarranted; the word is derived, in slightly adapted form, from the verb *bastırmak*, "to press."

19 Ali Seydi Bey, *Teşrifat ve Teşkilatımız* (Istanbul, n.d.), p. 92.

20 Ismail Hakki Uzunçarşılı, *Osmanli Devletinin Saray Teşkilatı* (Ankara, 1945), pp. 380, 382.

21 Ibid., p. 379; H. A. R. Gibb and Harold Bowen, *Islamic Society and the West* (London, 1950), I:1, pp. 357-358.

22 The former figure is taken from Uzunçarşili, *Saray Teşkilatı*, p. 379; the latter from Reşad Ekrem Koçu, *Topkapu Sarayı* (Istanbul, n.d.), p. 52.

23 Uzunçarşılı, *Saray Teşkilatı*, p. 381; Koçu, *Topkapu Sarayı*, p. 52.

24 Uzunçarşılı, *Saray Teşkilatı*, pp. 381, 458; Emin Cenkman, *Osmanli Sarayı ve Kiyafetleri* (Istanbul, 1948), pp. 145-155.

25 Uzunçarşılı, *Saray Teşkilatı*, p. 460.

26 Koçu, *Topkapu Sarayı*, p. 52.

27 Ibid., p. 50.

28 Gibb and Bowen, *Islamic Society and the West*, I:1, pp. 319-321.

29 Evliya Çelebi, *Seyahatname*, ed. Zuhuri Danışman, (Istanbul, 1969), II, pp. 231-258. Part of the relevant section has been translated by Bernard Lewis in his *Istanbul and the Civilization of the Ottoman Empire* (Norman, 1963), pp. 120-121.

30 Turkish miniature painters created pictorial records of some of these parades. See Richard Ettinghausen, *Turkish Miniatures* (New York, 1965), plates 18-28.

31 See Roger Mantran, *Istanbul dans la seconde moitié de la xviie siècle* (Paris, 1962), pp. 331-335.

32 See E. J. W. Gibb, *A History of Ottoman Poetry* (London, 1902), II, pp. 319, 334-335.

33 *Kaygusuz Abdal, Hatayi, Kul Himmet (Türk Klasikleri:20)*, ed. Abdülbaki Gölpınarlı (Istanbul,

1953), p. 48. For German translations of some of his verse, see Annemarie Schimmel, *Aus dem goldenen Becher* (Istanbul, 1975), pp. 60–61.

34 E. K. Birge, *The Bektashi Order of Dervishes* (London, 1937), pp. 169–170.

35 Abdülbaki Gölpinarlı, *Mevlanadan sonra Mevlevilik* (Istanbul, 1953), pp. 417–419.

36 Birge, *The Bektashi Order*, p. 254.

37 Hamit Zübeyr, "Mevlevilikte Mutfak Terbiyesi, *Türk Yurdu*, V:28 (March 1927), pp. 280–286; Gölpinarlı, *Mevlevi Adab ve Erkani*, (Istanbul, 1963), pp. 27, 41.

38 See Schimmel, *The Triumphal Sun*, p. 144.

39 Mehmed Şemseddin, *Yadigar-i Şemsi* (Bursa, 1332/1914), p. 220.

40 İsmet Efendi, *Risale-i Kudsiyye* (Istanbul, n.d.), p. 41.

41 For full information on the food consumed during Ramadan, particularly in Istanbul, see Musahipzade Celal, *Eski Istanbul Yaşayışı* (Istanbul, 1940), pp. 93, 125–127; Ali Riza Bey, *Bir zamanlar Istanbul* (Istanbul, n.d.), p. 168; Halit Fahri Ozansoy, *Eski Istanbul Ramazanları* (Istanbul, 1968), pp. 6, 17–18; and Samiha Ayverdi, *Ibrahim Efendi Konağı* (Istanbul, 1973), pp. 87–88.

42. Celal, *Eski Istanbul Yaşayişi*, p. 125; Ali Riza Bey, *Bir zamanlar Istanbul*, p. 166.

43 For these and other details, see a mid-eighteenth-century book of verse, the *Ramazanname* of Emir Mustafa (ed. Amil Çelebioğlu [Istanbul, n.d.]), which is predominantly concerned with food. With minor variations, a similar itinerary could profitably be undertaken in Istanbul today.

44 Celal, *Eski Istanbul Yaşayışı*, p. 130.

45 Ibid., pp. 123–124.

46 Fazil Yenisey, *Bursa Folkloru* (Bursa, 1955), p. 88.

47 Celal, *Eski Istanbul Yaşayışı*, pp. 90–91, 99–100.

48 Rodinson, "Recherches," p. 105.

49 V.S. Leclant, "Le café et les cafés à Paris, 1644–1693," *Annales: Economies, Sociétés, Civilisations*, VI:1 (January–March 1951), pp. 2–4.

AMERICAN NAMES FOR SOME INGREDIENTS AND THEIR BRITISH EQUIVALENTS

active-dry yeast: dry yeast

all-purpose flour: use plain white flour unless strong plain flour (or strong white flour) is specifically recommended. For the recipes in the section on böreks, strong plain flour is preferable. (See note on flour on page 232). There are a few other recipes where use of strong flour has been indicated. Otherwise, all references to all-purpose flour apply to British plain white flour.

almond meal: unblanched ground almonds

beet: beetroot

bell peppers: sweet peppers

bulgur: cracked wheat or burghul

Chinese parsley: fresh coriander

cornstarch: cornflour

eggplant: aubergine

fava beans: broad beans

grape leaves: vine leaves

great northern beans: dried haricot beans

ground beef: minced beef

ground lamb: minced lamb

half-and-half: single cream

Japanese eggplant: small, slender aubergine (Dutch aubergine)

kasseri cheese: aged Greek, Turkish or Bulgarian cheese

mastic: gum arabic

phyllo pastry: fila or strudel pastry

powdered sugar: icing sugar

*US cups and spoons are standard measuring utensils; all measurements made with them are level, not heaped.

SELECTED DRY MEASURES:

USA	UK
Butter:	
1 tablespoon	1/2 oz
1/2 cup (1 stick)	4 oz
1 cup (2 stick)	8 oz
Dried beans:	
1 cup	61/2 oz
Flour	
1 teaspoon	1/8 oz
1 tablespoon	1/3 oz
1 cup	5 oz
Lentils:	
1 cup	7 oz
Nuts:	
1 cup	51/2 oz
Rice:	
1 cup	7 oz
Sugar (castor):	
1 cup	71/4 oz
Sugar (icing):	
1 cup	41/2 oz

Temperatures are all degrees F.

AMERICAN AND BRITISH MEASURES
(All conversions are approximate)

FLUID MEASURES:

USA	UK
1 US quart (4 cups)	32 fluid oz
1 US pint (2 cups)	16 fluid oz
1 US cup (16 tablespoons)	8 fluid oz
1 US tablespoon (3 teaspoons)	1/2 fluid oz

Soups

Soups have a well-established place in Turkish cuisine. Especially during the cold months of winter, a pot of soup can be found simmering in almost every Turkish home. Throughout the year, soups are generally served as the first course of a meal. This holds true even of formal dinners. Soups not only are inherently enjoyable but are also believed to help digestion, particularly if the soup is a light one. A good soup served at the beginning of a meal can also make up for the scantiness of the main dish in poorer households.

There are two fundamental types of soup: a light soup, generally served as a first course, and a substantial soup, made with grains, legumes, and vegetables. The latter variety makes a small meal in itself and will often be served as a lunch or light supper, to be eaten with an abundance of good fresh bread.

Yogurt and mint soup is a guaranteed favorite with everyone. In eastern Turkey, especially Erzurum, hulled wheat is commonly substituted for the rice generally used in this soup, and *reyhan* (Chinese parsley) for mint leaves. Red lentil soup is a surprise for most people in the West, since they are not familiar with red lentils. The lentils are actually reddish orange in color, and when cooked they turn to a beautiful shade of yellow, creating a very wholesome and tasty soup. Fish soups, vegetable soups, especially the spinach soup and carrot soup have also been very popular with my guests. Finally, do not overlook the finishing sauce made with egg yolk and lemon juice prescribed for certain soups; it enriches the texture and flavor.

Yogurt Soup with Mint
Naneli Yoğurt Çorbası

Everyone's favorite.

1. Put the meat stock and rice in a pan, cover and simmer until the rice is soft, about 30 minutes.

2. In a mixing bowl, beat the egg yolks with the yogurt and flour. Add the water and blend to the consistency of a thin batter. Gradually add this to the soup through a sieve, stirring constantly. Cover and simmer 10 to 15 minutes. Remove from heat.

3. Melt 4 tablespoons butter in a saucepan, stir in the mint leaves and cayenne or paprika, and cook until bubbly. Gently stir this mixture into the hot soup. Serve immediately.

8 Servings

2 quarts beef or chicken stock
1/2 cup rice
4 egg yolks
3 cups yogurt
6 tablespoons all-purpose flour
1 1/2 cups water
4 tablespoons butter
3–4 tablespoons dried mint leaves, crushed
1/2 teaspoon or more cayenne or paprika

Red Lentil Soup
Kırmızı Mercimek Çorbası

Red lentils are sold in bulk in stores that stock a variety of grains. They are actually reddish orange in color and turn beautifully yellow when cooked. It is important to know that most lentils contain some small, hard particles almost like pebbles that must be carefully removed by spreading the lentils on a tray before washing. Red lentils are nourishing and create a wholesome, tasty soup.

1. Cook the lentils and rice together in the

stock or water until soft, about 45 minutes. Press through a sieve and set aside. Discard the residue remaining in the sieve.

2. Sauté the onions in 4 tablespoons butter in a large saucepan until golden brown. Blend in the flour and stir 2 to 3 minutes over medium heat. Slowly pour the hot lentil-rice mixture into the onions and flour, stirring briskly with a wire whisk to blend until thick and smooth. Cover and simmer gently 10 to 15 minutes, stirring occasionally.

3. Beat the egg yolks with the milk and stir into the soup. Bring just to a boil. Remove from heat. The consistency should be that of a cream soup. Hot water may be added if necessary to thin. Sprinkle croutons over individual bowls of hot soup.

CROUTONS:
Remove the crusts from the French bread. Cut into 1/4-inch cubes. Sauté in butter until golden brown.

8 Servings

**1 cup red lentils, picked over
and washed several times
2 tablespoons uncooked
short-grain rice
2 quarts meat stock or water
1–2 finely minced onions
4 tablespoons butter
6 tablespoons all-purpose flour
3 egg yolks
1 cup milk**

CROUTONS:
**2 slices French bread
Butter**

Red Lentil Soup with Mint
Ezo Gelin Çorbası

This is a delicious variation of the previous recipe, made by omitting the croutons and stirring mint-seasoned butter into the soup just before serving.

Melt 2 tablespoons butter in a small pan. Add the mint leaves; stir a few seconds. Add the pepper and cook a few seconds until bubbly. Stir this mixture into the hot Red Lentil Soup, mixing well to blend. Serve immediately.

8 Servings

Red Lentil Soup, p. 18
3 tablespoons butter
1/4 cup dried mint leaves,
    crushed
1 teaspoon cayenne or red
    pepper flakes (or more)
    to taste

Peasant Soup with Wheat and Yogurt
Yayla Çorbası

A healthy and delicious soup from eastern Turkey.

1. Soak the grain in hot water for 1 hour. Drain and set aside.
2. In a kettle or large saucepan, sauté the onion in butter until golden brown. Stir in the broth and wheat or barley; simmer until the grain is tender but not mushy, about 30 to 40 minutes.
3. In a mixing bowl, beat together the yogurt, flour, egg yolks, and 1 1/2 cups water until smooth.

Gradually add to the soup through a sieve, stirring constantly. Cover and simmer 10 to 15 minutes. Add the Chinese parsley; simmer 1 or 2 minutes longer. The consistency should be that of a cream soup. Let the soup stand 15 minutes. Just before serving, heat the soup and pour into individual bowls. Spoon some of the seasoned butter on top.

SEASONED BUTTER:
Melt the butter in a small pan. Stir in the paprika or cayenne and cook until bubbly without browning. Remove from heat.

8–10 Servings

2 quarts chicken or beef broth
10 tablespoons hulled wheat
   or barley
Hot water
1 large onion, minced
3–4 tablespoons butter
3 1/2 cups yogurt
6 tablespoons all-purpose flour
4 egg yolks
1 1/2 cups water
1 bunch Chinese parsley
   (coriander or cilantro),
   chopped

SEASONED BUTTER:
3–4 tablespoons butter
1 teaspoon paprika or cayenne
   (or more to taste)

Lentil Soup with Mint
Siyah Mercimek Çorbası

1. Sauté the celery and 1 chopped onion in 2

tablespoons butter in a large saucepan until golden brown. Add the tomato and sauté 2 or 3 minutes longer.

2. Stir in the stock and the lentils; cover and cook until the lentils are soft, about 40 minutes. Stir in the fettucine or Chinese noodles and continue to cook 5 to 20 minutes, until the pasta is done.

3. In a small pan, sauté 1 chopped onion in 3 tablespoons butter until golden brown. Add the mint leaves and cook a few seconds longer. Stir into the hot soup. Serve immediately.

8 Servings

2 quarts meat stock
1 cup chopped celery with
    leaves
2 large onions, chopped
5–6 tablespoons butter
1 medium tomato, chopped
1 1/2 cups lentils, soaked
    in water overnight
3/4 cup fresh or packaged
    fettucine or fresh Chinese
    noodles
1/3 cup dried mint leaves,
    crushed

Tomato and Rice Soup
Domatesli Pirinç Çorbası

Cook the tomatoes in a large saucepan until they reach the consistency of a sauce. Add the rice and the stock and cook, covered, for 20 to 30 minutes or until the rice is soft. Stir in the parsley; continue to cook 1 or 2 minutes longer. Serve.

6 Servings

6–7 cups of beef or
   chicken stock
2 minced tomatoes
1/2 cup uncooked short
   grain rice
1/2 cup chopped parsley

Coil Capellini and Lemon Soup
Terbiyeli Şehriye Çorbası

1. Melt the butter in a pan; add the tomatoes and cook until soft. Stir in the chicken stock.

2. Bring the mixture to a boil. Add the capellini, stir to separate the strands, and cook about 5 minutes, until it is soft. Stir in the parsley.

3. Beat the egg yolks with the lemon juice; mix in a little of the liquid from the soup. Gradually add this mixture to the soup, stirring constantly. Bring just to the boiling point. Remove from heat.

4–6 Servings

2 tablespoons butter
1 large tomato, diced
4 cups chicken stock
3/4 cup slightly crushed coil
   capellini
1/2 cup parsley, finely chopped
2 egg yolks
Juice of 1/2 lemon

Wedding Soup
Düğün Çorbası

1. Place the lamb in a large kettle or stockpot

with the carrot, onion, salt, peppercorns, and water. Bring to a boil. Remove the froth that forms on the surface. Cover and simmer until the meat is tender, 1 hour or longer.

2. Remove the bones and discard. Cut the meat into small bite-sized pieces and reserve. Strain the stock, measure out 2 quarts and keep it at a gentle simmer over low heat.

3. Melt 6 tablespoons butter in a large pot. Blend in the flour and stir 2 to 3 minutes over medium heat. Gradually pour in the hot stock, stirring briskly with a wire whisk to blend until thick and smooth. Add the meat pieces to the soup, cover and simmer gently 10 minutes.

4. Beat the egg yolks together with the lemon juice. Stir in 2 cups of the hot soup, then return all to the pan. Bring just to the boiling point; remove from heat. The consistency should be that of a cream soup. If necessary, add a little hot water to thin.

5. Melt 2 tablespoons butter and stir in the paprika. Cook until bubbly without browning. Pour the soup into individual bowls and spoon the seasoned butter on top.

8–10 Servings

**2 lbs. lamb shoulder or neck
   slices, with bones**
1 chopped carrot
1 chopped onion
Salt
10 peppercorns
2 1/2 quarts water
8 tablespoons butter
**1/2 cup plus 2 tablespoons
   all-purpose flour**
3 egg yolks
Juice of 1 lemon
1 teaspoon paprika

Tripe Soup
İşkembe Çorbası

A celebrated, traditional soup. In Istanbul there are small restaurants that serve nothing but this. They are frequented all night into the early hours of the morning by men, for tripe soup is reputed to be a good cure for a hangover.

1. Wash the tripe thoroughly. Place in a large pan with 2 1/2 quarts water and some salt. Bring to a boil. Remove the foam that forms on the surface. Cover and cook until the tripe is soft, 2 hours or longer. Remove the tripe from the pan. Allow the tripe and the cooking liquid to cool.

2. Remove all fat from the tripe and the liquid. Measure out 2 quarts of the liquid; discard the rest of it. Cut the tripe into very small pieces and return to the liquid. Simmer.

3. Blend the flour into 4 tablespoons melted butter and stir 2 to 3 minutes over medium heat. Gradually pour in 2 cups hot liquid from the tripe, stirring briskly with a wire whisk until smooth and bubbling. Return the thickened liquid to the soup, blend well. Cover and simmer 15 minutes.

4. In a mixing bowl, beat the egg yolks with the lemon juice and gradually stir into the soup. Cook just to the boiling point. The consistency should be that of a cream soup. If necessary, a little hot water may be added to thin.

5. Melt 2 tablespoons of the butter in a small pan. Stir in the cayenne or paprika; cook until bubbly. Remove from heat.

6. Combine the vinegar and the garlic in a small serving dish. Pour the soup into individual bowls. Top with a spoonful of the seasoned butter and serve with the vinegar-garlic sauce, to be added to individual taste.

8 Servings

3–4 lbs. honeycomb tripe, cut
   into large pieces
2 1/2 quarts water
Salt
1/2 cup all-purpose flour
6 tablespoons butter
3 egg yolks
Juice of 1 lemon
1 1/2 teaspoons cayenne
   or paprika
1 cup vinegar
5 cloves garlic, mashed

Chicken Soup
Tavuk Çorbası

1. Blend the flour into the melted butter in a large pan and stir 2 to 3 minutes over medium heat. Gradually add the chicken stock, stirring briskly with a wire whisk to blend until smooth. Blend in the chicken, cover and simmer 15 minutes over low heat.

2. Beat the egg yolks with the cream or milk and a little liquid from the soup. Slowly add this mixture to the soup, stirring constantly. Bring just to a boil. The consistency should be that of a cream soup. If necessary, a little hot liquid may be added to thin. Serve the soup with croutons if you wish. For croutons see page 19.

6–8 Servings

2 quarts chicken stock
1/2 cup plus 2 tablespoons all-
   purpose flour
6 tablespoons melted butter
2 cups cooked chicken meat, cut
   into bite-sized pieces

3 egg yolks
3/4 cup cream or milk

Chicken and Lemon Soup
Terbiyeli Tavuk Çorbası

Heat the chicken stock. Beat the egg yolks with the lemon juice. Beat in 1 cup of the hot stock. Slowly add this to the hot stock, stirring constantly. Bring just to the boiling point. Serve with parsley sprinkled on top.

6 Servings

6 cups clear chicken stock
3–4 lightly beaten egg yolks
4 tablespoons lemon juice
2 tablespoons chopped parsley

Fish Broth
Balık Suyu

A good, hearty fish stock is essential for making authentic fish soup. The best fish stocks are those made with fish scraps—the head, tail, and bones—remaining from fileted bass, cod, haddock, halibut, and similar fish. Of course, fish itself can be substituted; either a number of small fish used whole or one large fish cut into slices, including head and tail, would be appropriate.

Place all ingredients in a kettle or stockpot, bring to a boil; remove the froth that forms on the surface. Cover and simmer 1 1/2 hours. Strain.

Yields about 2 quarts

2 1/2 quarts water
4 lbs. fish scraps (heads, tails,
  bones) or 2 lbs. fish
1 large carrot, chopped
1 large onion, chopped
1 chopped leek
3 ribs celery with leaves,
  chopped
1/2 bunch parsley, chopped
2 cloves garlic, mashed
1/2 teaspoon peppercorns
Salt
2 bay leaves

Fish Soup with Tomatoes
Domatesli Balık Çorbası

Blend the flour into the melted butter and stir 2 to 3 minutes over medium heat. Add the tomatoes and cook 3 to 4 minutes longer. Stirring briskly with a wire whisk gradually add the hot Fish Broth. Continue stirring until the soup is smooth and bubbling. Simmer 10 minutes. Correct the salt. If necessary, a little hot liquid may be added to this. Serve with lemon wedges.

8 Servings

2 quarts Fish Broth, p. 27, hot
1/2 cup all-purpose flour
4 tablespoons butter
5 large ripe tomatoes, chopped
  and mashed
Salt
Lemon wedges

Fish and Lemon Soup
Balık Çorbası

1. Melt the butter or heat the olive oil in a large saucepan; blend in the flour and stir 2 to 3 minutes over medium heat. Stirring briskly with a wire whisk, gradually add the hot Fish Broth. Keep stirring until the soup is thick and smooth. Cover and simmer 10 minutes.

2. Beat the egg yolks with the lemon juice and the water. Pour slowly into the soup, stirring constantly. Bring just to a boil. Remove from heat and serve. Sprinkle with croutons if you wish. For croutons see p. 19

8 Servings

2 quarts Fish Broth, p. 27, hot
6 tablespoons butter or olive oil
1/2 cup all-purpose flour
3 egg yolks
Juice of 1 lemon
1/4 cup water

Fish Soup with Vegetables
Sebzeli Balık Çorbası

1. Bring the Fish Broth to a boil in a large pan. Add the onion, potatoes, celery root, carrot, parsley, and rice. Cover and simmer until the vegetables are almost tender, about 20 minutes. Add the parsley and cook 10 or 15 minutes longer until the vegetables are tender.

2. In a mixing bowl, beat the egg yolks with the lemon juice. Stir in the cold water and flour; blend. Slowly pour in 2 cups liquid from the soup, stirring briskly. Gradually stir this mixture into the soup. Adjust with salt. Bring just to the boiling point, sprinkle parsley on top, and serve.

8 Servings

2 quarts, Fish Broth, p. 27
1 chopped onion
1 cup diced potatoes
3/4 cup peeled and diced
   celery root
1 medium carrot, diced
2 tablespoons uncooked rice
1/2 cup chopped parsley
4 egg yolks
Juice of 1 large lemon
1/2 cup cold water
1/4 cup all-purpose flour
2 tablespoons minced parsley

Potato Soup
Patates Çorbası

1. Sauté the onion in 1 tablespoon butter until soft. Add the potatoes and 5 cups of the stock; cover and cook until the potatoes are tender. Put this mixture in a blender in batches and blend 10 seconds. Set aside.

2. Melt 5 tablespoons butter in a large pan; blend in the flour and stir over medium heat 2 to 3 minutes. Gradually add the potato mixture, stirring briskly with a wire whisk until smooth and thick. Blend in enough additional stock to give the consistency of a cream soup.

3. Beat the egg yolks with the milk and gradually stir into the soup. Bring just to the boiling point. Remove from heat. Correct the seasoning.

2 quarts beef stock
1 chopped onion
6 tablespoons butter
4 large potatoes, finely
   chopped (1 lb.)
1/4 cup all-purpose flour
3 egg yolks
1 cup milk
Salt and pepper

Vegetable Soup
Sebze Çorbası

1. In a large pan, sauté the onion, garlic, carrots, and parsley in the butter 5 to 8 minutes. Add the tomatoes and cook 2 or 3 minutes longer. Add the stock and bring to a boil.

2. Add all the remaining vegetables, the rice, and salt to taste. Cover and simmer 30 to 40 minutes, until the vegetables are tender. Stir in the dill and remove from heat.

8–10 *Servings*

2 quarts beef stock
1 large onion, chopped
4 cloves garlic, minced
2 small carrots, diced
1 cup chopped parsley
3 tablespoons butter
4 diced tomatoes
2 celery ribs with leaves,
   chopped
1/4 cup uncooked rice
4 diced potatoes

1 small celery root, diced
5 cabbage leaves, shredded
2 diced leeks
1 cup fresh dill, chopped, or
  1 tablespoon dried dill weed

Spinach Soup
Ispanak Çorbası

1. Put 6 cups of the beef stock in a large pan with the carrots and the celery root; simmer until the vegetables are tender. Wash the spinach several times; shred finely, and add to the pan of soup. Bring to a boil and simmer 10 to 15 minutes until the spinach is cooked.

2. Melt the butter in a large saucepan. Blend in the flour and stir over medium heat until smooth and bubbly. Heat and stir in 2 cups remaining stock, mixing with a wire whisk. Gradually pour this mixture into the soup and simmer 10 minutes. Beat the egg yolks with the lemon juice, gradually stir 1 cup of the hot soup into the mixture and blend well. Return this into the soup stirring constantly. Add the dill and parsley. Bring just to the boiling point and remove from heat. Correct the salt.

8 Servings

2 quarts beef stock
3 medium carrots, cut into
  shoestring pieces
1/2 cup celery root (optional), cut
  into shoestring pieces
3/4 lb. spinach
4 tablespoons butter
6 tablespoons all-purpose flour
4 egg yolks
Juice of 1 lemon

1/2 cup chopped fresh dill
1/2 cup chopped parsley
Salt

Carrot Soup
Havuç Çorbası

1. Sauté the carrots with 1 tablespoon butter. Stir in 4 cups beef stock, cover, and cook until the carrots are tender. Put this mixture in a blender in batches and blend. Gradually stir in the remaining stock and keep hot.

2. Melt 5 tablespoons butter in a large pan; blend in the flour and stir 2 to 3 minutes over medium heat. Gradually add the carrot mixture, stirring constantly with a wire whisk until smooth and bubbling. Add some hot water to thin if necessary.

3. Beat the egg yolks with the milk and gradually stir into the soup. Bring just to the boiling point. Remove from heat. Adjust with salt.

6–8 Servings

2 quarts beef stock
4–5 medium carrots, chopped
  (2/3 lb.)
6 tablespoons butter
6 tablespoons all-purpose flour
3 egg yolks
3/4 cup milk
Salt

Tarhana (a soup mix)

The mix is traditionally prepared in the summer

or fall to be used for soup in the winter. Because the mix is made from a fermented dough, the soup it produces has a slightly sour flavor and is excellent for the stomach.

1. Mix the tomatoes, onions, and bell peppers and the yogurt in a blender in batches.

2. Dissolve the yeast in the tepid water; add the sugar and let stand 10 minutes.

3. Combine all the ingredients except the flour and mix well. Gradually add enough flour to make a stiff dough. Because the amount of dough is very large, you may find it easier to divide the dough into halves and work with one piece at a time.

4. On a floured board, knead 5 to 10 minutes, until the dough is smooth and elastic. Place it in a very large glass, enamel, or plastic bowl; cover with wax paper and let stand, at room temperature, 10 to 12 days. Every day punch it down a little. If the dough becomes watery, knead in additional flour. Let stand until the dough ceases to rise and is no longer elastic. It is ready when you pull on a small piece of dough and it breaks rather than stretches.

5. Spread out a clean sheet; outdoors is best because the entire drying process will take more than a week. Break off small pieces of dough and spread them out on the sheet. When they have dried slightly, break them still smaller. Then, when the dough gets drier and almost reaches the point of hardening, crumble it as fine as you can, rubbing it between your hands. Dry still longer. When completely dry, grind it into powder in a blender, a small quantity at a time. Place the powdered soup mix in a clean cloth bag (like a rice sack), a plastic freezer bag, or large jars. Close tightly. Store in a cool place or refrigerate. Use it to make Tarhana Soup.

Yields about 24 cups soup mix

Note: This amount of soup mix is meant to last through the winter. Feel free to reduce it.

4 lbs. ripe, very juicy tomatoes
3 large onions, chopped
3 green bell peppers, chopped
2 red bell peppers, chopped
6 cups yogurt
2 packages dry-active yeast
1/2 cup tepid water
1 teaspoon sugar
1 tablespoon red pepper flakes
2 tablespoons paprika
Salt
All-purpose flour

Tarhana Soup
Tarhana Çorbası

1. If you are using ground beef, brown it in 2 tablespoons butter in a large pan; add the tomatoes or tomato paste. If not using beef, simply sauté the tomatoes in 4 tablespoons butter 5 minutes or stir the tomato paste in the butter 2 to 3 minutes. Stir in the flaked red chili pepper. Cook a few seconds longer.

2. Stir the Tarhana into 3 cups meat stock or water. Pour into the pan of tomato sauce. Gradually add enough additional meat stock or water to make a fairly thick soup of cream-soup consistency. Cook 15 to 20 minutes. Remove from heat. Pour into individual bowls and if desired, garnish with either croutons or seasoned butter or both.

For Croutons, see p. 19. For Seasoned Butter, see p. 21.

1/3 **lb. ground beef (optional)**
2 large tomatoes, grated, or
   2 tablespoons tomato paste
7–8 cups meat stock or water
1 cup Tarhana, p. 33
2–4 tablespoons butter
1/4–1/2 **teaspoon flaked red chili**
  pepper

Mezes

As you sit waiting for your fish to be cooked and brought to the table at one of the fish restaurants that jut out over the flowing waters of the Bosporus, you will be served a seemingly endless variety of small dishes called *mezes* (very roughly, hors d'oeuvres), following upon each other in a delightful display. Every restaurant has its own specialties determined by its own character, so the range of *mezes* encountered will vary in sophistication and elaboration in different restaurants.

The simplest *meze* might be a slice of sweet, fragrant melon accompanied by a few slabs of creamy white cheese, or a plateful of thin slices of smoked sturgeon. An example of the more complex would be a dazzling arrangement of platters filled with a variety of *dolmas*—green peppers, eggplants, and vine leaves all stuffed with mixtures of rice, onions, currants, and pine nuts, moistened with olive oil and lemon juice—shiny black mussels, also stuffed; hot, flaky golden pastries filled with cheese and dill; and Circassian chicken.

If you go to one of the unpretentious fish restaurants under the Galata Bridge, the only *meze* you should count on is a plate of salad. This, however, is nothing to look down upon, for the tomatoes, cucumbers, green peppers, and onions that are set before you—dressed with olive oil and lemon juice and accompanied by half a loaf of fresh, crusty bread—will indeed sharpen your appetite for the fish course that follows.

It should be pointed out that *mezes* may not only serve as hors d'oeuvres or side dishes but also—when grouped together in an array of dishes—make an elegant, distinctive, and attractive buffet.

Finally, the number of servings given in most recipes in this section applies to the use of *mezes* as side dishes. When *mezes* are used as an appetizer, the recipe yields more servings.

Vine-Leaf *Dolmas* in Olive Oil
Zeytinyağlı Yaprak Dolması

This is one of the most refined and exquisite dishes in Turkish cookery.

1. Place vine leaves in a large bowl. Rinse, one at a time, under running water and cut off the stems. Leave them to drain in a colander.

2. In a heavy pan, heat 3/4 cup olive oil. Add the onions and pine nuts and cook over medium heat 15 to 20 minutes, stirring frequently. Add the rice; cook another 10 or 15 minutes, stirring almost constantly. Add the tomatoes, mix, and continue to cook 5 minutes more. Turn the heat to low. Add the dill, mint leaves, cinnamon, allspice, cloves, nutmeg, 1 teaspoon salt, sugar, juice of 1 lemon, currants, and 3/4 cup hot water. Mix well, cover, and cook 5 to 10 minutes over low heat. Remove from heat, cool.

3. On a dinner plate, spread out 1 vine leaf, shiny side down, with the stem end toward you. Spoon 1 to 3 tablespoons filling, depending on the size of the leaf, onto the leaf near the stem, 1 inch away from the three edges. Fold the left and right sides over to seal, fold the stem edge over the filling, and roll what is now a rectangular packet toward the point of the leaf firmly, but not too tightly. Proceed in the same manner, making a roll 1 1/4 to 1 1/2 inches in diameter out of each grape leaf, until you run out of filling.

4. In the bottom of a heavy pan, place a few unfilled leaves. In layers on top of these, arrange the stuffed leaves, seamside down. Pour in a mixture of 1 cup hot water, 1/4 teaspoon salt, 2 tablespoons olive oil, and the juice of 1 lemon. Place a plate upside down on top of the mound of *dolmas* to add some extra weight. Cover and cook over low heat for 50 minutes. Usually there is no need to add more water. If at any time while cooking the liquid in the pan is absorbed, add 2 or 3 tablespoons hot water. When the *dolmas* are cooked, there should be no more than 1 or 2 tablespoons water left in the pan. Remove the pan from heat and leave until cool. Remove the inverted plate. Arrange *dolmas* on a serving dish and chill. Serve cold, garnished with lemon wedges. Makes 1 1/2–2 dozen or more large *dolmas*.

8 Servings

1 8-oz. jar vine leaves
3/4 cups plus 2 tablespoons
    finest virgin olive oil
5 medium onions, finely
    chopped
2 heaping tablespoons
    pine nuts
1 cup uncooked long-grain rice
2 small tomatoes, cubed
    and mashed
3 tablespoons chopped fresh
    dill or 1 teaspoon dried
    dill weed
3 tablespoons fresh mint leaves,
    chopped, or 1 tablespoon
    dried mint leaves, crushed
1/2 teaspoon cinnamon
1/8 teaspoon allspice
Pinch cloves
Pinch nutmeg
Salt
1 tablespoon sugar
Juice of 2 lemons
2 heaping tablespoons currants
Water
Lemon wedges for garnish

Circassian Chicken
Çerkez Tavuğu

Circassian Chicken looks and tastes as regal as its origins.

1. Place the chicken in a pan with 3 to 4 cups water, 1 tablespoon salt, the small whole onion, and the carrot; bring to a boil. Cover and simmer 45 minutes or until the chicken is done. Cool the chicken in its stock. Remove it from the pan; bone and tear into bite-sized pieces. Discard the skin and bones. Set aside and reserve the stock.

2. Remove the crust from the bread. Put the slices of bread in a bowl with water to barely cover; let stand 5 minutes. Squeeze dry with your hands and set aside.

3. Prepare the Walnut Sauce.

MEAT GRINDER METHOD: Put the walnuts through a meat grinder using the finest blade. In a bowl, combine the ground nuts with the chopped onion, garlic, bread, salt, paprika, and cayenne; then put this mixture through the meat grinder. Gather up the walnut oil produced during this process.* Take 2 tablespoons of this oil and set aside to use for garnish later. In a bowl, combine the walnut mixture with about 2 cups chicken stock and the remaining walnut oil and blend well to make a thick sauce. Add a little more chicken stock if the sauce seems too thick.

BLENDER METHOD: This is easier, but produces no walnut oil for garnish. Grind the walnuts in the blender in thirds. In a bowl, combine the ground nuts with the onion, garlic, bread, salt, paprika, and cayenne. Again in thirds, mix this in the blender with portions of 2 cups chicken stock. Blend well to make a thick sauce.

4. Take half the walnut sauce and mix with the chicken pieces. Transfer this to a serving dish and spread the remaining sauce on top. Garnish with the walnut halves. If you used the blender method, garnish with paprika oil. ** If you used the meat grinder method and gathered some walnut oil, drizzle it over the top. Chill.

6-8 Servings

*As the walnut mixture is put through the meat grinder, some walnut oil will drip from the meat grinder. Gather this oil by placing a saucer underneath the place where the oil is dripping.

** Paprika oil: Heat 3 tablespoons fine vegetable oil in a small saucepan. Blend in 2 teaspoons Hungarian paprika and stir over medium heat only a few seconds until the paprika is well blended with the oil.

1 chicken, about 2$1/2$ **lbs.**
3-4 cups water
1 tablespoon salt
1 small onion
1 carrot

WALNUT SAUCE:
3$3/4$ **cups ground walnuts**
1 small onion, chopped
4-5 teaspoons minced garlic
3 slices French bread
$1/4$ **teaspoon salt**
1$1/2$ **tablespoons paprika**
1 teaspoon cayenne
About 2 cups chicken stock
10 walnut halves for garnish

PAPRIKA OIL:
3 tablespoons fine vegetable oil
2 teaspoons Hungarian paprika

Stuffed Mussels
Midye Dolması

1. Well before cooking time, sprinkle the mussels with 2 to 3 tablespoons of salt and set aside. This will make the job of cleaning them easier.

2. Wash the mussels thoroughly, by scrubbing them with a brush and rinsing them in cold water several times. Discard the ones that are already open. Pull and remove the beards. Cover the mussels with warm, salted water; let stand 5 minutes and drain. With a bowl underneath to catch all the liquid, open the mussels by inserting a sharp knife between the shells, running it along the flat edge and taking care not to break the hinge. Open the shells until they are loosened but not separated. Strain and measure the liquid from the mussels and if necessary, add water to make 1 1/2 cups. Set aside.

3. In a heavy pan, heat 3/4 cup plus 2 tablespoons olive oil. Add the onions and pine nuts and cook over medium heat 20 minutes, stirring frequently. Add the rice and cook 15 minutes longer, still stirring. Stir in the tomatoes and cook 5 minutes longer. Reduce heat to low. Add the currants, sugar, salt, pepper, allspice, cinnamon, cloves, nutmeg, and 3/4 cup of the mussel liquid; mix, cover, and simmer 10 minutes. Remove from heat; let stand, covered, for 20 minutes. Mix well.

4. Using a small spoon, fill the shells lightly, allowing room for the rice to expand. Close the shells as far as possible and arrange in a shallow pan in layers. Place a piece of wax paper over the mussels and an inverted plate over that to add some weight. Add the remaining 3/4 cup of mussel liquid to the pan, bring it to a simmer, cover and cook for 35 minutes over medium heat. Check the liquid content occasionally and add hot water in very small quantities if needed. Remove from heat. Cool thoroughly in the pan. Chill. To give a polished appearance, wipe the surface of the shells with a cloth and rub with a little olive oil. Serve cold with lemon wedges.

40 mussels, large (about 4 lbs.)
Salt
Lemon wedges for garnish
3/4 cup plus 2 tablespoons
   finest virgin olive oil
5 medium onions, finely
   chopped
2 heaping tablespoons pine nuts
1 cup uncooked rice
2 small tomatoes, mashed
2 heaping tablespoons currants
1 tablespoon sugar
Freshly ground pepper to taste
1/8 teaspoon allspice
1/2 teaspoon cinnamon
1/8 teaspoon cloves
Pinch nutmeg

Fried Mussels
Midye Tavası

1. Wash the mussels, rinsing them in cold water several times. Pull and remove the beards. Discard the ones that are already open. Cover the mussels with warm, salted water; let stand 5 minutes and drain. Open the mussels by inserting a sharp knife between the shells and running it along the flat edge. Remove the meat, discard the shells. Place the mussels on a clean towel and pat gently to dry. Place them in a bowl and sprinkle with a little salt and lemon juice.

3. Put the flour in a bowl and the bread crumbs in another. Break the eggs into a small bowl and beat them with a fork until well blended.

Dip each mussel into the flour, then into the egg, and finally into the bread crumbs. Arrange the breaded mussels side by side on a tray.

4. Heat the oil until hot in a pan for deep-frying and drop in a few mussels. Fry 2 to 3 minutes, until golden in color. Using a slotted spoon, place them on a paper towel. Continue cooking, a few at a time. Arrange them on a serving platter. Place a toothpick in each. Serve hot or cold with lemon wedges or tarator sauce, p. 58.

10 Servings

40 mussels, large (about 4 lbs.)
Salt
1 cup all-purpose flour
2 cups bread crumbs
4 eggs
1 1/2 cups oil for frying
Lemon wedges for garnish
Toothpicks

Sautéed Brains
Beyin Tavası

1. Wash the brains under running water and soak 1 hour in cold water mixed with 1 tablespoon vinegar. Remove the membrane and veins carefully under running water.

2. In a saucepan, bring to a boil 4 cups water to which 1 tablespoon vinegar and 1 teaspoon salt have been added. Add the brains and simmer about 20 minutes. Remove from the pan. Cool, pat dry, and cut crosswise into 1/2-inch slices.

3. Beat the eggs in a bowl with 1 tablespoon of the flour or potato starch. Put the remaining flour or potato starch on a plate. Heat the oil in frying pan over high heat. Dredge the slices of brain with flour or potato starch and lay on a paper towel. Then dip each slice in the egg mixture and fry in the oil until golden brown on both sides, about 2 minutes on each side. Arrange slices on a serving platter, sprinkle with parsley, and add some lemon wedges. Serve hot.

8 Servings

2 sets calf's or lamb's brains
Cold water
2 tablespoons vinegar
4 cups water
1 teaspoon salt
3 eggs
1 cup all-purpose flour or
    potato starch
3/4 cup oil for frying
Chopped parsley and lemon
    wedges for garnish

Tarama Salad
Tarama

Tarama is salted carp roe. It is light orange in color. It comes in tiny jars and can be found in specialty stores. Prepared according to the following recipe, it makes an excellent dip or appetizer.

1. Remove the crusts from the bread. Soak in the milk a few minutes; squeeze dry. Discard the milk.

2. Put 1/4 of each of the ingredients (except the parsley) in a blender; blend a few seconds. Add and blend the rest of these ingredients in 3 successive stages until the consistency of thick mayonnaise. Place in a serving dish; garnish with parsley.

VARIATION: Blend in 2 teaspoons onion juice and 1 teaspoon cayenne. For onion juice, see p. 79.

8–10 Servings

4 slices stale French bread
1/3 cup hot milk
1 4-oz. jar tarama caviar
1/2 cup fine olive oil
1/4–1/3 cup lemon juice
Parsley for garnish

Albanian Liver
Arnavut Ciğeri

1. Clean the liver and cut into 1/2-inch cubes. Season with salt and 1/2 to 1 tablespoon paprika. Roll in flour and fry in smoking hot oil, a small amount at a time, 3 to 4 minutes, turning them constantly with a slotted spoon.

2. When all the liver has been fried, remove all but 1/4 cup of the oil from the frying pan; stir 1 tablespoon paprika into that and pour over the fried liver cubes. Arrange them on a serving platter. If you are serving them as appetizers, place a toothpick in each. Garnish with the onion slices mixed with parsley.

4 Servings

1 lb. calf, lamb, or beef liver
Salt to taste
2 tablespoons paprika
1/2 cup flour
1 cup olive oil or salad oil
1 onion, sliced paper-thin, and
  1 cup chopped parsley

for garnish
Toothpicks

Raw Kibbe
Çiğ Köfte

This is a Turkish version of an originally Arab dish.

1. Rinse the bulgur and squeeze dry with your hands. Mix in the salt; cover and let it stand in the refrigerator 25 minutes.

2. Combine the meat, bulgur, onions, cinnamon, and cumin and knead five minutes, dipping your hands frequently in cold water.

3. Grind this mixture in a meat grinder three times through a fine blade. Mix in the cayenne or pepper flakes, chili sauce, green onions, and lemon juice. Adjust with salt and knead again to a smooth paste. Form into thumb-sized shapes and arrange on a plate lined with romaine leaves. Sprinkle parsley and serve with lemon wedges.

8 Servings

1 lb. very fresh, extra lean lamb
(freshly butchered lamb
works best)
1 cup extra fine grain bulgur
2 medium onions, grated
1 teaspoon salt
1/8 teaspoon cinnamon
1 teaspoon cumin
1–2 teaspoons or more cayenne
or red pepper flakes
2 tablespoons hot, red Mexican
chili sauce
Freshly ground pepper
Juice of 1/2 lemon

5 minced green onions,
   including tops
1/2 cup minced parsley
Lemon wedges
Romaine leaves

Cheese-Filled Triangles
Muska Böreği

1. Soak the feta cheese in water for 1 hour if it is very salty. Drain well and crumble. Mix with the egg yolks and parsley or dill.

2. Melt the butter; have a pastry brush ready.

3. Preheat oven to 400°.

4. Take the phyllo pastry out of the box; remove the plastic bag and paper, but do not unroll the pastry. Cut the roll into two equal pieces. Wrap one piece carefully and return to the refrigerator or freezer for another use. Cut the remaining half roll into 2 equal pieces, giving 2 rolls of strips approximately 3 1/2 inches wide. Unroll 1 roll and remove 1 pair of strips Work with 1 pair only at a time, keep all the rest well covered to prevent pastry from drying. Place one strip directly on top of the other. Brush the surface with melted butter. Place 1 teaspoon cheese filling at one end. Fold one corner across over the filling, forming a triangle. Continue folding as you would fold a flag, until you reach the other end of the strip. When all the strips have been filled and folded, arrange the triangles in a lightly greased baking pan about 1/2 inch apart. Brush the tops generously with the melted butter. Bake 10 to 15 minutes or until the triangles are puffed and golden brown. Serve hot or cold.

3 Dozen

2/3 lb. feta cheese
Cold water
4 lightly beaten egg yolks
1/2 cup chopped parsley or
    fresh dill
1/2 lb. thin phyllo pastry
1/2–3/4 cup butter

Beans Plaki
Zeytinyağlı Fasulye Plâkisi

A very popular dish. It is frequently served as a side dish in Turkish homes, but it makes a fine appetizer.

1. Soak the beans in plenty of water overnight. Place in a pan with cold water to cover; boil, covered, 20 minutes and drain.

2. Heat the olive oil in a heavy pan; cook the onions, garlic, and carrots 20 minutes, stirring frequently. Stir in the tomatoes and cook 3 more minutes. Add 2 cups hot water, salt, paprika, and sugar; bring to a boil and stir in the beans. Simmer, covered, 1 1/2 hours or longer. Add small quantities of hot water to maintain the water level if needed. When the beans are tender, add the parsley and continue to cook 10 minutes. Remove from heat. Transfer to a large serving dish, chill for several hours. Serve sprinkled with parsley and garnished with lemon wedges.

6 Servings

2 cups pinto beans
Water
1/2 cup plus 1 tablespoon
    finest virgin olive oil
2 large onions, finely sliced
6 large garlic cloves, each cut
    into 4–6 slivers
2 carrots, quartered lengthwise
    and then cut in 1/8-inch slices
3 ripe tomatoes, chopped and
    mashed, or 1 1/2 cups canned
    tomatoes with juice
1 lemon
2 teaspoons paprika
3 tablespoons sugar
1 cup chopped parsley
Chopped parsley and lemon
    wedges for garnish

Fava Bean Purée
Fava, Kuru Bakla Ezmesi

1. Soak the beans in plenty of water overnight. Drain.

2. Heat the olive oil in a large skillet; sauté the onion until golden brown. Stir in the beans and sauté a few minutes. Add 3 cups water, salt, and sugar; cover and cook, stirring frequently, until the beans are tender (about 2 hours). Add small quantities of hot water as needed. The water should be well absorbed when the beans are cooked. Stir in the dill and remove from heat.

3. Mash the beans with a potato masher or put them in a blender. Let cool and stir in the lemon juice. Mix well. Mound the bean purée onto a serving plate and chill. Dribble 1 tablespoon olive oil on top and garnish with dill, black olives, and lemon wedges.

1 1/2 cups dry fava beans
Water
1/2 cup finest virgin olive oil
1 chopped onion
Salt to taste
2 teaspoons sugar
1/2 cup chopped fresh dill, or
    2 teaspoons dried dill weed
6 tablespoons or more
    lemon juice
1 tablespoon olive oil
Chopped dill, black olives, and
    lemon wedges for garnish

Hummus
Humus

Drain the chick-peas, reserving 3 tablespoons of the liquid. Put this liquid, the salt, the lemon juice, and the garlic in the blender. Blend 10 seconds. Add the chick-peas a few at a time and blend to a creamy mixture. Add and blend in the tahini. Place in a serving dish and decorate with paprika, pars ley and olives.

8–10 Servings

2 cans (15 ounces each)
  chick-peas
3 tablespoons chick-pea liquid
1/2 cup tahini
1 tablespoon mashed garlic
1/2 teaspoon salt
7 tablespoons lemon juice
Paprika, parsley, and black
  olives for garnish

Lentil *Köfte*
Mercimekli Köfte

1. Cook the lentils in 2 1/2 cups water until tender. Add more water if necessary. When they are almost soft and the water is nearly all absorbed, stir in the bulgur and boil 2 or 3 minutes. Remove from heat. Allow the bulgur to soften.

2. Sauté the onion in olive oil; stir in the tomato paste and remove from heat.

3. Combine all the ingredients and knead into a paste. When the mixture has cooled and reabsorbed all its moisture, form tablespoonfuls into thumb-sized *köftes*. Arrange on a platter and sprinkle with parsley. Serve cold as an appetizer.

10 Servings

1 cup red lentils
Water to cover
3/4 cup fine-grain bulgur
1 minced onion
1/4 cup olive oil
1 1/2 tablespoons tomato paste
1 cup minced green onions,
    including tops
1 cup finely chopped parsley
2 1/2–3 1/2 cups water
2–3 teaspoons cumin
2 teaspoons or more paprika
Salt and cayenne to taste
Chopped parsley for garnish

Artichokes in Dill
Zeytinyağlı Enginar

1. Mix the juice of 2 lemons and 2 tablespoons flour in a large bowl. Add 2 quarts of water, mix thoroughly. Wash the artichokes. Bend back and snap off the tough, outer leaves, leaving the meat at the bottom of the leaves attached to the artichoke base, until only the tender inner leaves remain. Slice off these leaves just above the heart. With a teaspoon, scoop out the fuzzy choke and remaining pinkish leaves. Cut off the steam and, using a vegetable peeler, trim around the base. With smaller artichokes, trim just enough to smoothen the base. Do not overtrim. However, with the very large ones, peel around the base as if peeling an apple until you reach the whitish, tender part. As you trim each artichoke, take a lemon half, sprinkle it with salt, and rub the whole artichoke with the lemon. Then drop the finished artichoke into the lemon-water mixture.

2. When all the artichokes have been prepared, pour some of the lemon-water out, leaving just enough to cover the artichokes. Cover and simmer 10 minutes.

3. Remove the artichokes from the pot and drain. Arrange them in a heavy, shallow pan stem side down. Spread the onions over the artichokes. Mix the remaining flour, juice of 1 lemon, olive oil, sugar, and salt in a small bowl. Pour this mixture over the artichokes. Sprinkle the dill on top. Add water to within 1 inch of the tops of the artichokes. Cover and cook over medium heat about 35 minutes or until the artichokes are tender. As they cook, add small portions of hot water if needed. Cool and transfer into a serving platter. Serve cold.

8 Servings

8 artichokes
3 lemons
3 tablespoons all-purpose flour
Water

4–5 lemons, cut into halves
Salt
2 medium onions, minced
1/2 cup fresh dill, chopped, or
   2 teaspoons dried dill weed
1/2 cup finest virgin olive oil
1 teaspoon sugar

Pan-Fried Eggplant and Peppers with Yogurt
Yoğurtlu Patlıcan Biber Kızartması

1. Cut the stem off the eggplant. Using a vegetable peeler, and peeling lengthwise, remove a strip of skin; leave the next strip on. Continue to peel in this striped fashion. Cut the eggplant in half lengthwise. Then cut each half crosswise into 1/4-inch slices. Spread the slices in a large baking pan, sprinkle generously with 2 1/2 tablespoons salt, and set aside at least 3 hours. Rinse thoroughly with cold water. Using a clean old kitchen towel, squeeze each slice gently to get all the water out without tearing.

2. Mix together the yogurt, garlic, and a little salt. Beat to a creamy consistency; if too thick, blend in a little water. Set aside.

3. Heat 1/2 cup oil in a heavy skillet and brown the slices of eggplant, in a single layer, on both sides over high heat. Place on a paper towel to drain off the excess oil. When all the eggplant has been cooked and removed from the pan, add the bell peppers and cover the pan to prevent the hot oil from splattering. Fry the peppers on both sides until golden brown. Arrange the fried eggplant and bell peppers on a large platter. The yogurt sauce may be spooned over all or passed in a separate serving dish.

6 Servings

1 large eggplant
Salt
1/2 cup finest virgin olive oil
2 cups yogurt
1–2 teaspoons mashed garlic
4 bell peppers, cut in quarters
   lengthwise

Roast Peppers
Izgara Yeşil Biber Salatası

If you like hot peppers, *chiles pascillas* are wonderful fixed this way.

1. Place the peppers directly on a gas burner over a high flame or over a charcoal fire. (If you must use an electric stove, cook them in an ungreased cast-iron skillet over medium heat.) Turn frequently to cook on all sides. They are done when the skins are charred and black and the peppers are limp. Remove from heat.

2. To make it easier to peel your peppers after charring them, put them into a large plastic bag and seal it closed. Cover with a towel. Let them sit 30 minutes before starting to peel them. Peel off the skin and rinse the peppers in cold water. Pat dry. Cut off the tops and remove the seeds. Cut lengthwise into quarters and place in a serving dish.

3. Prepare a marinade with the oil, garlic, vinegar, and salt. Pour over the peppers. Allow them to marinate several hours. Serve at about room temperature.

6 Servings

6 bell peppers or hot green
   peppers

1/2 cup olive oil
4 cloves garlic, mashed
3–4 tablespoons vinegar
Salt

Eggplant Salad with Tahini
Patlıcan Salatası

1. Place the unpeeled eggplant directly on a gas burner over a high flame or over a charcoal fire. Turn frequently to cook on all sides. It is done when the skin is charred and black and the eggplant is thoroughly soft. Cool slightly. Peel the eggplant, carefully removing all the pieces of burnt, black skin, and wipe it clean with wet hands. Squeeze out all the water.

2. Place the eggplant in a bowl with the lemon juice and 1 tablespoon olive oil; mash well. Stir in the tahini; blend. Mix in the mashed garlic, minced parsley, and salt. Adjust with more lemon juice and blend thoroughly. Chill. Mound in a serving dish; garnish with lemon wedges.

6 Servings

1 medium eggplant (1 lb.)
1/4 cup lemon juice
4 tablespoons tahini (sesame
  butter)
2 teaspoons garlic, mashed
Salt
1 tablespoon olive oil
1/4 cup minced parsley
Chopped parsley and lemon
  wedges for garnish

Eggplant Salad with Yogurt
Yoğurtlu Patlıcan Salatası

This is an excellent eggplant salad with an unexpected taste.

1. Place the unpeeled eggplant directly on a gas burner over a high flame or over a charcoal fire. Turn frequently to cook on all sides. It is done when the skin is charred and black and the eggplant is thoroughly soft. Cool slightly. Peel the eggplant, carefully removing all the pieces of burnt, black skin, and wipe it clean with wet hands. Place it in a bowl with the lemon juice. Let stand 20 minutes.

2. Roast the bell and chili peppers also by placing them directly on a gas burner or on a charcoal fire, turning them frequently. They are done when the skins are charred and black and the peppers are limp. Place the peppers in a plastic bag and seal it closed. Let them sit for 30 minutes. Remove them from the bag, peel, and rinse with water. Remove and discard the stems and seeds.

3. Squeeze out all the moisture from the eggplant. Using a fork or a wooden pestle, mash the eggplant in a bowl; stir in the walnuts and blend. Stir in the yogurt and olive oil and blend. Put the garlic and the roasted peppers in a mortar with a little salt and mash together until they are roughly blended. Stir this into the eggplant mixture, add the vinegar, and blend thoroughly. Place in a serving dish and chill.

6 Servings

1 large eggplant (1 1/4 lbs.)
Juice of 1/2 lemon
2 bell peppers or pascillas
2 small, green hot chili peppers
1/4 cup ground walnuts

1/2 cup plus 2 tablespoons
    yogurt
1–2 tablespoons olive oil
1 1/2–2 teaspoons mashed garlic
Salt
4 teaspoons vinegar
Tomato slices, olives, and
    paprika for garnish

Tarator Salad
Tarator Salatası

Grind the walnuts in parts in a blender. Put them
in 2 parts in a mortar with a little salt and the
garlic; pound and mash together. Combine in a
mixing bowl with all the other ingredients and
blend thoroughly. Place in a serving dish and decorate with the olives and lemon wedges. Serve
as a salad or spread.

Yields 1½ Cups

1 cup walnuts
Salt
2–4 cloves garlic
1/3 cup tahini
2/3 cup lemon juice
1 cup chopped parsley
Black olives and lemon wedges
    for garnish

Tarator Sauce
Tarator

A nut and garlic sauce, good on boiled vegetables
and fried mussels.

1. Remove the crusts from the French bread. Soak in water and squeeze dry.

2. Place 1/3 the nuts in a blender with 1/3 of the olive oil and half the softened bread; turn the blender on and off several times. Add half of the remaining nuts, oil, remaining bread, salt, and garlic. Turn the blender on low for 5 seconds; turn it on and off several times. Add the vinegar and blend until smooth. It may be thinned with a little water, if needed.

Yields 1½–2 Cups

Note: Use lemon juice with pine nuts or almonds; vinegar with walnuts.

4 slices French bread
1 cup pine nuts, walnuts,
  or almonds
1 cup olive oil
1 teaspoon salt
2–4 large cloves garlic, mashed
1/2 cup vinegar or lemon juice

Potato *Köfte*
Patates Köftesi

1. Boil the potatoes until tender. Drain and cool.

2. Mash the potatoes very well or put them through a meat grinder. Add the coconut, salt, pepper, one egg yolk, 1 egg, and the cheese and mix thoroughly with your hands. Sprinkle the flour on a plate. Use your hands to make thumb-sized shapes out of the paste, each about a large tablespoonful in volume. Coat them lightly with flour.

3. Heat the oil over high heat. In a small

bowl, beat 2 eggs with a fork until well blended. Put the bread crumbs on a plate. Dip each *köfte* in the beaten eggs, then roll in the bread crumbs, and fry in hot oil until golden brown.

6 Servings

1 lb. potatoes
1 egg yolk
3 eggs
1 tablespoon grated coconut,
   unsweetened
Salt and pepper to taste
1 cup grated kasseri or Romano
   cheese
2 tablespoons all-purpose flour
1 cup oil for frying
1 cup dry bread crumbs

Russian Salad
Rus Salatası

1. Cook the potatoes and carrots in salted water until soft. Cook the beet separately. Drain all the vegetables and cool.

2. Combine all the ingredients; add most of the mayonnaise and blend well. Arrange on a serving platter and dab on the remaining mayonnaise.

4 Servings

2–3 medium potatoes, diced
2 small carrots, diced
Salted water
1 medium beet, diced
1 small dill pickle, diced
3/4 cup cooked peas ·
2 hard-boiled eggs, diced
About 1 cup mayonnaise

Eggs

Eggs are used abundantly in Turkish cooking, particularly in different types of *börek*, desserts, and sauces. For breakfast they are served either hard or soft-boiled, but never fried or scrambled. Children are particularly encouraged to eat eggs for their breakfast.

In addition, egg dishes may constitute the main course at lunchtime. A simple but attractive meal consists of eggs fried simply in butter and served in individual little copper or enamel dishes called *sahan*, accompanied by fresh bread and salad.

Eggs Fried in Butter
Sahanda Yumurta

Each serving of fried eggs is individually cooked in a 5-inch skillet.

Heat the butter until bubbly. Break the eggs into it. Sprinkle a little salt over them. Cover and cook 3 to 5 minutes over low heat until the white of the egg is cooked through. Sprinkle pepper on top of the eggs and remove them from the heat. You may put a little butter on top. Serve with fresh French bread.

1 Serving

2 eggs
1 tablespoon butter
Salt and pepper to taste

Eggs with Pastırma
Pastırmalı Yumurta

Pastırma is made of beef highly seasoned and cured with cumin, garlic, and red peppers.

In a skillet, sauté the onions in butter for 8 minutes. Cover and steam over low heat for 2 or 3 minutes. Stir in the *pastırma* and cook another 2 or 3 minutes. Clear 4 spaces among the meat and onions. Break the eggs into the spaces. Sprinkle a little salt and pepper over them. Cover and cook 3 to 5 minutes until the egg whites are cooked through. Serve with fresh French bread.

2 Servings

1/2 lb. *pastırma*, sliced very thin
1 onion, halved and then sliced
   paper-thin
2–3 tablespoons butter
4 eggs

Eggs with Turkish Sausage
Sucuklu Yumurta

Sauté the sausage in butter for 2 to 3 minutes. Clear spaces among the meat slices for the eggs. Break 1 egg into each space. Cover and cook 5 minutes until the whites are cooked through. Serve with fresh French bread.
VARIATION: Beat the eggs in a mixing bowl with a fork. Sauté the sausage in butter, then pour in the beaten eggs. Cook, stirring constantly, until the eggs are cooked through.

2–3 Servings

1/2 lb. Turkish Sausage, p. 145,
    sliced very thin
4 tablespoons butter
4–6 eggs

Eggs with Ground Beef
Kıymalı Yumurta

Sauté the onion in butter for 10 minutes. Add the ground beef and cook it, stirring constantly, until it browns. Stir in the green pepper and tomato; cook 2 minutes longer. Add the parsley and a little salt and pepper. Mix well, cover, and simmer 5 to 8 minutes. Clear spaces in the meat mixture for the eggs. Break 1 egg into each space. Sprinkle with more salt and pepper. Cover and cook 5 minutes until the whites are cooked through. Serve with fresh French bread.

3 Servings

1/2 lb. ground beef
1 small onion, finely chopped
2 tablespoons butter
1/2 green pepper, diced
1 diced tomato
2 tablespoons parsley
Salt and pepper to taste
6 eggs

Eggs with Spinach
Ispanaklı Yumurta

1. Wash and drain the spinach. Chop it finely. Bring 2 cups water to a boil, add the spinach, and cook until wilted. Drain and squeeze out all the moisture.

2. Melt the butter in a skillet and sauté the onion for 5 minutes. Add the spinach; cook 10 minutes, stirring frequently. Blend in some salt and pepper. Clear spaces in the spinach for the eggs. Break 1 egg into each space. Sprinkle with more salt and pepper. Cover and cook 5 minutes until the whites are cooked through. Serve with fresh French bread.

2–3 Servings

1 lb. spinach
Water
4–6 tablespoons butter
1 small onion, chopped
Salt and pepper to taste
4–6 eggs

Eggs with Potatoes
Yumurtalı Patates

Pan-fry the potatoes in 4 tablespoons or more butter. When golden brown, add a little salt and then pour in the beaten eggs. Cook, stirring constantly, until the eggs are cooked through. Sprinkle pepper on top and serve.

2 Servings

2 potatoes, cut as for French fries
4 tablespoons or more butter
Salt
4 eggs, beaten
Pepper

Eggs with Tomatoes and Peppers
Domatesli Yeşil Biberli Yumurta

Sauté the tomatoes and peppers in butter until they are soft. Sprinkle with some salt and stir in the beaten eggs. Cook, stirring constantly, until the eggs are cooked through.

2-3 Servings

2 large ripe tomatoes, chopped
1 bell pepper or 2 hot chili
  peppers, chopped
2 tablespoons butter
Salt
6 eggs, beaten

Eggs with Yogurt Sauce
Çilbir

1. Beat the salt into the yogurt with a wire whisk. Set it somewhere to warm up slightly.

2. Poach the eggs. Place them on a heated plate and pour the yogurt over the top.

3. Melt the butter in a small pan. Stir in the paprika or cayenne and heat until bubbly. Pour over the eggs and yogurt. Serve immediately.

VARIATION: 1 clove mashed garlic may be added to the yogurt.

2 Servings

1 cup yogurt
Salt to taste
4 eggs
2 tablespoons butter
1/4 teaspoon paprika or cayenne

Fish and Seafood

Perhaps the simplest fish dinner to be found in Istanbul is that offered by the fishermen themselves, perched in their boats tied up at the side of the Galata Bridge, a pontoon bridge built in 1913 that somehow defies all predictions of imminent collapse. The fishermen fry their catch in a pan of sizzling oil, sandwich pieces of fish in half a loaf of fresh warm bread, and reach up to pass this simple but nourishing meal to eager customers waiting on the pier. They provide one of the most colorful sights in the bustling district of Galata, which is possibly the liveliest area in all Istanbul.

One step up in the hierarchy of places to eat fish are the modest restaurants hidden beneath the Galata Bridge. For a reasonable sum, the diner at one of these restaurants can have his pick of the ten to fifteen varieties that make up the day's catch. As he eats he can watch the steamers coming in and heading for the Asiatic shore of Istanbul and the islands in the Sea of Marmara.

People requiring a greater degree of sophistication must travel to one of the fish restaurants that line the shore of the Bosporus from Bebek to the mouth of the Black Sea. When the weather is warm, the customers are served outdoors, and the pleasure of a leisurely meal in one of these restaurants is enhanced by the matchless view of the sparkling waters of the Bosporus and the green hills of Anatolia beyond.

At such a fine restaurant, dinner begins with a good variety of *mezes*: sizzling hot pieces of cheese *börek*, fragrant crescents of melon, *dolmas* stuffed with rice, pine nuts, and currants and, glistening with olive oil and lemon juice, perhaps some paper-thin slices of smoked sturgeon. Then comes the main course, the fish: *uskumru*, dipped in eggs and flour and pan-fried, then served on a bed of onions and parsley; or juicy pieces of swordfish charcoal-broiled on skewers; maybe milky fillets of sea bass, steamed and masked with a béchamel sauce, given a light topping of grated cheese, and held under the broiler just long enough for the cheese to melt. The famous fish delicacies available in Istanbul number in the hundreds. The variety, indeed, seems unlimited; the Bosporus alone is said to contain sixty varieties of fish, among them some of the best fish in the world.

No discussion of the pleasures of fish in Istanbul would be complete without mentioning the fish markets. Again, the simplest are situated along the Golden Horn, close to the Galata Bridge. They consist of little more than a series of open stalls offering their wares on large trays painted bright red and green and set at an angle in vivid rows. These stalls are close to other markets and the baritone voices of the fish vendors proclaiming the merits of their fish are intermingled with a lively cacophony of urban noise.

But wherever bought or consumed, fish in Turkey is a food unbelievably tasty to those who encounter it for the first time.

Among the recipes offered in this chapter, those for grilled fish, fish plaki (fish simmered with vegetables), mussel plaki, and baked bass masked with béchamel sauce will probably give the best results. Recipes for fish soup and different fish sauces, like garlic sauce, are also particularly worth trying.

Cold Prawns in Lemon Dressing
Karides Limon Salçalı

1. Bring to a boil 2 to 3 cups water and 1 teaspoon salt. Add the prawns. Cook 4 to 8 minutes, depending on the size of the prawns. Do not overcook. Cool in cooking liquid. Drain, shell, and devein the prawns. Place them on a platter and allow them to cool.

2. In a bowl, blend together the olive oil, lemon juice, mustard, and salt to taste. Mix well with a fork. Pour over the prawns. Sprinkle with parsley. Serve cold.

3–4 Servings

1 1/2 lbs. raw prawns, unshelled
Salt
1/3 cup olive oil
1/3 cup lemon juice
1/2 teaspoon dry mustard
1/2 cup chopped parsley

Mussels Plaki
Midye Plâkisi

1. Scrub the mussels with a brush and rinse in cold water several times. Pull and remove the beards. Discard the ones that are already open. Cover the mussels with warm, salted water; let stand 5 minutes and drain. With a bowl underneath to catch all the liquid, open the mussels by inserting a sharp knife between the shells and running it along the flat edge. Remove the mussels, discard the shells. Strain and measure the mussel liquid, add water, if necessary, to make 1 cup.

2. Heat the oil in a heavy pan; sauté the onions until they are just beginning to brown. Add the carrots, potatoes, celery root, and garlic and sauté 2 or 3 minutes. Add 1 cup of mussel liquid, sugar, and salt. Cover and simmer until the vegetables are tender. Add more mussel liquid if necessary to cook the vegetables. Remove the lid. Add the tomatoes, sprinkle in the flour, and blend well. Cook until almost all liquid is absorbed. Stir in the mussels and cook 5 minutes more. Stir in the parsley and remove from heat. Serve cold, sprinkled with lemon juice.

6 Servings

50–60 mussels (about 4 1/2 lbs.)
1/2 cup finest virgin olive oil.
2 small onions, finely chopped
1 cup diced carrots
1 cup diced potatoes
1 cup peeled and diced celery
  root
4–6 cloves garlic, cut
  lengthwise into quarters
1 teaspoon sugar

Salt to taste
Water
1 large or 2 medium tomatoes,
** diced**
1 teaspoon all-purpose flour
1 cup chopped parsley

Fish Plaki
Balık Plâkisi

1. Wash and drain the fish steaks. Sprinkle with a little salt and set them aside.

2. Heat the olive oil and sauté the onions 3 or 4 minutes. Add the celery root, potatoes, carrot, and garlic; sauté 7 to 10 minutes. Stir in the tomatoes and cook 2 minutes longer. Add the bay leaves, 1 teaspoon salt, sugar, and 1/4 cup water. Cover and simmer 20 minutes or until the vegetables are barely tender. Check the level of the liquid occasionally and add more hot water, a small amount at a time, if necessary.

3. Place the fish steaks in a large pot. Spoon the vegetables and all their oil and sauce over the fish. On top, sprinkle half the parsley and arrange the lemon wedges. Pour about 1/2 cup hot water over all. Cover and simmer 20 to 25 minutes or until the fish and vegetables are done. Remove from heat. Sprinkle the juice of 1 lemon and the remaining parsley over the top. Serve warm or cold with lemon wedges.

6 Servings

2 lbs. striped bass or grey
** mullet, or any good fish, cut**
** into steaks 1-inch thick**
Salt
1 1/2–2 onions, sliced paper-thin

1/2 cup olive oil
3/4 cup cubed celery root
2 new potatoes, peeled and
  cubed
1 diced carrot
5 cloves garlic, cut lengthwise
  into quarters
2 ripe tomatoes, diced
2 bay leaves
1/2 teaspoon sugar
Water
1 cup chopped parsley
Juice of 1 lemon
1 lemon, cut in wedges

Poached Fish Masked with Mayonnaise
Mayonezli Balık

For a very special presentation of poached fish, prepare homemade mayonnaise and give the fish and mayonnaise an elegant shape. Then decorate it fancifully with pipings of mayonnaise forced through a pastry bag, tiny pieces of pimento, black olives, and parsley. The egg yolks, olive oil, and lemon juice must be at room temperature before you start to make the mayonnaise.

1. Clean the fish without removing head and tail. Wash, pat dry, and cut into 2 pieces. Put the fish in a bowl, sprinkle with a little salt and the lemon juice and set aside 30 minutes.

2. Put the fish in a pan with the onion, carrot, garlic, salt, peppercorns, bay leaves, and enough water to barely cover the fish. Cover; bring it to a boil and simmer 7 to 8 minutes or until the fish is cooked. Remove the pan from the heat and cool the fish in the fish stock. When cool, drain first, then skin and bone the fish, keeping it in large flakes.

3. Shape the pieces of fish into the form of a whole fish and spread the mayonnaise evenly over it, keeping some of it for decoration. Decorate as desired.

MAYONNAISE:
Rinse a mixing bowl in hot water and dry it. Measure out the lemon juice and olive oil. Put the egg yolks, mustard and salt in the warm bowl and beat them with a wire whisk until they are thick. Beat in half of the olive oil, very slowly, dripping it in from the point of a fork. Still beating constantly, add the remaining olive oil alternately with the lemon juice. Do not stop beating until you have a thick mayonnaise.

4 Servings

2 lb. halibut, seabass, or turbot
Salt
Juice of 1 lemon
1 onion, cut into halves
1 carrot, cut into halves
2 cloves garlic
1/2 teaspoon peppercorns
2 bay leaves

MAYONNAISE:
1/2 cup lemon juice
1 cup olive oil
3 egg yolks
1/2 teaspoon dry mustard
1/2 teaspoon salt

Fish Baked with Tomatoes and Garlic
Domatesli Balık Fırında

1. Wash the fish and drain it. Sprinkle it with a little salt and lemon juice. Set it aside for 30 minutes.

2. Sauté the onions and garlic lightly in 1/4 cup of the olive oil. Add the tomatoes and parsley and continue cooking for 2 or 3 minutes. Stir in the bay leaves, paprika, salt, and sugar and set aside.

3. Butter a baking dish and arrange half the sautéed vegetables on the bottom. Arrange the fish on top of the vegetables. Spread the remaining vegetables over the fish. Combine the 1/4 cup olive oil, and lemon juice and pour over all. Bake, covered, at 350° for 30 minutes. Uncover and continue baking 10 minutes or until the fish is done.

4–6 Servings

**2 lbs. cod, halibut, or haddock
   fillets or steaks**
Salt and lemon juice
2 chopped onions
2–3 cloves garlic, mashed
1/2 cup olive oil
4 chopped tomatoes
1/2 cup chopped parsley
2 bay leaves
1 teaspoon paprika
1/2 teaspoon sugar
Juice of 1 lemon

Sea Bass Masked with Sauce

Beyaz Salçalı Levrek

Individual baking dishes of sea bass, shrimp, and mushrooms in cheese sauce, topped with melted cheese and served sizzling.

1. Clean the fish and cut into 2 fillets. Reserve the head, tail, and bones. Grease a small saucepan or pot with 1 tablespoon butter and arrange the fillets in it. Sprinkle with a little salt. Set aside.

2. Put the fish head, tail, and bones in a pan with the carrot, onion, parsley stems, bay leaves, and some salt. Add just enough water (about 3 cups) to cover. Simmer, uncovered, for 1 hour. Strain the stock and set aside.

3. Spread the mushrooms on top of the fish fillets. Pour in the fish stock and cook over medium-high heat 15 to 20 minutes. Remove the fish from the pan and set aside. Boil the fish stock and mushrooms until the liquid is reduced to 1/2 cup. Strain and reserve the stock and the mushrooms.

4. Melt 2 tablespoons butter in a saucepan. Blend in the flour and stir 2 to 3 minutes over medium heat. Gradually pour in the hot milk and the fish stock, stirring vigorously with a wire whisk, until the sauce thickens. Reduce the heat to low. Cut the remaining butter into pieces the size of chick-peas. Add them, one at a time, to the sauce, stirring well after each addition. Blend in 1/4 cup of the cheese. Add salt to taste and remove from heat.

5. Break the fish into small pieces and combine it with the mushrooms, shrimp, and half the sauce and place in a buttered casserole or in 4 buttered individual baking dishes. Spread the remaining sauce over the fish. Sprinkle 1/4 cup cheese evenly on top. Immediately before serving, place it under the broiler just long enough for the cheese to melt and turn golden brown.

4 Servings

1 2- or 3-lb. bass (or any good
**   white fish)**
1/2 cup plus 1 tablespoon butter
Salt
1 small carrot, chopped
1 small onion, chopped
Stems of 1 bunch parsley
2-3 bay leaves
Water
1/4 lb. mushrooms, chopped
2 tablespoons all-purpose flour
1 cup hot milk
1/3 cup grated kasseri or
**   Romano cheese**
1/4 lb. cooked shrimp

Stuffed Mackerel
Uskumru Dolması

To prepare this delicacy the fish has to be eviscerated without cutting the belly and then the flesh and the bones have to be squeezed out carefully so that the skin is left intact.

1. Clean the fish, cut the heads off behind the gills, and remove the entrails by inserting two fingers through the opening made where the head was removed. Wash the fish several times and dry. Break the back bones 1/2 inch above the tail. Rub the fish firmly upward from the tail between the thumb and forefinger trying to loosen its skin from the flesh. Finally, when the flesh is loose, squeeze out the flesh and bones by forcing them upward from the tail. The aim is to leave the skin intact. Remove the bones, mince the fish meat and set aside. Reserve the skins.

2. Heat the olive oil in a pan and cook the onions 15 to 20 minutes. Stir in the pine nuts, walnuts, raisins, set aside fish meat, cinnamon, allspice, salt, and pepper, and cook 5 minutes longer stirring over medium heat. Stir in the dill and parsley, and remove from the heat and cool.

3. Stuff the emptied fish skin firmly with the filling described above. Coat each one first with flour, dip in the eggs, coat with the bread crumbs, and place on a platter.

4. Heat the oil until hot. Fry the fish until nicely brown on all sides. Place on a paper towel to drain the excess oil. Transfer on to a serving platter. Serve cold.

6 Servings

3 lbs. whole mackerel
1/2 cup finest virgin olive oil
5 small onions finely chopped
4 heaping tablespoons pine nuts
1/4 cup ground walnuts
4 tablespoons raisins
1/2 teaspoon cinnamon
1/2 teaspoon allspice
Salt and freshly ground pepper
1/4 cup fresh dill, finely chopped
1/4 cup parsley, finely chopped
1 cup all-purpose flour
4 eggs
1-2 cups bread crumbs
Oil for frying

Fried Fish
Balık Kızartma

Arrange the fish on a bed of paper-thin onion slices blended with chopped parsley and pass the sauce of your choice. Those who like garlic will especially enjoy the excellent garlic sauce.

Clean the fish and drain it. Dip it in flour and fry it in hot olive oil. Serve it hot with either of the following two sauces.

GARLIC SAUCE:
Soak the French bread in water and squeeze it dry. Set aside. Peel the garlic cloves. Pound them in a mortar with some salt until thoroughly mashed. Combine them with the olive oil. Stir in the vinegar. Add the bread. Blend thoroughly. This makes almost 2 cups sauce. It can be kept in the refrigerator for several days.

LEMON SAUCE:
Combine all the ingredients and blend well.

4–6 Servings

2 lbs. fish of your choice
Flour
Olive oil for frying
2 large onions, thinly sliced
1 cup chopped parsley

GARLIC SAUCE:
5 slices French bread, crusts
  removed
1 whole head garlic
1 teaspoon salt
1 cup olive oil
1/4 cup vinegar

LEMON SAUCE:
1/4 **cup olive oil**
1/4 **cup lemon juice**
1/2 **cup chopped parsley**
Salt to taste

Grilled Fish
Izgara Balık

Mackerel, cod steaks, butterfish fillets, and king fish are all delicious prepared this way. Whichever you use, serve it hot on a bed of paper-thin onion slices mixed with plenty of chopped parsley.

1. Clean the fish. Sprinkle it with a little salt and set it aside.

2. Using a fork, mix the olive oil with the lemon juice and salt. Brush the fish generously, inside and out, with the sauce. Place it in a non-metal dish and pour the remaining sauce over it. Arrange the onion rings and bay leaves on top. Marinate 1 hour or longer.

3. Arrange the fish on a well-greased grill 3 inches above a hot charcoal fire. Cook, basting frequently with the marinade, 5 to 10 minutes on each side, just until the fish flakes easily. If desired, sprinkle it with additional lemon juice and olive oil immediately before serving.

4–6 Servings

2 lbs. fish
Salt
1 onion, sliced in rings
3–4 bay leaves

LEMON OLIVE OIL MARINADE:
1/3 **cup olive oil**
Juice of 1 lemon
1/4 **teaspoon or more salt**

Grilled Whole Sea Bass or Perch
Levrek Izgara

1. Combine the olive oil with lemon juice, thyme leaves and salt. Add enough bread crumbs to make a thick paste. Blend well. Coat the fish evenly with this paste, put it in a deep dish, and allow to stand 3 or 4 hours in the refrigerator.

2. Light a charcoal fire and when the coals are red-hot, spread them out. Set the grill high above the fire and cook the fish very slowly, about 30 minutes on each side. Serve hot.

3–4 Servings

1 whole sea bass or perch,
   2–3 lbs., cleaned
3/4 cup olive oil
Juice of 1 lemon
1 teaspoon thyme leaves
1 teaspoon salt
Bread crumbs

Grilled Swordfish
Kılıç Balığı Izgara

1. Clean the fish. Sprinkle it with a little salt and set it aside.

2. Using a fork, mix together the olive oil, lemon juice, onion juice, paprika, and salt.

3. Place the fish in a nonmetal dish and pour the marinade over it. Arrange the bay leaves on top. Marinate 5 or 6 hours.

4. Put the fish steaks on a well-greased grill 3 inches above a hot charcoal fire. Cook, basting frequently with the marinade, 5 minutes on each side or just until the fish flakes easily. Serve hot with Lemon Sauce, p. 77.

4 Servings

Note: To obtain onion juice, slice 1 or 2 onions. Put the slices in a bowl, sprinkle with salt, and let stand 10 minutes. Squeeze the slices by the handfuls to press out the onion juice. Strain, discard the onion slices.

2 lbs. swordfish steaks,
  1/2-inch thick
Salt
Lemon Sauce, p. 77

LEMON-ONION MARINADE:
1/3 cup olive oil
1/3 cup lemon juice
4 tablespoons onion juice
2 teaspoons paprika
1/2 teaspoon salt
8 bay leaves

Grilled Swordfish on Skewers
Kılıç Balığı Şişte

1. Prepare the Lemon-Onion Marinade, p. 78
2. Marinate the cubes of swordfish in the sauce for 5 hours or longer.
3. Thread the fish on skewers alternately with the tomatoes, pieces of pepper, and little onions. Place the skewers on a well-greased grill 3 inches above a hot charcoal fire. Cook, basting frequently with the marinade, 5 minutes on each side. Serve with Lemon Sauce.

4 Servings

2 lbs. swordfish, cut into
  1 1/2-inch cubes

Cherry tomatoes
Bell peppers, cut into squares
Stewing onions
Lemon-Onion Marinade, p. 79
Lemon Sauce, p. 77

Sardines Grilled in Bay Leaves or Vine Leaves
Balık Asma Yaprağında Izgara

1. Clean the sardines. Sprinkle them with salt and set aside.

2. Prepare the marinade and pour it over the sardines. Arrange the onion rings on top. Set aside for at least 1 hour.

3. If using grape leaves, rinse them and pat dry. Brush with the marinade. Roll one roughly around each sardine. Brush with marinade.

4. Set a greased grilling rack 3 inches above a hot charcoal fire. Cook the sardines in leaves on it 5 minutes on each side or until done. Serve hot with lemon juice.

4 Servings

2 lbs. fresh sardines
Salt
Lemon-Olive Oil Marinade, p. 77
1 onion cut into rings
1/2 jar vine leaves or a handful
    bay leaves

Sea Bass en Papillote
Levrek Kağıtta

1. Blend together the olive oil, lemon juice,

onion juice, garlic, parsley, thyme, and salt. Place the fish in a non-metal dish and pour the marinade over it. Marinate it for 3 hours.

2. Spread out a sheet of parchment or a double-layer of wax paper. Place the fish in the center and pour some of the marinade over it. Fold carefully into a package to seal the fish and sauce inside. Place on a baking sheet; sprinkle with a little water. Bake at 375° for about 30 to 40 minutes until the fish is done.

3-4 Servings

Note: See page 79 about ob-
taining the onion juice.

1 whole sea bass, 2 lbs., cleaned
1/3 cup olive oil
1/4 cup lemon juice
2 tablespoons onion juice, page 79
2 cloves garlic, mashed
1/2 cup chopped parsley
1/4 teaspoon thyme leaves
Salt to taste

Sea Bass Fillets en Papillote
Levrek Pandeli

This simple dish is prepared at the famous Pandeli restaurant in Istanbul's spice bazaar. Home-grown tomatoes should really be used here because they have so much more flavour than the common grocery-store variety.

Butter a sheet of parchment or a double-layer of wax paper. Arrange the fish fillets in the center; sprinkle them with salt and pepper. On top of each fillet, set a pat of butter and a thick slice of tomato. Fold carefully into a package so that the fish and all the juices will be sealed inside. Place on a baking sheet; sprinkle with a little water. Bake at 400° for 20 minutes.

Sea bass fillets
Butter
Tomatoes, very red and juicy
Salt and pepper

Meats

Contrary to popular notions in the West, *kebabs* come in about fifty different varieties, including broiled, roasted, baked, and stewed meat dishes. *Tandır kebab, döner kebab, kuzu çevirme,* and *şiş kebab* are only a few of the dishes that go by the name of kebab. The first of these, *tandır kebab,* probably originated in Central Asia; now it is prepared chiefly in Anatolia, where many restaurants even specialize in it. The meat is cooked in a special oven called a *tandır,* essentially a pit with a charcoal fire burning in the bottom and walls coated with baked clay. Once the meat has been placed inside, the top of the pit is covered, so that the meat gradually cooks to a matchless degree of succulence.

Döner kebab is beginning to become known in the West, but the *döner* served abroad never tastes quite the same as in Turkey. To prepare *döner,* various cuts of lamb interspersed with layers of suet are marinated in onion juice and a variety of spices and then wrapped around a vertical spit that rotates next to a charcoal fire. (In the West, and recently in many places in Turkey, a vertical electrical or gas fire has taken the place of the charcoal, but it never gives the same result.) Thin slices are shaved off the kebab as it cooks and served on individual beds of *pide* (flat bread) or rice, topped with a roasted long, green pepper.

Kuzu çevirme, as its name suggests, consists of a spring lamb roasted whole on a spit turned slowly over a smoldering charcoal fire.

Şiş kebab, the best known of all Turkish kebabs, is, of course, cubes of meat threaded on skewers with tomatoes, onions, and green peppers and cooked over charcoal.

Still other kebabs require the meat to be chopped up finely (not ground), using two sharp knives moving over the meat in opposite directions. This method of chopping the meat gives it a special and succulent flavor. Once chopped, the meat is mixed with different spices broiled and served in different ways according to the kind of kebab desired, such as *Adana kebab* or *Urfa kebab.*

Another important class of kebab consists of what might be called meat stews: meat chopped into small cubes and stewed with different vegetables, such as eggplant kebab. In some cases, egg and lemon sauce may be added to the stew.

In preparing the stews, the cook always follows three basic rules; failure to do so would significantly alter the result. First, the meat is never left in large chunks; it is cut into small cubes no larger than one inch. Second, the meat is first covered with a little butter and onions and then cooked without any liquid added for about twenty or thirty minutes over medium heat. This permits the meat to release all its natural juices and then to reabsorb them, so that it begins to brown in its own fat and juice. If a longer cooking time is needed, additional liquids are added at this point. (Such liquids must be hot and are always added in small quantities, while the meat is simmering over low heat.) Third, the meat and vegetables are never left swimming in water, which would cause them to boil while cooking. Instead, they simmer in a small amount of liquid, which may be supplemented only gradually.

Next in our survey of meat dishes come several categories of dish involving the use of minced meat. The first is *köfte*: minced meat mixed with spices before being grilled, fried, or steamed, and—in some cases—served with different sauces. Another category comprises *dolmas*: different vegetables stuffed with a mixture of minced meat, chopped onion, rice, and herbs and spices and simmered. Finally, there is minced meat cooked with different legumes or vegetables, a very big category that includes *musakka* and *karnıyarık*.

A final word concerning meat is that in Turkey lamb is the most favored meat, and it certainly tastes different from its counterpart in Europe and the United States. In fact, foreigners have been heard to joke that Turkish lamb is a quite different species. A pair of Turkish spring lamb chops, sprinkled with salt, pepper, and a whiff of thyme, then broiled or grilled on charcoal, can be an unexpected delight. In accordance with the Turkish preference for lamb, most recipes in this section of the book specify the use of lamb. Beef, however, is an acceptable second choice, and needless to say, one can always experiment with different cuts of meat.

The dishes covered in this section all contain meat to widely varying degrees. Nevertheless, irrespective of the amount of meat used, they are usually served as main dishes accompanied by bread, pilav, or pasta (See section on Pilav, page 204, and Pasta, page 222) and salad, and they are always served hot. Very often, they are followed by an olive oil dish (see section on *Mezeler*, page 37 and Vegetables, page 161), which is always served cold, or a *börek* (see section on *Böreks*, page 230).

Finally, I should like to point out that most of these dishes, with the exception of broiled kebabs, can be reheated the next day and will taste even better.

Kebab with Yogurt
Yoğurtlu Kebab

Succulent cubes of lamb on a bed of flat bread

with tomato sauce, pepper-seasoned butter, and yogurt—this dish is worth all the effort it calls for. If you have the time, do prepare the authentic *pide* dough on page 260 and ignore the instructions below about the frozen loaves. Either bread may be prepared in advance and warmed up while the meat is cooking. Authentically, for this kebab, the meat is threaded on skewers and charcoal broiled like Şiş kebab for best results. However, for a faster and simpler version, it can be stir-fried and will still taste very good.

1. Put the onion slices in a bowl; sprinkle them with a little salt. Squeeze them, a handful at a time, in the palm of one hand to press out the onion juice. Add the lamb cubes, the olive oil, vinegar, thyme, more salt, and pepper to taste and mix well. Refrigerate overnight, if possible, or 4 to 5 hours. Leave at room temperature for 2 hours before cooking.

2. Prepare the bread. Preheat the oven to 550° for 20 minutes. Also preheat the pan(s) in which the bread will bake in the lower-middle section of the oven. An earthenware baking surface works best; if not available, use two shallow aluminum pans, about 10 inches by 14 inches. Make sure that the bread is completely thawed.

3. Take the preheated pan(s) from the oven; quickly sprinkle with cold water. Place one piece of dough in the pan, moisten your fingertips, and quickly flatten and enlarge it with swift jabs of the fingers distributed all across the dough. You want to end up with a thin, oval-shaped sheet of dough that nearly fills the pan. It will be marked with craterlike mounds and hollows left by your fingerprints. (These hollows should be as deep as possible without actually making holes in the dough, and the mounds should be no higher than 1/5 inch. Spread out the other piece of dough using the same process, in a separate pan. Bake only about 4 minutes. The flat breads should come out soft and pale in color. Cool for 5 to 10 minutes, then cut the bread into bite-sized pieces. Divide the bread among 4 serving plates. Cover the plates with foil and keep in the warm oven until everything else is ready.

4. Cut the meat into 3/4-inch cubes and thread it on skewers, if you will be cooking over charcoal.

5. Prepare the tomato sauce in a saucepan, melt 1 tablespoon butter. Cook the diced tomatoes, gently mashing them with a fork while they simmer. After about 5 minutes, add the tomato paste and the water to make a sauce; stir a few minutes. Add the garlic and continue stirring and cooking 1 minute. Add the vinegar and remove the pan from the heat. Cover and keep very warm.

6. Melt 6 tablespoons butter. Remove from heat. Have the paprika or cayenne next to the pan.

7. Melt the remaining 9 tablespoons butter in a small saucepan. Keep warm.

8. Beat the yogurt to a creamy consistency. Keep it on the stove near the two pans of melted butter and the tomato sauce.

9. Cook the lamb. If you are using a charcoal fire, broil 3 inches away from red coals, only 2 to 3 minutes on each side. Turn frequently, avoiding flames. Do not overcook or the meat will dry out and lose all its flavor. It should be juicy, tender, and pinkish inside.

If cooking on top of the stove, heat a wok or heavy skillet over high heat; butter it just to coat. Add the meat and stir-fry in the Chinese manner, allowing it to cook very fast. This should take 5 to 7 minutes. It should be well browned but pinkish inside.

10. Take the plates containing the bread from the oven. Spoon equal amounts of the 9 tablespoons of melted butter over the bread. Then pour equal amounts of the tomato sauce over the buttered bread. Pour some of the yogurt over the sauce, but don't use quite all the yogurt. Place the meat on the yogurt. Now pour 1 or 2 tablespoons yogurt over each serving of meat. Add the paprika or cayenne to the 4 tablespoons melted butter; heat until bubbly and pour over the yogurt. Serve immediately, or you may place the plates under the broiler for a second, just long enough to make the yogurt sizzle.

4 Servings

2 lbs. boneless leg of lamb, cut into 1/2-inch cubes (for stir-frying), or 3/4-inch cubes (for charcoal broiling)
1 onion, sliced paper-thin
Salt
1/4 cup olive oil
1 tablespoon vinegar
1/4–1/2 teaspoon dried thyme leaves
Coarsely ground pepper to taste
2 loaves frozen white bread dough (1/3-lb. each), thawed
1 cup butter
4 large ripe tomatoes, diced
1/2 cup water
4 tablespoons tomato paste
2 large cloves garlic, mashed
2 teaspoons vinegar
Paprika or cayenne to taste
2 cups yogurt, at room temperature

Lamb in Phyllo
Talaş Kebabı

Talaş kebabı is truly traditional and elegant. It is a perfect choice for dinner guests, for it is also relatively easy to prepare.

1. Trim the meat, discarding fat. Cut it into very thin strips 1/4 inch by 1/2 inch by 1/4 to 1/8 inch thick. Cut the onions into halves, then slice them very thinly.

2. Heat a heavy skillet or wok over high heat until hot. Stir in the meat, onions, and shallots with 2 tablespoons butter. Stir-fry 3 to 4 minutes or a little longer, until the meat releases its moisture, reabsorbs it, and browns lightly in its own juice and fat. Stir in the tomatoes and mashed garlic; cook 1 to 2 minutes. Remove from heat. Add the minced garlic, parsley, thyme, salt, and pepper. Mix thoroughly.

3. Melt the rest of the butter. Have a pastry brush ready. Preheat the oven to 400°.

4. Unfold the phyllo sheets. Take 16 sheets; rewrap and store the rest. Work with 2 sheets at a time, keeping the other sheets well covered to prevent them from drying out. Spread 2 sheets open in a double layer on a flat surface; brush with melted butter. Lay another double layer directly on top of the first; brush with butter. Fold in half to form a rectangle that is nearly equilateral. Brush the new top layer with butter. Spread 1/4 of the meat filling in the middle covering an area about 4 inches by 5 inches. As if you were wrapping a package, fold one longer side of the pastry over the filling, brush with butter. Fold the opposite side over and brush with butter. Fold over one end, butter; fold over the other and butter it too. Place seam side down on a baking dish and brush the top with generous amounts of butter. Repeat the process with the remaining 12 sheets and filling. Glaze the tops with the egg yolk. Bake 20 minutes. If the tops are browning too rapidly, cover with a sheet of foil during the last 5 to 10 minutes of baking. Serve hot.

2–4 Servings (4 packages)

1 1/2 lb. boneless lamb (sirloin
   part of the leg)
1/2 cup plus 4 tablespoons butter
2 medium onions
4–5 shallots (optional)
2 medium tomatoes, chopped
2 cloves garlic, mashed
2 cloves garlic, minced
1 cup chopped parsley
1 1/2–2 teaspoons thyme
Salt and pepper to taste
16 sheets thin phyllo pastry
1 egg yolk, lightly beaten
   for glaze

Sultan's Delight
Hünkâr Beğendi

This celebrated dish features a simple lamb stew
served together with an elegant eggplant purée.
It is reputed to have been created for Sultan
Murad IV. Leg of lamb may be used if you cannot
obtain lamb shoulder.

1. Cut the lamb into 3/4-inch cubes and sauté
in 2 tablespoons butter for 3 or 4 minutes over
high heat. Add the onions, cover, and cook over
medium heat, stirring frequently, until the meat
releases its moisture, reabsorbs it, and browns in
its own juice and fat 20 minutes. Stir in the tomatoes. Turn heat to low. Add some salt and pepper.
Stir in 3/4 cup hot meat stock or water. Cover and
simmer for 1 to 1 1/2 hours, until the meat is tender.
As it cooks, check the liquid occasionally. Small
amounts of hot water, 1/3 cup at a time, may be
added if needed. The meat should be moist and
in ample sauce, but the mixture should not be
runny and watery.
2. Place the unpeeled eggplants directly on a

gas burner over a high flame or over a charcoal fire. Turn frequently to cook on all sides. They are done when the skin is charred and black and the eggplants are thoroughly soft when pierced with a fork. Cool slightly. Peel them, carefully removing all the pieces of burnt black skin. Wipe the eggplant clean with wet hands. Place them in a bowl.

3. Melt 4 tablespoons butter in a saucepan; blend in the flour and stir 2 to 3 minutes over medium heat. Take small pieces of the eggplant by hand and squeeze out all the water. Stir into the butter and flour mixture. Finish adding the eggplant and beat with a fork over low heat until smooth. Gradually add the hot milk, beating briskly with a wire whisk until smooth and bubbling. When the mixture becomes a smooth paste, stir in the cheese. Correct the seasoning. Remove from heat. Keep warm.

4. Transfer the meat mixture to a platter and serve the eggplant purée next to it.

4 Servings

2 lbs. boneless lamb shoulder
2 tablespoons butter
2 chopped onions
3 diced tomatoes or 1 lb. canned
    tomatoes, drained and
    chopped
Salt and freshly ground pepper
    to taste
2 cups hot meat stock
    or water
2 medium eggplants
3 tablespoons lemon juice

4 tablespoons butter
3 tablespoons all-purpose flour
1 1/2 cups hot milk
1/2 cup grated kasseri cheese
  (if unavailable, substitute
  Roquefort, Romano, or
  Gruyère)

Eggplant Kebab
Patlıcan Kebabı

If lamb shoulder is unavailable, meat from the leg may be used.

1. Cut the stems off the eggplants. Using a vegetable peeler, and peeling lengthwise, remove a strip of skin. Leave the next strip on and continue to peel in this striped fashion. Repeat with the second eggplant. Cut both into 1/2-inch to 3/4-inch cubes. Sprinkle them generously with salt and set aside for at least 3 hours.

2. Cut the lamb into 3/4-inch cubes. In a heavy pot, brown the lamb in butter over high heat. Remove from the pan.

3. Sauté the onions in the same pan. Add the tomatoes and return the meat to the pan. Stir in 1/2 cup hot meat stock, water, or a combination of both and salt and pepper to taste. Cover and simmer over low heat until the meat is tender (1 to 1 1/2 hours, depending on the cut of the meat). As it cooks, check the liquid occasionally. Small amounts of hot water or meat stock, 1/3 cup at a time, may be added if needed.

3. Rinse the eggplant cubes in cold water. Squeeze them in the folds of a clean old kitchen towel, pressing out as much moisture as possible without tearing them. Sauté the eggplant in 1/4 cup or more oil over high heat until golden brown.

Place on a paper towel to drain off the excess oil.

4. Check the meat to make sure it is tender. Stir in the eggplant and the bell pepper. Continue cooking at a simmer 30 to 40 minutes or until the eggplant is tender, adding to the liquid if necessary as before. The dish should be moist and have ample sauce without being runny and watery. Correct the seasoning. Serve with rice pilav.

6 Servings

2 lbs. boneless lamb shoulder
2 medium eggplants
Salt
1–2 tablespoons butter
1 1/2 chopped onions
2 large tomatoes, chopped, or
    1 lb. canned tomatoes,
    drained and chopped
2–2 1/2 cups meat stock or water
Salt and pepper to taste
1/4 cup oil for frying
1 large or 2 medium bell
    peppers, chopped

Eggplant Roulade
Patlıcan Kebabı II

This version of the dish is the way they used to prepare it at the famous Konyalı restaurant in Sirkeci, Istanbul. Again, leg of lamb may be used if lamb shoulder is not available.

1. Cut the stems off the eggplants. Using a vegetable peeler, and peeling lengthwise, remove a strip of skin. Leave the next strip on. Continue to peel in this striped fashion. Repeat with the second eggplant. Cut both in slices, lengthwise,

1/4 inch thick. Cut slices into strips about 1 inch wide. Sprinkle the strips generously with salt and let stand for at least 3 hours.

2. Melt 1 tablespoon butter in a heavy skillet and sauté the lamb for 3 to 4 minutes. Add the chopped onions, cover, and cook over medium heat, stirring frequently, until the meat releases its moisture, reabsorbs it, and browns in its own juice and fat about 20 to 30 minutes. Stir in the chopped tomatoes. Add salt and pepper to taste and 1/2 cup hot meat stock or water, or a combination of the two. Cover and simmer over low heat until the meat is tender (1 to 1 1/2 hours, depending on the cut of the meat). As it cooks, check the liquid occasionally. Small amounts of hot water or meat stock, 1/3 cup at a time, may be added if needed. The meat should be in ample sauce, but the mixture should not be runny.

3. Rinse the eggplant strips in cold water. Dry them in a clean old towel, pressing out as much moisture as possible without tearing. Fry the strips in the oil over high heat or butter until golden brown on both sides.

4. Working on a plate, take 2 strips of eggplant and place one on top of the other to form a cross. Place a tablespoon of the lamb with a little sauce right in the center. Fold the four ends of the eggplant strips over the meat filling, creating a small packet. Place seam side down in a large rectangular baking dish. Repeat the process until all the meat and eggplant have been used. Set a green pepper ring and a tomato slice on top of each packet and pour the remaining tomato sauce over all. Cover and bake at 350° for 30 to 40 minutes. Check occasionally and add small amounts to the liquid if necessary. Serve with pilav.

6 Servings

2 lbs. boneless lamb shoulder, cut into 3/4-inch cubes

2 medium eggplants
Salt
1 tablespoon butter
2 chopped onions
2 tomatoes, chopped, or 1 lb.
  canned tomatoes, drained
  and chopped
Salt and freshly ground pepper
2 cups hot meat stock
  or water
1/4 cup or more oil or butter
  for frying
2 slices tomatoes
2 green peppers, sliced into
  rings

Shish Kebab
Şiş Kebabı

Rice pilav customarily accompanies this well-known dish. Cutting the lamb into smaller-sized cubes, as the Turks do, results in shorter cooking time and vegetables that are not overdone and mushy.

1. Put the lamb cubes in a bowl. Put the onions on top and sprinkle salt over them. Squeeze the onions by the handful to press out their juice. Add the olive oil, vinegar, pepper, and thyme; mix thoroughly. Put the pieces of bell pepper on top, cover with wax paper, and refrigerate overnight. Remove the meat from the refrigerator 1 hour before cooking. Mix well.

2. Thread the meat on the skewers alternately with the pearl onions or onion chunks, green pepper pieces, and tomatoes. Broil over charcoal, 3 inches from red-hot coals, turning the skewers frequently. If the fire is hot enough, cooking takes just 4 to 6 minutes. Be careful not to overcook or the meat will be dry and flavorless. It should be very juicy and pinkish on the inside. Serve immediately. Serve with pilav.

4 Servings

3 lbs. boneless lamb shoulder
   or leg, cut into 1-inch cubes
1 onion, sliced paper-thin
1 1/2 teaspoons salt
1/4 cup olive oil
1 tablespoon vinegar
1 teaspoon coarsely ground
   pepper
1/2 teaspoon thyme leaves
2 green bell peppers, cut into
   1-inch squares
8–16 pearl onions or quarters
   of large onions
8–16 cherry tomatoes

Roast Leg of Lamb
Kuzu Fırında

Serve this with Pilav with Currants and Pine Nuts (page 210) or oven-roasted potatoes.

Let the meat stand at room temperature 2 hours before cooking. Preheat the oven to 450°. Rub the lamb with the cut garlic, salt, pepper, and thyme. Using a thin, sharp knife, insert slivers of garlic deep into the meat. Spread yogurt over the outside in a film. Place meat, fat side up, on a rack in an uncovered pan. Put in the oven and reduce the temperature to 350°. Bake 25 minutes to the pound, or until the internal temperature reaches between 160° and 165°.

6 Servings

1 leg of lamb, about 5 lbs.
3–4 cloves garlic, cut into
  slivers
Salt and coarsely ground
  pepper
2 teaspoons thyme leaves
2 tablespoons yogurt

Loin of Lamb in Phyllo
Kuzu Yufka İçinde

A truly gourmet choice! In some areas, this cut of meat is known as one split half of a saddle of lamb.

1. Mix together the olive oil, lemon juice, and a dash of salt and pepper. Place the lamb in a small bowl and pour the marinade over it. Slice the 1/2 onion, sprinkle it with salt, and squeeze the slices by the handful over the meat to obtain all the onion juice possible; and mix thoroughly. Place the onions on top of the meat. Allow the meat to marinate, refrigerated, 5 to 6 hours or overnight.

2. Briefly sauté the spinach leaves in 1 tablespoon butter just until limp (3 minutes or less); set them aside.

3. Sauté 1 onion, the garlic, and the shallots in 1 or 2 tablespoons butter; cook 5 to 7 minutes and stir in the parsley, thyme, and salt and pepper to taste. Set aside.

4. Sauté the loin of lamb in a little butter until medium-rare. Cut the long piece of meat in two crosswise and set aside.

5. Melt the rest of the butter. Have a pastry brush ready. Preheat the oven to 400°.

6. Unfold the sheets of phyllo dough. Work with 2 sheets at a time, keeping the other sheets covered with a towel to prevent their drying out.

Pick up 2 sheets of the phyllo dough and spread them open in a double layer on a flat surface; brush with melted butter. Lay another double layer directly on top of the first; brush with melted butter. Fold in half to form a rectangle that is nearly equilateral. Brush the new top layer with butter. Spread 4 spinach leaves in the center, covering an area about 3 inches square. Spoon half the onion-parsley mixture over the spinach. On top of that, place 1 piece of the loin of lamb. As if you were wrapping a package, fold one longer side of the pastry dough over the filling; brush with melted butter. Fold the opposite side over and brush with more butter. Fold over one end and butter it, then the other end and butter it, too. Place seam side down on a baking sheet. Brush the top generously with butter. Repeat the process to make an identical packet with the remaining 4 sheets of phyllo dough, spinach leaves, onion-parsley mixture, and piece of lamb loin. Bake in the pre-heated oven for 20 minutes. Serve hot. Leave whole for 2 hungry adults or slice 1/2-inch thick to feed more.

2 Servings

1 loin of lamb (if unavailable, substitute 4 extrathick loin lamb chops), boned and trimmed of fat
1 tablespoon olive oil
1 tablespoon lemon juice
Salt and pepper
1/2 onion
8 leaves fresh spinach
1/2 cup plus 2 tablespoons butter
1 small onion, diced
4 cloves garlic, mashed
4 diced shallots (optional)
1/4 cup chopped parsley
1/2 teaspoon thyme
8 sheets thin phyllo pastry

Lamb Baked on Skewers
Çöp Kebabı

1. Cut the stems off the eggplants. Using a vegetable peeler, and peeling lengthwise, remove a strip of skin; leave the next strip on. Continue to peel in this striped fashion. Repeat with the second eggplant. Cut both eggplants into 3/4-inch cubes. Sprinkle generously with salt and let stand for at least 3 hours.

2. Melt 2 tablespoons butter in a heavy pan and sauté the lamb cubes and onions 2 to 3 minutes over high heat. Add salt to taste. Cover and cook 20 to 30 minutes over medium heat, stirring occasionally, until the meat releases its moisture, reabsorbs it, and browns in its own juice and fat. Chop 2 tomatoes. Add the chopped tomatoes and 1/2 cup hot meat stock or water to the meat. Cover and simmer over low heat until the meat is tender, about 1 to 1 1/2 hours. Check the liquid occasionally and add small quantities, 1/3 cup at a time, hot stock or water as needed. Remove the meat and set aside. Measure the sauce and increase with water or stock to 1 1/2 cups.

3. Rinse the eggplant cubes in cold water. With a clean old kitchen towel squeeze each cube to get out all the water without tearing. Fry in 1/2 cup hot oil over high heat until golden brown on all sides. Remove from pan. Sauté the pieces of green pepper very briefly.

4. Have a large baking dish ready. Assemble the meat, eggplant, green pepper, and tomato sauce next to each other in separate dishes. Cut 2 tomatoes into thin slices. Thread a cube of meat on a skewer, followed by a piece of eggplant and a piece of green pepper. Continue skewering the meat and vegetables and place in the baking dish. Pour the sauce over. Place slices of tomato on top of the skewers, cover, and bake at 400° for 20 minutes, or until the eggplant is tender. Once or twice during that time, open the oven and turn the skewers and baste them with the sauce; add to the liquid if necessary. Finally uncover and bake 5 minutes longer.

3–4 Servings

1 1/2 lbs. boneless lamb
  shoulder, cut into 3/4-inch
  cubes
2 medium eggplants
Salt
2 tablespoons butter
1 1/2 chopped onions
3–4 tomatoes
2 1/2–3 cups hot meat stock
  or water
1/2 cup oil or butter for frying
2 green bell peppers, cut into
  1-inch squares
Salt and pepper to taste
10 bamboo skewers

Lamb with Chard and Dill in Lemon Sauce
Kuzu Kapama

1. Arrange the chard leaves in the bottom of a heavy pot. Spread the onions, carrot, and scallions or green onions on top of the chard. Arrange the meat on top of the vegetables. Mix together 1 cup water, the sugar, salt, and pepper; pour over the vegetables. Dot with the butter. Sprinkle half the dill on top. Cover and cook over low heat 1 to 1 1/2 hours or until the meat is tender.

2. Blend together the egg yolks and flour. Stir in the lemon juice and 1/2 cup broth from the meat and vegetables. Beat well. Stir the lemon sauce and the remainder of the dill into the pot of lamb and vegetables. Cook 5 minutes longer. Serve hot.

3–4 Servings

**2 lbs. lamb shoulder, cut in
  2-inch chunks, or 2 large
  lamb shanks, each cut in half
1 bunch of chard, washed and
  drained
1 onion, cut into eighths
1 carrot, cut into 4 chunks
1 bunch scallions or green
  onions, chopped
1 1/2 cups water
1 teaspoon sugar
Salt and pepper to taste
3 tablespoons butter
1 bunch fresh dill, chopped, or
  1 tablespoon dried dill weed
2 egg yolks
1 tablespoon all-purpose flour
Juice of 1 small lemon**

Lamb in Paper
Kağıt Kebabı

Paper packets of savory lamb, herbs, and vegetables. If you like this dish, you might want to try cooking veal or beef sirloin the same way.

1. Melt 3 tablespoons butter in a heavy skillet and add the meat, onions, and carrots. Cover and cook over medium heat stirring frequently, until the meat releases its moisture, reabsorbs it, and browns in its own juice and fat 20 minutes. Stir in the tomatoes; cook 2 or 3 minutes longer. Blend in the vinegar and half the dill. If the meat is not yet tender, add 1/2 cup hot meat stock or water, cover, and simmer until it is tender.

2. Sauté the potatoes in a small amount of oil until tender. Remove from heat. Mix in the peas, remaining dill, and thyme. Combine the peas and potatoes with the meat. Adjust the seasoning. The mixture should not be runny,but it should have plenty of sauce. If necessary, add a little stock or water.

3. Preheat oven to 375°. Tear off 8 16-inch lengths of wax paper. Fold each in half and have several sheets in front of you. Place one-eighth of the meat and vegetable mixture together with some sauce in the middle of each paper rectangle. Fold closed as you would wrap a package, making firm, secure bundles. Place them on a baking sheet that has been sprinkled with a few tablespoons water. Make sure the sauce will not leak out. Sprinkle water on the tops of the packages and bake for 20 to 25 minutes. Serve still wrapped and hot.

6–8 Servings

**2 lbs. boneless lamb, boned and
  cut into less than 1/2-inch
  cubes**
3 tablespoons butter
2 onions, sliced paper-thin
2 small carrots, diced
3–4 diced tomatoes
1 tablespoon vinegar
**1 bunch fresh dill or
  1 tablespoon dried dill weed**
**3 potatoes, diced
  1/2-inch cubes**
2 tablespoons oil
1 cup slightly cooked peas
1 1/2 cups meat stock or water
2 teaspoons thyme leaves

Lamb with Lemon Sauce
Terbılyeli Haşlama

A very tasty, Turkish version of boiled beef and vegetables.

1. Place the lamb shanks or shoulder in a pan with the onions, carrots, peppercorns, and salt to taste. Add water and bring to a boil. Remove the froth that forms on the surface. Cover and simmer 1 to 1 1/2 hours, until the meat is almost tender. Add the potatoes and cook until tender.

2. Melt 3 tablespoons butter in a saucepan. Stir in the flour and cook over medium heat 3 minutes, stirring constantly. Measure out 3 cups broth from the lamb and vegetables. Gradually add to the flour paste, beating briskly with a wire whisk. Cook until smooth.

3. Beat the egg yolks in a mixing bowl with the lemon juice and about 1 cup of the lamb broth. Slowly add this to the thickened sauce. Heat just to the boiling point and then pour slowly into the lamb and vegetables; blend well. Serve immediately in large individual bowls.

2–3 Servings

2 large lamb shanks (2 1/2 lbs.),
  each cut in half, or lamb
  shoulder, bone in, cut into
  2-inch chunks
1 onion, cut into eighths
3 carrots, cut in half
25 peppercorns
Salt
6 cups water
5 small potatoes
3 tablespoons butter
3 tablespoons all-purpose flour

3 egg yolks
Juice of 1 lemon

Steamed Kebab
İslim Kebabı

1. Cut the stem off the eggplant. Using a vegetable peeler, and peeling lengthwise, remove a strip of skin; leave the next strip on. Continue to peel in this striped fashion. Cut into 1-inch cubes.

2. Arrange the chunks of lamb in the bottom of a heavy pan with a tight-fitting lid. Place the onion chunks over the meat. Add the eggplant cubes. Place the bell pepper over the eggplant and top with the tomatoes. Mix together salt and pepper and 3/4 to 1 cup water. Pour the water over; dot with butter. Cover so that no steam will escape and cook over low heat about 2 hours, until the meat is tender. Serve hot.

4 Servings

2 lbs. lamb shoulder, bone in,
  cut into 6 or 7 pieces
1 medium eggplant
3 onions, quartered
3 bell peppers, chopped
3 chopped tomatoes
Salt and pepper to taste
Water
4 tablespoons butter

Grilled Lamb Chops
Kuzu Pirzolası

1. Pound the lamb chops with a mallet until

they are about 1/5 inch thick. Place in a small bowl.

2. Sprinkle the onion slices with some salt; squeeze in the palm of one hand to release the juice.

3. Place the chops on a plate. Moisten with the olive oil and onion juice, sprinkle with thyme, cover with onions, and let stand 2 hours.

4. Discard the onions. Grill the chops over charcoal, cooking about 2 to 3 minutes on each side. Transfer to a platter and season with salt. Serve hot with fried potatoes or pilav.

4 Servings

2 lbs. loin lamb chops
1 sliced onion
Salt
1 tablespoon olive oil
1 tablespoon thyme leaves

KÖFTES

Grilled *Köfte*
Izgara Köfte

Serve these tiny meat patties with flat bread and thin slices of onion mixed with chopped parsley.

Grind the meat twice if you have a meat grinder. Mix the meat with the egg, onion, salt, and pepper. Knead with your hands for 5 to 10 minutes, until the consistency of a paste. Take walnut-sized pieces, shape into round balls, and flatten them. Grill over charcoal, 2 inches from the coals, turning the *köftes* once or twice. Serve immediately.

3 Servings

1 lb. medium-fat ground lamb,
  or 1/2 lb. each lean ground beef
  and medium-fat ground lamb,
  or 1 lb. ground chuck
1 egg
1 small onion, grated
Salt and freshly ground pepper

Köfte on Skewers
Şiş Köfte

You will need flat skewers for these. Serve with flat bread and thin slices of onion mixed with chopped parsley.

Grind the meat twice if you have a meat grinder. Mix the meat with the egg, onion, salt, and pepper. Knead with your hands for 10 minutes, until the consistency of a paste. Take an egg-sized piece of meat and wrap it around a skewer to form a roll rather like a hot dog. With wet hands, squeeze the meat gently against the skewer to make it stick. Prepare about 6 skewers in all. Cook over charcoal 3 to 4 minutes, turning the skewers to cook the *köfte* evenly. Sprinkle with sumac, if desired. Serve immediately.

3 Servings

1 lb. medium-fat ground lamb,
  or 1/2 lb. each ground beef and
  medium-fat ground lamb,
  or 1 lb. ground chuck
1 egg
1 small onion, grated

Salt and freshly ground pepper
2–3 tablespoons sumac
   (optional)
Thinly sliced onion and
   chopped parsley for garnish

Köfte in Broth
Sulu Köfte

1. Mix together the meat, rice, onion, salt, and pepper. Knead with your hands for 5 minutes. Shape this mixture into little balls, 1/2 inch in diameter.

2. Spread the parsley on a plate. Roll the meatballs to coat them with the parsley flakes.

3. In a large saucepan, bring to a boil the water, 1 teaspoon salt, and the butter. Add the meatballs and potatoes. Cover and simmer 20 minutes or until done. Remove from heat and serve in soup bowls.

3 Servings

3/4 **lb. lean ground beef**
1/3 **cup uncooked rice**
1 small onion, grated
Salt and freshly ground pepper
   to taste
1 cup finely chopped parsley
4 cups water
1 tablespoon butter
3 potatoes, peeled and cut into
   1/2-**inch cubes**

Köfte with Lemon Sauce
Terbiyeli Sulu Köfte

1. Mix together the meat, rice, onion, salt, and pepper. Knead with your hands for 5 minutes. Shape this mixture into little balls, 1/2 inch in diameter.

2. Spread the parsley on a plate. Roll the meatballs to coat them with the parsley flakes.

3. In a large saucepan, bring to a boil 2 1/2 to 3 cups water, 1 teaspoon salt, and the butter. Drop in the meatballs, cover, and simmer 20 minutes or until done.

4. Beat the egg yolks with the lemon juice. Gradually add 1/2 cup broth from the meatballs. Slowly pour the sauce into the simmering meatballs and mix. Bring just to the boiling point. Remove from heat and serve in soup bowls.

3 Servings

3/4 lb. lean ground beef
1/3 cup uncooked rice
1 small onion, grated
Salt and freshly ground pepper
1 cup parsley, finely chopped
2 1/2–3 cups water
1 tablespoon butter
4 egg yolks
Juice of one lemon

Gardener's *Köfte*
Bahçıvan Köftesi

Frozen peas may be used instead of fresh ones. Add them in the last few minutes of cooking instead of with the other vegetables.

1. Cut the stem off the eggplant. Using a vegetable peeler, and peeling lengthwise, remove a strip of skin; leave the next strip on. Continue to peel in this striped fashion. Cut into 3/4-inch cubes. Sprinkle generously with salt and set aside at least 3 hours.

2. Soak the bread in water. Squeeze it dry and crumble. Add it to the meat along with the onion, eggs, allspice, dill or parsley, salt, and pepper. Knead with your hands for 5 minutes. Take walnut-sized pieces, shape into round balls, and flatten them.

3. Heat the oil in a frying pan. Fry the potatoes briefly; remove from pan and set aside.

4. Rinse the eggplant in cold water. Using a clean old kitchen towel, squeeze out all the water without tearing. Fry in the hot oil over high heat until golden brown; remove from pan and set aside.

5. Fry the little meat patties in the same skillet until golden brown. Add a liitle more oil if needed.

6. In a second pan, cook the tomatoes, mashing them, until they soften and form a sauce. Add the cooked meat patties and vegetables, fresh peas, tomato paste, water, butter, salt, and pepper. Blend well and cook until everything is done, about 30 to 35 minutes. Add small amounts of water as it cooks if needed.

4 Servings

1 lb. ground meat—half lean
   beef and half lamb, or all lean
   beef
1 small eggplant
Salt
2 slices stale French bread,
   crusts removed
1 large onion, grated
2 eggs
1/2 teaspoon allspice

1/2 cup fresh dill or parsley, or
   1 teaspoon dill weed
Salt and freshly ground pepper
   to taste
3 tablespoons or more oil
2 large new potatoes, peeled
   and diced
2 large ripe tomatoes, cubed
1 tablespoon tomato paste
1 cup water
2 tablespoons butter
1 cup fresh peas

Fried *Köfte*
Kuru Köfte

In Turkey, these are served with French-fried
potatoes.

   Grind the lamb and beef together twice if you
have a meat grinder. Soak the bread in water.
Squeeze it dry and crumble. Add it to the meat
along with the onion, eggs, parsley, allspice, salt,
and pepper. Knead with your hands 5 to 10 minutes, until the consistency of a paste. With wet
hands, form the meat into thumb-like shapes. Roll
in flour to coat lightly. Fry in hot oil. Serve hot.

   3 Servings

1/2 lb. ground chuck
1/2 lb. ground lamb
Or 1 lb. ground chuck
2 slices stale French bread,
   crusts removed
1 small onion, grated
2 eggs, lightly beaten
1/2 cup finely chopped parsley

1/2 **teaspoon allspice**
Salt and freshly ground pepper
1/2 **cup all-purpose flour**
1/2–1 **cup oil for frying**

Stuffed Kibbe
İçli Köfte

This dish is Arab in origin but also enjoyed in Turkey.

1. Wash the bulgur and drain. Squeeze dry with your hands and set aside.

2. Combine the bulgur, the extra lean lamb or beef, the small onion, 1/2 teaspoon salt and 1/2 teaspoon cinnamon. Grind this mixture 3 times through the fine blade of a meat grinder. Put some cold water in a small bowl. Each time you put some of the mixture in the meat grinder, dip fingers in the cold water. This additional moisture helps soften the mixture.

3. Put the mixture in a bowl and knead 5 minutes to a smooth paste, wetting your hands frequently with cold water. The paste should be soft but not soggy. Cover and chill until required.

4. Put the (regular) ground lamb and the 2 medium onions in a skillet and cook over medium heat until the meat releases its moisture, reabsorbs it, and browns in its own juice and fat. Stir in some salt, freshly ground pepper, 1/2 teaspoon cinnamon, the allspice, and the nuts; remove from heat. Set aside.

5. Mix the cornstarch with 3/4 cup water in a small bowl. Take egg-size lumps of the meat and bulgur paste, shape into balls. Pick one and roll in your palms until very smooth. Hold one ball in the palm of one hand; thrust the thumb of your other hand into the ball and begin to hollow it out. As your thumb presses against the sides of the hollow, the ball turns slowly in your palm and the hollow becomes larger. Continue until you have a smooth shell with a uniform thickness of about 1/8 inch (and a sizable hole). Spoon some of the filling into the hollow. Pressing the sides in gently, close the hollow and smooth with fingers, frequently dipping them in the cornstarch and water mixture. Complete the shape to make it resemble an egg.

6. Heat the oil and deep fry the kibbes until a rich brown. Fry a few at a time and remove from oil with a slotted spoon. Drain on paper towels. Keep warm in low oven until the remainder are cooked. Serve hot.

VARIATION: Kibbes can also be boiled instead of fried. They are gently cooked in simmering salted water. As they are done, they rise to the surface and float. Some people boil them in salted water 5 minutes, dip them in eggs and fry them.

4 Servings

**1 cup extra lean ground lamb
  (from leg) or ground round
1 cup ground lamb
1 cup fine-grain bulgur
1 small onion, minced
Salt
Cinnamon
2 medium onions, minced
1/2 teaspoon allspice
1/3 cup minced walnuts or
  almonds or pine nuts
Cold water
1 tablespoon cornstarch
Oil for frying**

"Lady's Thigh" *Köfte*
Kadın Budu Köfte

These are usually eaten hot, but they are also good chilled, as part of a buffet supper.

1. Melt the butter in a saucepan and sauté the onions until they are just beginning to brown. Stir in the rice, 1 teaspoon salt, and the water. Cover and cook about 20 minutes over low heat until all the water is absorbed. Remove the pan from heat and cool.

2. Sauté half the meat until it releases its moisture, reabsorbs it, and browns. Remove from heat and cool. Combine it with the uncooked meat and run through a meat grinder or knead with your hands to the consistency of a paste.

3. Beat 2 eggs lightly. Add to the meat along with the salt, pepper, dill, cheese, and the cooked rice. Knead with your hands for 5 minutes. Wet your fingers and shape tablespoonfuls into slightly flattened oval forms.

4. Spread the flour on a large plate. Beat 2 or 3 eggs lightly in a small bowl. Heat the oil over high heat in a heavy pan or wok. Dip the meatballs into the flour first, then into the egg, and fry 3 to 5 minutes on each side in hot oil. Serve hot.

3–4 Servings

1/2 **lb. lean ground beef**
1/2 **lb. lean ground lamb**
Or 1 lb. lean ground beef
2 tablespoons butter
2 finely chopped onions
1/3 **cup uncooked rice**
Salt
1 1/2 cups water
4–5 eggs
Salt and pepper to taste

1/2 **cup fresh dill, chopped, or**
   2 teaspoons dried dill weed
1/2 **cup grated Romano or**
   kasseri cheese
1 **cup all-purpose flour**
1 **cup oil for frying**

MEAT DOLMAS
Etli Dolmalar

Meat *dolmas* are colorful, very nutritious, and delicious vegetables stuffed with meat. Each of the following recipes uses different vegetables. In Turkey, however, especially in the summer when an abundant variety of vegetables is available, two or more of these vegetables are stuffed and cooked together so that the different flavors, aromas, and colors of these vegetables blend, making a unique meal.

In Turkey, one simply goes to a butcher and asks for meat for making *dolmas (dolmalık et)*. The butcher combines rather fatty ground lamb with some ground veal for this purpose. Here, however, after many experiments, I came to the conclusion that medium-fat ground lamb works best. I buy leg of lamb, leg of spring lamb when available, and grind it myself with quite a bit of its fat. Lamb mixed with lesser amount of beef or veal is also very good. Needless to say one can also use ground beef alone. Ground chuck works especially well for *dolmas*.

There are two basic methods of preparing most meat *dolmas*. In the longer version, some ingredients of the filling are cooked before the vegetables are stuffed. This way produces better-tasting results. Still, for all but the most special occasions, today's Turkish cooks prefer to skip the precooking step and use the shorter method.

Meat-Stuffed Vine Leaves

Etli Yaprak Dolması

1. Rinse the vine leaves under running water and cut off the stems. Let drain in a colander.

2. In a saucepan, sauté the onions in 2 tablespoons butter and 1 tablespoon oil until just beginning to brown. Add the rice and 1 1/2 cups water. Cover and simmer 10 minutes or until the water is absorbed. Remove from heat, and cool.

3. In a large bowl, mix together the onions and rice and the meat, tomatoes, tomato paste, parsley, dill, lemon juice, salt, and pepper. Knead with your hands for 5 minutes.

4. Spread 1 vine leaf open on a dinner plate, shiny side down, with the stem end toward you. Put 1 to 3 tablespoons filling, depending on the size of the leaf, near the bottom of the leaf, about 1 inch in from the 3 edges. Fold the stem end of the leaf over the filling. Fold the 2 sides over to seal. Roll toward the point of the leaf, being careful to allow a little room for the rice to expand as it cooks. Repeat with the other leaves until you have used all the filling.

5. Lay a few unstuffed vine leaves in the bottom of a heavy pot. Spread the parsley and dill stems over the leaves if you have them. Place the stuffed vine leaves on top of them, seam side down; arrange them close together in layers. Dot with butter if the meat is lean. Stir 1/4 teaspoon salt into 1 cup water; pour over the stuffed grape leaves. Spread a sheet of wax paper over them and place a plate upside down on top of that to add some weight. Cover and simmer about 1 hour. Check the level of the liquid occasionally and add more hot water, a small amount at a time, if necessary. Serve hot with either of the sauces below.

SHORTER VERSION: Prepare the vine leaves as in step 1. Skip step 2. Move on to step 3 and add 1 1/2 cups of water to the ingredients in the bowl. Knead 5 minutes and proceed as above beginning with step 4.

LEMON SAUCE:
Beat the egg yolks with the lemon juice. Still beating, gradually add the hot broth. Heat just to the boiling point. Pour the sauce over the hot *dolmas* and serve immediately.

YOGURT SAUCE:
Whip the ingredients together until creamy. Pour over the hot *dolmas* or pass at the table.

4 Servings

1 lb. medium-fat ground lamb,
   or 1 lb. each ground lamb
   and ground chuck, or 1 lb.
   ground chuck
8 oz. jar vine leaves
2 large onions, finely chopped
2–4 tablespoons butter
1 tablespoon oil
1/3 cup uncooked rice
Water
2 ripe tomatoes, diced, or 1 cup
   canned tomatoes with juice
1 tablespoon tomato paste
1 cup chopped parsley
1/2 cup fresh dill, chopped, or
   1 tablespoon dried dill
Juice of 1 lemon
Salt and freshly ground pepper
   to taste

LEMON SAUCE:
4 egg yolks
Juice of 1 lemon
3/4 cup cooking liquid from the
   stuffed leaves

1–1 1/2 **cup(s) yogurt**
Scant 1/4 cup water
2–4 cloves garlic, mashed
1 teaspoon salt

Stuffed Cabbage
Etli Lahana Dolması

1. Wash the cabbage. With a long, pointed knife, cut around the core and remove it. Insert the knife deep inside the core area of the cabbage head to loosen the leaves. Place the whole head in a large pot with 2 to 3 cups water and simmer about 5 minutes until the outermost leaves become soft enough to be pliable (except at the core end). Take the cabbage out of the pot and detach any leaves that can be removed without being torn. Set them aside to drain and cool. Return the cabbage to the pot and simmer a few minutes longer. Remove more outer leaves and continue in this manner until almost all the leaves have been detached. The leaves should be softened without being soft, or they will lose their flavor.

2. In a saucepan, sauté the onions in 2 tablespoons butter and 1 tablespoon oil until just beginning to brown. Add 1 1/2 cup water and the rice. Cover and simmer 10 minutes or until the water is absorbed. Remove from the heat and cool.

3. In a bowl, combine the onions and rice with the meat, tomatoes, tomato paste, parsley, dill, allspice, salt, and pepper; knead with your hands for 5 minutes.

4. Spread 1 cabbage leaf open on a plate, the core end toward you. Cut off the hard area that is attached to the core. Place 2 to 4 tablespoons filling —depending on the size of the leaf—along the core edge of the leaf, 1 inch in from 3 edges. Fold over the 2 sides to seal; fold the core edge over the filling, and roll toward the pointed end of the leaf. Repeat with the other leaves until you have used all the filling.

5. Place a few unstuffed cabbage leaves in the bottom of a heavy pot. Spread the parsley and dill stems over the unstuffed leaves, if you have them. Arrange the stuffed cabbage in layers over the leaves. Dot with butter if the meat is lean. Stir 1/4 teaspoon salt into 1 cup hot water; pour over the cabbage rolls. Spread a sheet of wax paper over them and place a plate upside down on top of that to add some weight. Cover and simmer about 50 minutes until the cabbage is cooked. Check the level of the liquid occasionally and add more hot water, a small amount at a time, if necessary. Serve hot.

SHORTER VERSION: Prepare the cabbage as in step 1. Skip step 2. Combine the uncooked onions and rice with the meat, tomatoes, tomato paste, 1 1/2 cups water, parsley, dill, allspice, salt, and pepper; knead with your hands for 5 minutes. Proceed as above beginning with step 4.

4 Servings

**1 lb. medium-fat ground lamb,
  or 1/2 lb. each lean ground
  chuck and lamb, or 1 lb. lean
  ground chuck**
**1 medium head cabbage, about
  3 lbs.**
Water
3 large onions, finely chopped
2–4 tablespoons butter
1 tablespoon oil
1/3 cup uncooked rice
**2 ripe tomatoes, diced, or 1 cup
  canned tomatoes with juice**
1 tablespoon tomato paste
1 cup chopped parsley

1/2 **cup fresh dill, chopped, or**
  1–2 tablespoons dill weed
1/2 **teaspoon allspice**
Salt and freshly ground pepper
  to taste

Stuffed Bell Peppers
Etli Biber Dolması

1. Cut the tops off the peppers and reserve. Remove the seeds and white membrane from the peppers; wash and drain. Chop the parsley and dill and reserve the stems.

2. Sauté the onions in a saucepan with 2 table-spoons butter and 1 tablespoon oil. When just beginning to brown, add the rice and 1 1/2 cups water. Cover and simmer 10 minutes, until the water is absorbed. Remove from heat, and cool.

3. In a large bowl, combine the onion and rice with the meat, tomatoes, 2 tablespoons tomato paste, chopped parsley and dill, salt, and pepper. Knead with your hands for 5 minutes.

4. Fill each of the peppers with some of the meat and rice mixture, being careful to allow a little room for the rice to expand as it cooks. Place the pepper tops on the stuffed peppers.

5. Spread the parsley and dill stems in the bottom of a heavy pot. On top of them place the stuffed peppers, upright and close together. Dot with butter if the meat is lean. Stir 2 tablespoons tomato paste and 1/4 teaspoon salt into 3/4 cup hot water. Pour half of it over the stuffed peppers. Spread a sheet of wax paper over them and place a plate upside down on top of that to add some weight. Cover and simmer 45 minutes or longer, until the peppers are cooked. Check occasionally as they cook and add more of the hot water and tomato, just a little at a time, when the level of the liquid gets low. Serve hot.

SHORTER VERSION: Prepare the bell peppers, parsley, and dill as in Step 1. Skip step 2. Move on to step 3. and add 1 1/2 cups water to the ingredients in the bowl. Proceed as above beginning with step 4.

4 Servings

1 lb. medium-fat ground lamb, or 1/2 lb. each ground chuck and lamb, or 1 lb. ground chuck
2 lbs. green bell peppers
1/2–1 cup parsley
1/2 cup fresh dill or 1–2 tablespoons dill weed
2 large onions, finely chopped
2–3 tablespoons butter
1 tablespoon oil
1/3 cup uncooked rice
Water
2 ripe tomatoes, diced, or 1 cup canned tomatoes with juice
4 tablespoons tomato paste
Salt and freshly ground pepper to taste

Stuffed Tomatoes
Etli Domates Dolması

1. Cut off the tops of the tomatoes and save. Scoop out the insides with a spoon. Reserve the pulp from 6 tomatoes.

2. Sauté the onions in a saucepan with 2 tablespoons butter and 1 tablespoon oil until just beginning to brown. Add the rice and 3/4 cup water. Cover and simmer 10 minutes, until the water is absorbed. Remove from heat and cool.

3. In a large bowl, combine the onion and rice with the meat, tomato pulp, parsley, dill, mint, salt, and pepper. Knead with your hands for 5 minutes.

4. Fill each of the tomatoes with some of the meat and rice mixture. Replace the tops on the tomatoes.

5. Spread the parsley and dill stems in the bottom of a heavy pan. Arrange the stuffed tomatoes upright and close together in a heavy pot. Dot with butter, using more if your meat is lean. Pour 1/2 cup hot water over the stuffed tomatoes. Spread a sheet of wax paper over them and place a plate upside down on top of that to add some weight. Cover and simmer 30 to 35 minutes until everything is cooked. Check the level of the liquid occasionally and add more hot water, a little at a time, if necessary. Serve hot.

4–5 Servings

1 lb. medium-fat ground lamb,
   or 1/2 lb. each ground chuck
   and lamb, or 1 lb. ground
   chuck
10 large half-ripe tomatoes
2 chopped onions
2–3 tablespoons butter
1 tablespoon oil
1/3 cup uncooked rice
Water
1/2 cup chopped parsley
1/2 cup fresh dill, chopped, or
   2 tablespoons dried dill weed
1/4 cup fresh mint leaves,
   chopped, or 2 tablespoons
   dried mint
Salt and freshly ground pepper
   to taste

Stuffed Zucchini

Etli Kabak Dolması

1. Scrape the zucchini and wash. Cut off the stems. Cut the zucchini into halves and, using a vegetable peeler, or an apple corer, scoop out the insides and leave a 1/8-inch-thick shell; discard the pulp. Wash and drain well. Chop the parsley and dill and reserve the stems.

2. In a large bowl, blend together the meat, onions, tomatoes, tomato paste, rice, 1 1/2 cups water, garlic, parsley, dill, mint, salt, and pepper. Knead with your hands for 5 minutes.

3. Pack some of the filling into each of the zucchini, allowing a little room for the rice to expand as it cooks.

4. Spread the parsley and dill stems in the bottom of a heavy pot. On top of them stand the stuffed zucchini upright. Dot with butter, using more if your meat is lean. Stir 1/2 teaspoon salt into 3/4–1 cup water; pour over the zucchini. Spread a sheet of wax paper over them and place a plate upside down on top of that to add some weight. Cover and simmer 1 hour. Check the level of the liquid occasionally and add more hot water, a little at a time, if necessary. Serve hot with Yogurt Sauce (see p. 130).

Servings

**1 lb. medium-fat ground lamb,
or 1/2 lb. each ground chuck
and lamb, or 1 lb. ground
chuck**
2 lbs. zucchini
1 cup parsley
1/2 cup dill
2 large onions, finely chopped

2 ripe tomatoes, cubed
1 tablespoon tomato paste
1/3 cup rice
Water
2–3 large cloves garlic, mashed
1/2 cup chopped mint leaves
Salt and freshly ground pepper
   to taste
2–4 tablespoons butter
Yogurt Sauce, p. 130.

OTHER GROUND MEAT DISHES

Eggplant with Meat Filling
Karnıyarık

This is easy to make yet beautiful and interesting in both taste and appearance.

1. Cut the stems off the eggplants. Using a vegetable peeler, peeling lengthwise, remove a strip of skin. Leave the next strip on and continue to peel in this striped fashion until all the eggplants are peeled. Heat the oil and sauté the eggplant over medium-low heat 15 to 20 minutes, turning to cook on all sides until golden brown. Remove from heat and set aside.

2. Sauté the onion in 1 1/2 tablespoons butter until golden brown. Add the meat and cook, stirring often, until it releases its moisture, reabsorbs it, and browns. Stir in the chopped tomato and bell pepper and sauté 2 to 3 minutes. Add the tomato paste, parsley, salt, and pepper; blend well. Remove from heat.

3. Slit each eggplant open along one side from top to bottom, being careful not to cut all the way through. Use your hands to enlarge the openings as much as possible without tearing so that each will hold a maximum amount of filling. Pack equal amounts of the meat mixture into the eggplants and fill them to slightly heaping. Arrange in a single layer in a large cast-iron pot or heavy skillet. Place green peppers on top. Pour over 1/2 cup hot water and dot with the remaining butter. Place a sheet of aluminum foil loosely over the eggplant and cover. Cook over low heat or bake at 350- for 50 minutes or longer, until the eggplants are thoroughly cooked. Check the level of the liquid occasionally and add water, a small amount at a time, if needed. Remove the foil for the last 15 minutes or so of cooking. When ready, the eggplant and meat should be moist but there should be no more than 1/4 to 1/2 cup liquid in the pan. Serve with pilav.

3 Servings

1 1/2 **lbs. Japanese eggplant**
2–3 **tablespoons oil**
1/2 **lb. lean ground beef**
2 1/2 **tablespoons butter**
1 **small onion, finely chopped**
1 1/2 **tablespoons butter**
1 **minced tomato**
1/4 **cup chopped bell pepper**
1 **tablespoon tomato paste**
3/4 **cup chopped parsley**
1/2 **teaspoon salt**
1/2 **teaspoon freshly ground**
  pepper
1/2 **cup hot water**
1 **bell pepper, sliced in rings, or**
  4–5 long, slender green
  peppers

Moussaka
Musakka

1. Cut off the stems of the eggplants. Using a vegetable peeler, and peeling lengthwise, remove a strip of skin. Leave the next strip on and continue to peel in this striped fashion. Repeat with the other 2 eggplants. Cut all into 1/3 to 1/2-inch-thick slices. Sprinkle them generously with salt and set aside for 3 hours. Rinse well under cold water. Squeeze each piece in your hand and then in a clean old towel to get all the moisture out without tearing.

2. Heat the oil and fry the slices of eggplant and potato on both sides over high heat until nicely browned. Drain on paper towels.

3. Melt 2 tablespoons butter in a skillet and sauté the onions and garlic. Stir in the meat and brown. Drain off the excess fat. Stir in the tomatoes, tomato paste, water, oregano, salt, pepper, and water. Blend well. Cover and simmer 10 to 15 minutes.

4. Arrange half the eggplant and potato slices in a baking pan 10 inches by 14 inches by 21/4 inches. Spread the meat sauce over the vegetables and top with the remaining vegetables.

5. Preheat oven to 350°. Prepare the custard sauce. Simmer the cinnamon stick in the half-and-half 5 minutes. Remove the cinnamon stick and discard. Stir in a pinch of nutmeg. Melt 1/2 cup butter in a saucepan, blend in the flour, and stir 2 to 3 minutes over medium heat. Gradually blend in the hot half-and-half and, stirring with a wire whisk cook until thick and bubbling. Stir a small amount of sauce into the egg yolks, blend together, then return to the pan of sauce. Stir in the cheese. Cook a few seconds longer until smooth and thick. Adjust the seasoning. Pour over the vegetables and meat.

6. Bake 45 minutes. Check after about 35 minutes and, if already brown, cover with a sheet of foil for the last 10 minutes or so of baking. Remove from oven, let stand 10 minutes before cutting into squares. Moussaka can be reheated and served the next day.

8 Servings

3 medium eggplants (1 lb. each)
4 potatoes, peeled and sliced
   1/4-inch thick
Oil for frying
2 tablespoons butter
2 finely chopped onions
1/2 teaspoon minced garlic
1 lb. ground lamb
1 lb. ground beef
2 large tomatoes, chopped
2 tablespoons tomato paste
1/4 cup water
2 teaspoons oregano
Salt and pepper to taste
1/2 cinnamon stick, broken
   into pieces
5 1/4 cups half-and-half
Pinch nutmeg
1/2 cup butter
3/4 cup all-purpose flour
6 egg yolks, lightly beaten
1/3 cup grated kasseri or
   Romano cheese

Eggplant Layered with Ground Meat
Patlıcan Oturtması

1. Cut the stems off the eggplants. Using a vegetable peeler, and peeling lengthwise, remove a strip of skin. Leave the next strip on and continue to peel in this striped fashion. Repeat with the other eggplant. Slice both eggplants 1/3 inch thick. Sprinkle them generously with salt and set aside for 3 hours. Rinse well under cold water. Squeeze each piece in your hand and then in a clean old towel to get all the moisture out without tearing.

2. Sauté the onion in butter 2 to 3 minutes. Add the meat and cook over medium heat until it releases its moisture, reabsorbs it, and browns in its own fat and juice. Add the tomatoes, salt, and pepper; blend well. Remove from heat and set aside.

3. Heat oil in a skillet and lightly sauté the eggplant slices over high heat. Drain on paper towels. Arrange in a 9-inch-by-13-inch baking dish. Spread the meat mixture over the eggplant slices. Arrange the slices of tomato and green pepper on top of the meat. Sprinkle with salt; pour 3/4 cup hot water over all. Cover and bake at 350° for 35 minutes. Check the level of water occasionally; add water, a small amount at a time, if needed. Serve hot with pilav.

4–6 Servings

**1 lb. ground lamb or ground
  beef**
2 medium eggplants
Salt
1 finely chopped onion
2 tablespoons butter
2 minced tomatoes
Salt and pepper to taste

Oil for frying
1 sliced tomato
2 large bell peppers, sliced
   in rings
Water

Zucchini with Ground Beef
Kabak Oturtması

1. Scrape and wash the zucchini. Drain and cut crosswise into 1/2-inch-thick slices. Sauté on both sides in hot oil until golden brown. Set aside.

2. Sauté the onions in butter 2 to 3 minutes. Add the meat and cook over medium heat until it releases its moisture, reabsorbs it, and browns in its own fat and juice. Add the tomatoes, dill, paprika, salt, and pepper. Mix well.

3. Lightly butter a casserole dish or a heavy pan. Fill it with alternate layers of zucchini slices and the meat mixture, beginning with zucchini. Pour in about 3/4 cup hot water. Lay a sheet of foil over the top. Cover and bake at 350° or cook over low heat for 45 to 60 minutes. Check the level of the liquid occasionally and add more hot water, a small amount at a time, if needed. Serve with pasta or pilav.

4 Servings

1 lb. ground beef
2 1/2 lbs. zucchini
1/4 cup oil
2 finely chopped onions
4 tablespoons butter
3 cubed tomatoes or 1 lb.
   canned tomatoes
1 bunch fresh dill, chopped, or
   1 tablespoon dried dill weed

1/2 **cup fresh mint, chopped, or**
   1 tablespoon dry mint leaves
1 tablespoon paprika
1 teaspoon cayenne
Salt and pepper to taste
Water

Potatoes Layered with Ground Beef
Patates Oturtması

1. Peel the potatoes, wash, dry, and cut into 1/3 inch slices.

2. Heat the oil and sauté the potatoes on both sides until golden brown. Set aside.

3. Sauté the onions in butter, and add the meat. Cook over medium heat about 15 minutes, stirring often, until the meat releases its moisture, reabsorbs it, and browns. Add the cubed tomatoes, chopped peppers, thyme, salt, and pepper; blend well. Simmer for 5 minutes and remove from heat.

4. Spread half the potatoes in the bottom of a large casserole or a 9-inch-by-12-inch baking dish. Cover with half the meat mixture. Arrange the remaining potatoes over that and cover with the rest of the meat. Place slices of tomato and the whole green peppers or bell pepper slices on top. Add a little salt and pepper to 2 1/2 cups hot water and pour over all. Cover and bake at 350° for 30 minutes or until the potatoes are tender. Check the liquid content occasionally and add more water, if needed. Remove the cover during the last 5 minutes of baking. The potatoes should be very moist and in ample sauce but not watery.

8 Servings

1 1/2 lbs. ground beef or 1 lb.
  ground beef and 1/2 lb. ground
  lamb

1/4 cup oil
3 lbs. (9 medium) potatoes,
    peeled and sliced 1/2-inch
    thick
2 large onions, chopped
4 tablespoons butter
3 large tomatoes, cubed
1 green bell pepper, chopped
2 small hot chili peppers,
    chopped (optional)
1/2 teaspoon thyme
Salt and freshly ground pepper
    to taste
2–3 sliced tomatoes
4 long green peppers, if
    available, or 2 bell peppers,
    cut into rings
2–3 cups hot water

Spinach with Ground Beef
Kıymalı Ispanak

This also works well if you substitute 2 packages of frozen spinach for the fresh spinach.

1. Cut off spinach roots and chop the spinach finely. Wash several times and drain.

2. Sauté the onions in butter and add the ground beef. Cook about 15 minutes over medium heat, stirring often, until the meat releases its juice, reabsorbs it, and browns. Stir in the tomatoes or tomato paste diluted with 1/8 cup water and simmer 2 to 3 minutes. Add the spinach, cover, and cook for 10 to 15 minutes until the spinach is wilted and soft. Add the rice, salt, pepper, and 1 cup hot water; blend well. Cover and cook until the rice is tender, about 20 minutes. If needed, more hot water may be added, a small amount at a time, to maintain the level of the liquid as it cooks.

3. Pour Yogurt Sauce over individual servings of the dish.

YOGURT SAUCE:
Combine the yogurt with a little salt and the mashed garlic. Beat until smooth and creamy; if too thick to be a sauce, blend in a little water.

3–4 Servings

1/3 **lb. ground beef**
2 **small onions, finely chopped**
3 **tablespoons butter**
2 **large tomatoes, cubed, or**
   1 1/2 **tablespoons tomato paste**
2 **lbs. fresh spinach**
3 **tablespoons uncooked rice**
Salt and freshly ground pepper
1 **cup or more hot water**

YOGURT SAUCE:
2 **cups yogurt**
Dash salt
1 **teaspoon mashed garlic**
Water

Okra with Ground Beef
Kıymalı Bamya

You may substitute 2 packages frozen okra for the fresh okra. Serve with rice pilav.

1. Pare off the conical stems of the okra without cutting into the pods. Wash, drain, and cut any large ones in half. Place in a bowl with 2 tablespoons salt and 1/2 cup vinegar; mix well and set aside for 30 minutes.*
2. In a heavy pot, sauté the onions in butter

2 to 3 minutes. Add the meat and cook over medium heat for about 20 minutes until it releases its moisture, reabsorbs it, and browns. Add the tomatoes and cook 2 minutes longer. Drain the okra well and add to the meat mixture. Cover and cook over medium heat until it loses color and absorbs all the moisture. At this point, stir-fry the okra 2 or 3 minutes. Stir in 1 cup hot water, lemon juice, salt and pepper. Cover and simmer over low heat until the okra is tender, about 45 minutes. As it cooks, check occasionally and add more hot water, 1/3 cup at a time, if needed.

4–6 Servings

*Treating the okra with vinegar is necessary only if you wish to prevent it from becoming viscous during cooking.

1/2 **lb. ground beef**
2 **lbs. fresh okra**
Salt
1/4 **cup vinegar (optional)**
2 **small onions, chopped**
4 **tablespoons butter**
4 **tomatoes or 1 lb. canned**
   tomatoes, chopped
1 **cup or more hot water**
Juice of 1 small lemon
Salt and freshly ground pepper
   to taste

Green Beans with Ground Beef
Kıymalı Yeşil Fasulye

Sauté the onions in butter for 2 minutes. Add the meat and cook over medium heat, stirring frequently, until the meat releases its moisture, reabsorbs it, and browns lightly. Add the tomatoes or tomato paste, salt, and pepper; blend well. Stir in the beans. Cover the pan and cook, stirring occasionally, until the beans soften and begin to lose their color and all the moisture is absorbed. At this point, stir-fry the beans for 2 to 3 minutes. Add 1 cup hot water, freshly ground pepper, and salt, if needed. Cook until the beans are tender, about 30 or 40 minutes. Check the level of the liquid occasionally as it cooks and, if necessary, add more hot water, 1/3 cup at a time. Serve with pasta or pilav.

4 Servings

1/2 **lb. ground beef**
2 **chopped onions**
3–4 **tablespoons butter**
2–3 **cubed tomatoes or 1 lb.**
   canned tomatoes or 2
   tablespoons tomato paste
Salt and pepper to taste
2 **lbs. fresh green beans,**
   trimmed and cut in 2 or
   3 pieces
Water

STEWS

Güveç

A *güveç* is an unglazed earthenware pot. The dishes that take their name from the cooking vessel are usually different types of lamb stews, but Western cooks may want to try this one with beef. Serve it with pilav.

1. Cut the stem off the eggplant. Using a vegetable peeler, and peeling lengthwise, remove a strip of skin. Leave the next strip on and continue to peel in this striped fashion. Cut the eggplant into 1 inch cubes. Sprinkle generously with salt and set aside for 3 hours. Rinse well under cold water. Squeeze each piece in your hand and then in a clean old towel to remove as much water as possible.

2. Wash and drain the other vegetables. Chop the onions and tomatoes. Peel and cube the potatoes. Pare off the conical stems of the okra without cutting into the pods; Cut any large ones in half. Trim the beans and cut them into three pieces each. Cut the bell peppers into 1 1/2-inch squares. Scrape the zucchini and cut into 1-inch cubes.

3. Sauté the eggplant and the zucchini lightly in oil over high heat. Remove from heat.

4. Preheat the oven to 350°. You will need a large earthenware casserole with a lid. Place the meat in the bottom; sprinkle with salt and pepper. Arrange 1/4 of the bell peppers, onions, garlic, and tomatoes in layers on top of the meat. Spread the potatoes over the tomatoes; sprinkle with more salt and pepper and a little of the dill. The remaining vegetables should be added in layers in the following order: green beans, 1/4 of the bell peppers and tomatoes, 1/2 the onions and garlic; eggplant, zucchini, 1/4 of the tomatoes and bell pepper, rest of the onions and garlic, a sprinkling of salt, pepper, and dill; okra, rest of the tomatoes and bell peppers. Dot with butter. Pour 1/2 cup water over all. Cover and bake 1 to 1 1/2 hours until all the ingredients are tender. Check a few times as it cooks and add a little hot water if needed.

6 Servings

2 lbs. lamb, cut into 1-inch cubes

1 medium eggplant
Salt
2 onions
2–4 or more cloves garlic,
   mashed
4 very ripe tomatoes
2 medium potatoes
1/4 lb. okra
1/3 lb. green beans
4 large bell peppers
2 medium zucchini
1/2 cup fresh dill, chopped, or
   1 tablespoon dill weed
Black pepper to taste
Oil
4–6 tablespoons butter
Water

Lamb and Potato *Güveç*

Patatesli Kuzu Güveci

An easy, quick, and delightful dish!

1. Peel the potatoes, wash, drain and cut into 4 pieces. Remove the seeds from the bell peppers, wash and cut into eighths.

2. Preheat oven to 350°.

3. Combine the meat and all the vegetables and herbs in a large earthenware casserole or Dutch oven; mix well. Dot with butter; pour in 1/3 cup water. Cover and bake about 3 hours or until the meat is tender.

6 Servings

2 lbs. lamb with bones, cut into
   large chunks
6 medium potatoes

3 green bell peppers
2 large tomatoes, cut in chunks
2 onions, roughly chopped
8 green onions, cut into
   1 1/2-inch pieces
8 cloves garlic, halved
1 cup fresh dill, chopped, or
   2 tablespoons dried dill weed
2 bay leaves
Salt to taste
5 tablespoons butter
1/3 cup water

Lamb with Potatoes
Etli Patates

1. Peel the potatoes, wash, and cut into 1-inch cubes. Sauté very lightly in oil.

2. Melt 4 tablespoons butter in a heavy pot; sauté the onions and add the meat. Cover and cook over medium heat 20 to 30 minutes, stirring frequently, until the meat releases its moisture, reabsorbs it, and browns in its own fat and juice. Add the tomatoes, tomato paste, 1/2 cup hot water, salt, and pepper, reduce the heat, and simmer 1 1/2 hours. Add the potatoes, chili peppers, and 1 1/2 cups hot water; cover and cook until the meat and potatoes are tender, about another 30 minutes. Add more hot water, a small amount at a time, if needed. There should be ample sauce but it should be thick, not runny and watery.

6 Servings

2 lamb shanks or 1 lb. boneless
   lamb, cut into 1 1/2-inch
   chunks
2 lbs. potatoes

3 tablespoons oil
4–6 tablespoons butter
2 chopped onions
3 chopped tomatoes or 1 lb.
   canned tomatoes
2 tablespoons tomato paste
3 cups or more hot water
Salt and freshly ground pepper
   to taste
3 whole green chili peppers,
   hot or mild, seeded

Lamb and White Bean Stew
Etli Kuru Fasulye

A favorite dish for a cold winter's day. In Turkey it is always served with rice or bulgur pilav. If you like hot seasoning, replace the paprika called for with 2 or 3 red hot peppers or some red pepper flakes.

1. Soak the beans in plenty of water overnight. Drain. Boil them in fresh water for 30 minutes; drain and set aside.

2. In a large pot, sauté the onions in butter. Add the meat, cover, and cook 20 to 30 minutes over medium heat, stirring frequently, until it releases its moisture, reabsorbs it, and browns. Stir in the tomatoes, tomato paste, 1/2 cup meat stock or water, paprika, and salt. Cover and simmer for 20 minutes. Add the beans and meat stock or water to barely cover, and simmer gently until the meat and beans are very tender, about 1 1/2 hours. Add more hot water in small quantities, as needed to barely cover the beans. Serve in bowls.

6 Servings

4 lamb shanks or 2 lbs. lamb
   shoulder cut into 1 1/2-inch
   chunks, or 2 lbs. lamb neck, or
   combination of 1 lb. lamb
   neck and 1 lb. stewing beef,
   cut into 3/4-inch cubes
1 lb. dry Great Northern beans
3 chopped onions
6 tablespoons butter
3 cubed tomatoes
1 tablespoon tomato paste
4–5 cups beef stock or water
2 tablespoons paprika
Salt and pepper to taste

Chick-Pea Stew
Nohut Yahnisi

If you prefer, substitute 2 cans (15 oz. each) canned chick-peas for the dry ones. They should be added after the meat has been cooked in the tomato sauce until tender. Stir in the beans, undrained, and continue cooking about 20 minutes. If you like hot seasoning, replace the paprika with 2 or 3 red hot peppers or some red pepper flakes.

   1. Soak the beans in plenty of water overnight or for at least 8 hours. Drain. Boil in fresh water 15 minutes; drain.
   2. Sauté the onions in butter 1 or 2 minutes. Stir in the meat and cook about 20 minutes over medium heat until the meat releases its moisture, reabsorbs it, and browns. Add the tomatoes, tomato paste, 1/2 cup water, salt, and paprika. Cover and cook for 30 minutes over low heat.
   3. Add the beans and 1 cup hot water and cook until the meat and beans are very tender. Check occasionally and add more hot water, a small amount at a time, if necessary. Serve with rice pilav.

**2 lamb shanks or 1 lb. lamb
    shoulder bone in cut into
    1 1/2-inch chunks**
**1 lb. dry chick-peas (Garbanzo
    beans)**
**15 boiling onions, or 3 chopped
    onions**
6 tablespoons butter
3 cubed tomatoes
1 tablespoon tomato paste
Water
Salt to taste
2 tablespoons paprika

Cabbage with Lamb and Hot Pepper
Kapıska

Good cold winter dish.

1. Wash and cut the cabbage into 4 equal
pieces. Cut off the hard sections of the core and
shred coarsely.

2. Sauté the onions in butter 2 or 3 minutes.
Stir in the meat, cover, and cook over medium heat
until it releases its moisture, reabsorbs it, and
browns gently. Add the tomatoes or tomato paste,
red peppers, salt, and 1/2 cup hot water. Cover
and simmer until the meat is almost tender, about
35 minutes. Add the cabbage and 1 cup hot water
and cook covered until the meat and cabbage are
tender. Check occasionally and add more hot water,
a small amount at a time, if needed.

3. Transfer to a casserole and bake in a 350°
oven for 15 minutes. There should be ample sauce,
but it should be thick rather than watery.

2 lamb shanks or 1 lb. lamb
   shoulder, cut into 1 1/2-inch
   chunks
1 medium (3 lbs.) head cabbage
2 chopped onions
6–8 tablespoons butter
2 large tomatoes, 1 lb. canned
   tomatoes, cubed, or
   2 tablespoons tomato paste
Small red peppers, red pepper
   flakes, or cayenne to taste
Salt to taste
1–2 cups water

Celery Root with Lemon Sauce
Terbiyeli Kereviz

1. Using a vegetable peeler, pare the dark
outer skin from the roots until the white part is
reached. Wash and cut in halves. Slice 1/2-inch thick.
Place the slices in a bowl of cold water to prevent
discoloration and set aside.

2. In a heavy pan, sauté the onions in 1 tablespoon butter. Add the meat and stir a few minutes.
Sprinkle with a little salt, cover, and cook over
medium heat, stirring frequently, for 20 minutes.
Add 1/2 cup hot water and simmer 1 hour or until
the meat is tender. If necessary, add more water
in small quantities as it cooks.

3. Drain the slices of celery root and place
in a pan with 2 tablespoons butter and 1 cup
water. Simmer, covered, for 10 minutes. Set aside
uncovered.

4. Place the meat in the center of a large pan,
leaving a wide margin around it for the celery

root. Arrange the slices of celery root around the meat and on top of it. Measure out the cooking liquid from the celery root and add water to make 1 1/2 cups. Pour over the meat and vegetables. Cover with a sheet of wax paper and the pan lid and simmer 30 to 40 minutes. If all the liquid should be absorbed add 1 more cup hot water. When quite tender, remove from heat. Transfer the meat and roots gently into a serving platter without disturbing their arrangement. Keep hot.

5. Beat the egg yolks in a saucepan with the lemon juice. Gradually add 3/4 cup stock from the pan of meat and celery root. Simmer until the sauce thickens. Pour over the meat and celery root. Serve immediately.

4–6 Servings

1/2 **lb. stewing lamb or beef, cut**
    into 1/2-**inch cubes**
3 **lbs. celery roots**
1 **large onion, chopped**
5–6 **tablespoons butter**
Salt
2–3 **cups water**
2 **egg yolks**
Juice of 1/2 **lemon**
Salt and pepper to taste

Green Pea Stew
Etli Bezelye

Sauté the meat and onions in butter for 2 or 3 minutes. Add 1 teaspoon salt, cover, and cook over medium heat, stirring occasionally, about 20 minutes, until the meat releases its moisture, re-absorbs it, and browns lightly. Add the peas, dill, sugar, freshly ground pepper, and 1 1/2 cups hot water. Cover and simmer over low heat until the meat and peas are tender. Add more hot water, a small amount at a time, if necessary to maintain the level of the liquid.

If using frozen peas, simmer the meat, dill, and seasonings in 3/4 cup water until meat is tender before adding the peas. Simmer an additional 5 to 10 minutes to cook the peas. Add more water in small amounts as necessary. Serve with pilav.

4–6 Servings

1 lb. stewing lamb or beef, cut
   in 1/2-inch cubes
2 small onions
4 tablespoons butter
Salt
2 lbs. fresh peas, shelled, or
   2 10-oz. packages of frozen
   peas
1 bunch fresh dill, chopped, or
   1 1/2 tablespoons dill weed
1 teaspoon sugar
Salt and freshly ground pepper
   to taste
Water

Green Bean Stew
Etli Ayşe Kadın veya Çalı Fasulye

1. Remove strings from the beans, cut into 3 or 4 pieces, wash, and drain.

2. Sauté the onions in butter for 2 to 3 minutes over medium heat. Stir in the meat, cover, and cook about 20 minutes over medium heat, stirring occasionally, until the meat releases its moisture, reabsorbs it, and browns in its own juice and fat. Stir in the tomatoes or tomato paste, 1/2 cup hot water, salt, and pepper, cover, and cook for 20 minutes over low heat. Additional hot water may be added in very small amounts as it cooks, if necessary.

3. Stir in the beans, cover, and cook, stirring occasionally until the beans soften, begin to lose their color, and absorb all the moisture—about 15 to 20 minutes. When all the moisture is gone, stir-fry the beans 2 to 3 minutes. Add 1 cup hot water, cover and simmer over low heat, stirring occasionally, for 30 minutes or until the meat and beans are tender. Add more hot water, 1/3 cup at a time, as it cooks, if necessary.

If using frozen beans, simmer the meat, tomatoes, or tomato paste, in 1/2 cup or more water until the meat is tender before adding the beans. Add the beans and simmer an additional 15 or 20 minutes to cook the beans. Add more water in small amounts as the beans cook, if necessary.

6 Servings

**1 lb. stewing lamb or beef, cut
  in 3/4-inch cubes
2 lbs. fresh green beans
2 onions, finely chopped
4–5 tablespoons butter
2–3 medium tomatoes, 1 lb.
  canned tomatoes, chopped, or
  2 tablespoons tomato paste
Water
Salt and freshly ground pepper
  to taste**

Stew with Winter Vegetables
Kış Türlüsü

1. In a heavy pot, sauté the onions in 2 tablespoons butter. Add the meat, cover, and cook over medium heat 20 minutes, stirring occasionally, until the meat releases its moisture, reabsorbs it, and browns. Add salt and 1/2 cup hot water. Cover and simmer until the meat is tender, 1 to 1 1/2 hours. As it cooks, add more hot water as necessary.

2. Pare the dark outer skin from the celery roots until you reach the white part. Wash, drain, and cut into 1-inch cubes. Cut the roots off the leeks. Cut the leeks into 1-inch lengths, discarding the coarse outer leaves. Wash several times and drain. Wash the potatoes and carrots; dry; and cut into cubes.

3. In a saucepan, sauté the potatoes and carrots lightly in 2 tablespoons butter. Remove from the pan and set aside. Add another tablespoon butter to the pan. Stir in the leeks and celery root. Cover and cook over medium heat for 15 minutes, stirring occasionally.

4. Add all the vegetables to the meat mixture along with 1 1/2 cups water and salt and pepper. Cook covered until the meat and vegetables are tender. Add more water, a small amount at a time, if needed. Serve with French bread and salad.

4–6 Servings

**1 lb. stewing lamb or beef, cut
  into 1-inch long pieces**
**15 whole boiling onions, or
  2 onions, chopped**
5–6 tablespoons butter
Salt
Water
4 potatoes, peeled and cubed
2 cubed carrots

3 leeks
1 medium celery root
Freshly ground pepper to taste

Stew with Summer Vegetables
Yaz Türlüsü

1. Cut the stem off the eggplant. Using a vegetable peeler, and peeling lengthwise, remove a strip of skin; leave the next strip on. Continue to peel in this striped fashion. Cut into 1/2-inch cubes. Sprinkle generously with salt and set aside for 3 hours.

2. In a heavy pot, sauté the onions in 2 tablespoons butter for 2 or 3 minutes. Stir in the meat; add some salt, cover, and cook over medium heat about 20 or 25 minutes, stirring frequently, until the meat releases its moisture, reabsorbs it, and browns in its own juice and fat. Add 1/2 cup hot water; cover and simmer until the meat is almost tender.

3. Trim the beans and cut in 3 or 4 pieces. Scrape the zucchini and cut into 1/2-inch cubes. Cut the peppers into 1-inch squares. Wash all the vegetables and drain.Rinse the okra in cold water and drain well.

4. Rinse the eggplant well under running water. Squeeze each piece in the palm of your hand and then in a clean old towel to remove as much moisture as possible without tearing. Sauté the eggplant slices very lightly in hot oil over high heat.

5. Pare off conical stems of the okra without cutting into the pods. Wash, drain, and cut any large ones in half. Place in a bowl with 2 tablespoons salt and 1/4 cup vinegar. Mix well and set aside for 30 minutes.* (Optional) Drain well.

6. Add the beans to the meat, cover and cook over medium heat 20 to 30 minutes, until the beans lose their color and absorb all the moisture. At this point stir-fry the beans 2 to 3 minutes.

7. Add the eggplant, zucchini, okra, green pepper, and tomatoes, in that order. Add salt and pepper; dot with the remaining butter. Add 1/2 cup hot water; cover and simmer gently about 50 to 60 minutes until the meat and the vegetables are tender. As it cooks, add more hot water, a small amount at a time, if necessary. There should be ample sauce, but it should be thick rather than runny.

6 Servings

1 lb. stewing lamb or beef, cut
  in 3/4-inch cubes
1 medium eggplant
Salt
1/4 lb. okra
1/4 cup vinegar
1/2 lb. green beans
1/2 lb. zucchini
3 bell peppers
Oil for frying
2 chopped onions
6 tablespoons butter
3 large ripe tomatoes, cubed
Freshly ground pepper to taste
Water

    *Treating the okra with vinegar is necessary only if you wish to prevent it from becoming viscous during cooking.

Turkish Sausage
Sucuk

Turkish cooks would add a pound of fat from the tail of the lamb to the ground beef in this recipe.

It gives an excellent flavor, but I decided many people would be interested in a leaner sausage.* This is easy, nonfattening, and amazingly good.

If you have a meat grinder with a sausage attachment, buy an 8-foot length of natural casing and follow the traditional method. Otherwise, get one roll each of wax paper and aluminum foil and make the sausage another way. At home in Turkey, we used the traditional method, of course. We made sausage in the fall so we could hang it outside to dry when the days were clear but not too warm and have plenty on hand all winter. Now I usually use the freezer method.

1. Blend all the ingredients together with your hands. Run through a meat grinder twice or knead by hand 10 minutes or longer until it becomes a smooth paste.

2. *TRADITIONAL METHOD:* Soak the sausage casing for 1 hour in cold water to which you have added 1 or 2 tablespoons vinegar. Drain. Rinse it by fitting one end over the mouth of the water faucet and running water through it. Remove any damaged parts. Drain thoroughly. Cut in two. Remove the blade and disk from your meat grinder and attach the sausage funnel. Draw the casing over the funnel until you reach the last 3 or 4 inches of casing. Make a double knot there and leave the end hanging. Begin forcing the sausage mixture into the casing, easing the casing off the funnel as it is filled. Use a needle to pierce any air bubbles that form between the meat and the casing. Tie the sausage into 8-inch lengths. Then tie the ends of each individual sausage together, creating circles. Hang the sausages outdoors on a sturdy line and allow them to dry several days.

FREEZER METHOD: Place a handful of the meat mixture on a flat surface and form into firm rolls 1/2-inch in diameter. Roll each up tightly in a sheet of wax paper, then wrap in a sheet of aluminum foil, trying not to let any air in. Seal the ends and freeze at least a few days or up to 3 months. When needed, take a roll from the freezer and unwrap the foil. Cut the paper-wrapped roll into 1/4-inch slices. Peel off the paper. Brown in a skillet with a little butter, only a few minutes on each side. Serve with eggs or any way you like sausage. There is no need to thaw before using. Wrap any unused portion of the roll in foil and return to the freezer.

Yields 6 lbs. sausage

*If you wish to add the lamb fat, simply add it to the meat mixture. However, it is best not to add the fat if you are using the freezer method.

6 lbs. lean ground beef
1/3 cup finely mashed garlic
1/4 cup cumin
3 tablespoons paprika
3 tablespoons chili powder
4–5 teaspoons salt
1 tablespoon black pepper
1–2 tablespoons cayenne
1 teaspoon allspice

Grilled Kidneys
Böbrek Izgara

Split the kidneys lengthwise without severing the two halves. Spread them flat on a grill and cook over a charcoal fire, 3 inches from the hot coals. Grill on each side about 3 minutes. Sprinkle with salt and thyme leaves and serve immediately.

Allow 2 kidneys per serving

Lamb kidneys
Salt
Thyme leaves

Lamb Knuckles *Beykoz* Style
Beykoz Usûlü Paça

1. Put the lamb knuckles in a large pan with the water, 1 1/2 teaspoons salt, garlic, and olive oil. Bring to a boil, remove the froth that forms on the surface, and simmer 8 hours until the meat is tender. Remove from the pan and bone. Reserve 8 cups of the meat stock.

2. Sauté the bread slices on both sides in 5 tablespoons or more butter. Arrange them in a baking pan with the lamb knuckles on top. Set the pan in a warm oven or on a low burner to keep warm.

3. Melt 2 tablespoons butter in a saucepan over low heat. Mix the egg yolks, 1 teaspoon salt, the lemon juice, and the flour in a bowl; blend into the melted butter and stir with a wire whisk until smooth. Gradually stir in the hot meat stock and cook over medium heat, beating vigorously with the wire whisk until the sauce is thick and smooth. Pour over the meat and serve immediately.

4 Servings

12 lamb knuckles
3 quarts water
Salt
5 cloves garlic
1 tablespoon olive oil

12 slices French bread
5 tablespoons or more butter
3 tablespoons butter
5 egg yolks, lightly beaten
Salt
Juice of 2 lemons
1/4 cup all-purpose flour
6–8 cups stock from the cooked
   lamb knuckles

Lamb Knuckles with Chick-Peas
Nohutlu Paça

1. Put the lamb knuckles in a large pan with the water, garlic, olive oil, and 1 1/2 teaspoons salt. Bring to a boil. Remove the foam that forms on the surface. Simmer the lamb knuckles until tender, about 8 hours. Remove from the pan. Cut each piece in two and bone. Set aside the meat and reserve the cooking liquid.

2. Simmer the chick-peas in water to cover until barely cooked. Drain and set aside.

3. Melt the butter in a heavy pan and sauté the onions 5 minutes. Stir in the tomatoes, salt to taste, 5 to 6 cups of the cooking liquid, chick-peas, and the meat. Cover and simmer until the chick-peas are tender. Serve hot.

3–4 Servings

10 lamb knuckles
21/2 quarts water
5 cloves garlic
1 tablespoon olive oil
Salt
2/3 lb. chick-peas, soaked
   overnight and drained

6–7 tablespoons butter
2 chopped onions
2 chopped tomatoes

Lamb Knuckles with Lemon Sauce
Terbiyeli Paça Haşlaması

1. Put the lamb knuckles in a large pan with the water, olive oil, and 1 1/2 teaspoons salt and bring to a boil. Remove the foam that forms on the surface. Cover and simmer until the meat is tender, 8 hours. Remove from the pan. Bone the meat and divide it among individual serving bowls. Leave the pan of cooking liquid on the stove.

2. Combine the egg yolks, flour, garlic, and lemon juice; blend well. Stir in some hot cooking liquid from the lamb knuckles and blend. Stir this mixture into the pan of hot cooking liquid. Bring just to the boiling point.

3. Ladle the lemon sauce into the bowls of lamb knuckles. Melt the butter in a saucepan, add the cayenne or paprika, cook until bubbly. Dribble the butter over the tops. Serve hot.

3–4 Servings

10 lamb knuckles
2 1/2 quarts water
1 tablespoon olive oil
Salt
2 tablespoons butter
1 teaspoon cayenne or paprika
3 egg yolks, lightly beaten
Garlic
1/3 cup flour
Juice of 1 lemon

Lamb Knuckles with Yogurt and Garlic
Yoğurtlu Paça

1. Put the lamb knuckles in a pan with the water, olive oil, garlic, and salt. Bring to a boil. Remove the foam that forms on the surface. Simmer 8 hours until the meat is tender. Remove the meat from the pan, bone, and set aside. Reserve the cooking liquid.

2. Slice off 1/2-inch of the crust from the top and bottom of the loaf of French bread. Then cut each into fifths. Sauté the bread crusts on both sides in 4 tablespoons butter. Place in a large baking pan. Measure out 1/2 cup cooking liquid from the lamb knuckles and pour over the bread crusts. Place the pan over very low heat. Arrange the lamb knuckles on top of the bread. Cover and keep very warm.

3. Mix the yogurt with 2/3 cup hot cooking liquid and the mashed garlic. Beat until creamy and pour over the lamb knuckles.

4. Melt 4 tablespoons butter and stir in the cayenne or paprika. Heat until bubbly. Pour over the yogurt sauce. Serve hot.

3–4 Servings

10 lamb knuckles
21/2 quarts water
1 tablespoon olive oil
5 cloves garlic
11/2 teaspoons salt
1 loaf French bread
8 tablespoons butter
2 cups yogurt
4 cloves garlic, mashed
11/2 teaspoons cayenne or
  paprika

CHICKEN DISHES

Chicken in Phyllo
Tavuk Yufka İçinde

1. Heat the oil in a heavy skillet. Add the chicken pieces and brown on both sides about 10 minutes.

2. Cut the onions to halves, then slice them thinly. Add them to the chicken in the skillet and cook until soft, about 10 to 15 minutes. Stir in the tomatoes. Add salt, pepper, and water; cover and simmer about 1 hour or until the chicken is done. Remove from the heat and cool.

3. Take the chicken pieces out of the skillet and bone. Discard the skin and bones. Divide the chicken into bite-sized pieces and mix with the onions; tomatoes; and sauce that were left in the skillet.

4. Melt the butter in a saucepan. Preheat the oven to 400°.

5. Unfold the sheets of phyllo. Take 12 sheets; rewrap the rest to save for later use. Work with 2 sheets at a time, keeping the other sheets covered to prevent them from drying out. Spread the 2 sheets of pastry in a double layer on a flat surface; brush lightly with butter. Fold it in half, bringing the 2 shorter sides together, forming a nearly equilateral rectangle. Brush the top lightly with butter. Place 1/6 of the filling in the middle, covering an area about 3 inches square. Fold one longer side over the filling; brush with butter. Fold the opposite side over and brush again with butter. Fold over one end and butter lightly; fold over the end and butter it, too. Place seam side down on a baking pan. Repeat this process with the remaining sheets and filling; brush the tops lightly with butter. Bake 20 minutes. If the tops are browning too rapidly, cover them with a sheet of aluminum foil during the last 5 minutes of baking.

6 Servings

1 chicken (2 lbs.), cut into
   serving pieces
2 tablespoons vegetable oil
4 medium onions
4 medium tomatoes, chopped
1¼ cups water
Salt and pepper to taste
12 thin phyllo sheets
½ cup butter (1 stick)

Chicken Kebab
Şişte Tavuk

You will need skewers for this dish.

   Put the chicken cubes in a bowl. Mix together the oil, lemon juice, garlic, thyme, salt, and black pepper. Pour over the chicken and blend well. Refrigerate overnight. Thread the chicken on the skewers alternately with the cherry tomatoes, onions, and green peppers. Grill over a charcoal fire, turning and basting frequently. Be careful not to overcook.

4 Servings

2½–3 lbs. boned chicken, cut in
   1-inch cubes
½ cup olive oil
Juice of 2 lemons
3 cloves garlic, mashed

2 teaspoons thyme
1 teaspoon salt
1/2 teaspoon coarsely ground
    black pepper
8 cherry tomatoes
4–8 boiling onions, trimmed
    whole
1–2 green bell peppers, cut in
    1-inch squares

Marinated Chicken
Tavuk Izgara

Cut the chicken into small pieces. Cut the thighs and legs in half, the breast in similarly sized portions. Mix together the yogurt, onion, garlic, lemon juice, cumin, paprika, salt, and pepper. Put the chicken in a mixing bowl and pour the marinade over it. Mix to coat the chicken pieces well. Refrigerate overnight or 8 to 10 hours. Grill the chicken over a charcoal fire, turning and basting frequently. Allow 20 to 25 minutes cooking time.

4 Servings

1 frying chicken
1 cup yogurt
1/2 grated onion
3–4 cloves garlic, mashed
Juice of 1/2 lemon
1 tablespoon cumin
1 tablespoon paprika
Salt and pepper

Chicken with Eggplant
Patlıcanlı Tavuk

1. Cut the stem off the eggplant. Using a vegetable peeler, peeling lengthwise, remove a strip of skin; leave the next strip on. Continue to peel in this striped fashion. Cut the eggplant in eighths lengthwise. Sprinkle generously with salt and set aside for at least 3 hours.

2. In a heavy pan, melt the butter and sauté the chicken pieces on all sides. Remove from the pan and set aside.

3. Sauté the onions and green pepper in the same pan for a few minutes. Add the tomatoes and sauté a little longer. Add the chicken, chicken stock or water, salt, and pepper. Simmer 30 minutes or until the chicken is almost tender. Check occasionally as it cooks and add more hot stock or water, a small amount at a time, if needed.

4. Rinse the eggplant well under running water. Squeeze each piece in your hand and then in a clean old towel to remove as much moisture as possible without tearing. Fry the eggplant in oil until golden brown on all sides and drain the excess oil on paper towel. Stir it into the chicken mixture. Cover and simmer until the chicken and the eggplant are thoroughly cooked, 30 to 50 minutes.

4 Servings

1 chicken (2 1/2–3 lbs.), cut into serving pieces
1 medium eggplant
Salt
3–4 tablespoons butter
1 1/2 large onions, chopped
2 green bell peppers, diced
3 large tomatoes or 1 lb. canned tomatoes, cubed

1/4 cup or more hot chicken
   stock or water
Salt and freshly ground pepper
Oil for frying

Chicken with Peas and Potatoes
Patatesli Bezelyeli Tavuk

1. Sauté the potatoes in the oil. Set aside.
2. In a heavy pan, melt the butter and brown the chicken on all sides; remove from the pan and set aside. Add the onions to the pan and sauté. Add the tomatoes; sauté a few minutes. Stir in the chicken, 1/2 cup hot chicken stock or water, paprika, salt, and pepper and simmer 30 minutes. Stir in the peas and potatoes with an additional chicken stock or water, and simmer 20 minutes longer or until the chicken and the vegetables are tender.

3–4 Servings

1 chicken (21/2–3 lbs.), cut into
   serving pieces
3 potatoes, diced
2 tablespoons oil
4 tablespoons butter
11/2 large onions, chopped
3 large tomatoes or 1 lb. canned
   tomatoes, cubed
1/2 cup or more chicken stock
   or water
1–2 tablespoons paprika
Salt and freshly ground pepper
   to taste
1 cup peas

Chicken *Topkapı*
Topkapı Piliç

1. Brown the chicken in 1 tablespoon butter and 1 tablespoon oil. Cover and simmer 35–40 minutes. Set aside.

2. In a heavy pan, melt the rest of the butter and sauté the onions with the pine nuts for 10 minutes. Add the rice and sauté for 5 to 10 minutes. Stir in the tomatoes and cook 2 to 3 minutes. Add the chicken stock, sugar, allspice, salt, pepper, dill, currants, and chicken with its drippings. Cover and cook until all the moisture is absorbed. Remove from heat, cover, and let stand 20 minutes on a heat diffuser or somewhere warm.

4 Servings

8 or 9 chicken thighs or
  drumsticks
6 tablespoons butter
1 tablespoon oil
2 chopped onions
2 tablespoons pine nuts
2 cups uncooked rice
2 ripe tomatoes, grated
3 cups hot chicken stock
3/4 teaspoon sugar
1/2 teaspoon allspice
Salt and freshly ground pepper
  to taste
1/2 cup chopped dill
2 tablespoons currants

Stuffed Chicken
Tavuk Dolması

1. Remove the gizzard, heart, and liver; wash

the chicken and dry. Rub the chicken, inside and out, with the lemon juice, salt, and pepper. Sprinkle with the thyme. Set aside.

2. Cook first, then dice the gizzard, liver and heart and sauté in 1 tablespoon butter until just beginning to brown. Set aside.

3. Melt 3 tablespoons butter, add the onions and pine nuts, and cook, stirring frequently, for 15 minutes. Add the rice and sauté 10 minutes. Stir in the tomato and cook 5 minutes longer. Add 1 1/4 cups chicken stock, giblets, currants, dill, sugar, allspice, and pepper; mix well. Taste and adjust the seasoning. Simmer, covered, for 15 minutes or until all the liquid is absorbed. Remove from heat. Keep covered for 10 to 20 minutes.

4. Preheat the oven to 350°. Pack the stuffing firmly into the chicken. Leave any leftover rice mixture in the pan. Cover the cavity opening with a piece of aluminum foil. Rub the chicken with 2 tablespoons butter. Grease a roasting pan in which the chicken fits snugly. Place the chicken in the pan and bake, covered, 1 1/2 to 1 3/4 hours. Uncover and bake 30 minutes longer or until the chicken is done.

5. Add the remaining chicken stock to the leftover rice in the pan. Cover and cook until all the moisture is absorbed. Remove from heat, keep warm to serve for second portions.

4 Servings

1 3-lb. chicken, with gizzard
  heart, liver
Juice of 1 lemon
Salt and freshly ground pepper
  to taste
1/2 teaspoon thyme leaves
Water
6 tablespoons butter
1 small onion, finely chopped

1 1/2 tablespoons pine nuts
1 cup uncooked rice
1 large ripe tomato, mashed
1 1/2 cups chicken stock
1 1/2 tablespoons currants
1/3 cup fresh dill, chopped, or
   1 1/2 teaspoons dill weed
1/2 teaspoon sugar
1/2 teaspoon allspice
Salt and freshly ground pepper
   to taste

Poussin in Paper
Kağıtta Piliç

Preheat the oven to 375°. Place 2 sheets of wax paper, one directly on top of the other, on a flat surface. Coat lightly with the oil. Place one chicken half in the middle of the sheet. Sprinkle with salt, pepper, and thyme. Place 2 bay leaves on top; spread 1/2 cup mushrooms over the chicken. Place 2 sliced tomatoes over the mushrooms. Place the slices of 1/2 lemon on the tomatoes. Sprinkle lightly with salt. Dot with 1 tablespoon butter. Fold one edge of the wax paper over the chicken and vegetables. Fold over the opposite edge. Fold one end over, then the other end, forming a package. Repeat the same process with the other half of the ingredients. Place the packages in a baking pan. Sprinkle a little water over the packages; bake 1 to 1 1/4 hours.

2-4 Servings

1 poussin split into halves
Salt and pepper
2 teaspoons thyme
4 bay leaves

1 cup mushrooms, chopped
4 large ripe tomatoes, sliced
1 lemon, peeled and sliced
2 tablespoons butter
4 sheets wax paper (15 inches by 15 inches)
2 teaspoons oil

Rice Dolmas and Vegetables without Meat

There is a great abundance of vegetables in Turkey. More importantly, they taste unbelievably good. Tomatoes are so sweet and tasty that children eat them like apples, and they are generously used in cooking. Eggplant can be called the queen of vegetables in Turkey; people are very fond of it and use it in a seemingly infinite variety of ways. The eggplant used in Turkey resembles Japanese eggplant in its shape but is larger and tastes better. Bell peppers have tender skins and are very fragrant; they cook faster than their American counterparts. There is a long, delicate variety of green pepper (apparently unavailable in the West) that greatly improves the taste of many dishes and salads.

Vegetables are either cooked with meat (as in the case of meat *dolmas* and stews) or without. Many of those prepared without meat are cooked in olive oil and eaten cold, usually sprinkled with lemon juice. In Turkish cuisine, vegetables are never boiled and drained but cooked in their own liquid instead, thus retaining all their nutritive value and taste. Almost always, pure vegetable dishes are cooked in olive oil and eaten cold. Such olive-oil dishes are uniquely tasty, light, and refreshing, especially in summertime when meat dishes would prove too heavy.

As with so many of the meat dishes, the vegetables should simmer in small quantities of liquid and never be drowned in water or permitted to boil. The finished product should have some sauce and be moist but never watery.

I should also like to stress that the olive oil used in most of these recipes should be the finest virgin olive oil with the lowest level of acidity. A good olive oil has a very distinctive taste, color, and smell. Even though I am fortunate enough to have my personal supply from the shores of the Aegean, I recently discovered that California produces virgin olive oil of very good quality. This olive oil is also described as first press, or cold press, olive oil and can be found in specialty stores.

Finally, these vegetable dishes made with olive oil are served as appetizers or side dishes. A combination of them make a delicious and colorful buffet. Because they can be kept conveniently in the refrigerator for several days, in Turkey they are usually made to last more than one day.

Stuffed Artichokes in Olive Oil
Enginar Dolması

1. Mix the juice of 2 lemons and 2 tablespoons flour in a large bowl. Add 2 quarts water, mix thor-oughly. Wash the artichokes. Bend back and snap off the tough, outer leaves, leaving meat at the bottom of the leaves attached to the artichoke base, until only the tender, inner leaves remain. Slice off these leaves just above the heart. With a teaspoon, scoop out the fuzzy choke and remain-ing pinkish leaves. Cut off the stem and using a vegetable peeler, peel around the base, as if peeling an apple until you reach the whitish tender part. The artichoke, now, will look like a cup. As you trim each artichoke, take a lemon half, sprinkle with salt and rub it all around it, inside and outside the base. This will prevent discoloration. After rubbing it with lemon and salt, drop the artichoke into the lemon-water mixture.

2. If you are using fresh fava beans, remove the jackets. Sprinkle the beans with some salt and let them stand 5 or 10 minutes. Remove the skins of the beans. Rinse the beans and reserve. Discard the skins and jackets.

3. Heat 1 cup olive oil in a large pan. Add the onions and 1/2 teaspoon salt and sauté 5 minutes. Stir in the fava beans and rice; cook, stirring frequently, for 5 to 8 minutes. Add 1/2 cup water; cover and cook 5 minutes longer or until all the water is absorbed. Stir in the dill, salt and remove from heat. Let it stand covered 15 minutes.

4. Remove the artichokes from the lemon-water; reserve 41/2 cups of the liquid. Stuff the center cavity of the artichokes with the rice mixture. Place each one on a sheet of wax paper, sprinkle with a little water, and wrap as you would a package. Arrange them stems sides down side by side, in a heavy shallow pan. Add 1 1/2 cups of the reserved liquid, 1/4 cup olive oil, the juice of 1/2 lemon, and the sugar. Cover and cook over medium heat for 5 to 10 minutes. Reduce the heat to low and simmer for more than an hour. The liquid will continually be absorbed; check regularly and replenish it with some of the reserved liquid 1 1/2 cups at a time. When the artichokes are tender, remove the lid and cool them. Unwrap and arrange on a serving platter. Serve cold, garnished with lemon wedges.

6 Servings

6 large artichokes
Water
4 lemons
2 tablespoons flour
1 lb. fresh green fava beans, or
  1/2 package frozen baby lima
  beans (thawed)
1 1/4 cups finest virgin olive oil
3 finely chopped onions
Salt to taste
1/2 cup uncooked long-grain
  rice
2 teaspoons sugar
3/4 cup chopped fresh dill
Lemon wedges for garnish

Cabbage *Dolmas* in Olive Oil
Zeytinyağlı Lahana Dolması

1. Wash the cabbage. With a long, pointed knife, remove the core. Insert the knife deep inside to loosen the leaves. Put the whole head in a large pot with 2 to 3 cups water and simmer about 5 minutes or a little longer until the outermost leaves become soft enough to be pliable (except at the core end). Take the cabbage out of the pot and detach any leaves that can be removed without tearing. Set them aside to drain and cool. Return the cabbage to the pot and simmer a few minutes longer. Remove more outer leaves and continue in this manner until almost all the leaves have been detached. The leaves should be softened without being soft or they will lose their flavor.

2. In a heavy pot, heat 3/4 cup olive oil. Add the onions and pine nuts and cook 15 to 20 minutes, stirring frequently. Stir in the rice and cook 10 to 15 minutes stirring constantly. Stir in the tomatoes and cook 5 minutes longer. Reduce heat to low. Add the dill, mint leaves, sugar, salt, spices, currants, juice of 1 lemon, and 3/4 cup water. Mix well, cover, and simmer 8 to 10 minutes until all the water is absorbed. Remove from heat; cool.

3. Spread one cabbage leaf open on a plate, the core end toward you. Cut off the hard area that attached to the core. Place 1 to 3 tablespoons of filling—depending on the size of the leaf—along the core end of the leaf, 1 inch in from the 3 sides. Fold in the 2 sides to seal the edges. Fold the core end over the filling, and roll toward the pointed end of the leaf. Repeat with the other leaves until you have used all the filling. Your rolls should be 11/4 to 11/2 inches in diameter.

4. Place some loose cabbage leaves in the bottom of the same heavy pot. On top of them arrange the stuffed cabbage in layers. Blend together 1 cup hot water, 1/4 teaspoon salt, the remaining lemon juice, and 2 tablespoons olive oil. Pour over the cabbage. Place a plate upside down over the cabbage rolls to add some weight. Cover and cook over low heat for about 50 minutes or until the leaves are tender. If at any time while cooking the liquid in the pan is absorbed, add 2 or 3 tablespooons hot water. When the *dolmas* are cooked, there should be no more than 1 or 2 tablespoons left in the pan. Remove the pan from heat and leave until cool. Serve cold, garnished with lemon wedges.

6 Servings

1 large head cabbage
3/4 cup plus 2 tablespoons
  finest virgin olive oil
5 medium onions, finely
  chopped
2 heaping tablespoons pine
  nuts
1 cup uncooked long-grain rice
2 small tomatoes, mashed
3 tablespoons chopped fresh
  dill or 1 teaspooon dill weed
3 tablespoons chopped fresh
  mint or 1 tablespoon dry mint
1 tablespoon sugar
1 teaspoon salt
1/2 teaspoon cinnamon
1/8 teaspoon allspice
1/8 teaspoon cloves
Pinch nutmeg
2 heaping tablespoons currants
Juice of 2 lemons
Water
Lemon wedges for garnish

Stuffed Eggplant in Olive Oil

Zeytinyağlı Patlıcan Dolması

1. Cut 1/2 inch off the stem end of each eggplant. Wash and dry the eggplant. Gently rub each between the palms of your hands to soften the inside. Using a vegetable peeler or an apple corer, scoop out the inside leaving a shell 1/8 inch thick. Heat 1/4 cup of the oil; lightly sauté the eggplant 2 to 3 minutes on all sides.

2. In a heavy pan, heat 1/2 cup oil. Add the onions and pine nuts and cook 15 to 20 minutes, stirring frequently. Add the rice and cook 10 to 15 minutes stirring almost constantly. Stir in the tomatoes and cook 5 minutes longer. Add the sugar, currant, spices, mint, dill, and 1/3 cup water. Cover and simmer 10 to 15 minutes until all the water is absorbed. Remove from heat; cool.

3. Stir the filling. Stuff the eggplant, shaking them once or twice as you work to settle the filling. Place a sheet of wax paper in the bottom of a heavy pan. Stand the eggplant upright on top of it. Mix together the remaining olive oil, 3/4 cup hot water, and 1/4 teaspoon salt. Pour over the eggplant. Place a sheet of wax paper over the eggplant. Set a plate upside down on top to add some weight. Cover and cook over low heat 50 minutes. Allow to cool with the lid partially covering the pan. Serve cold.

6 Servings

**2 1/2–3 lbs. Japanese eggplants
(12 eggplants)
1 cup plus 2 tablespoons finest
virgin olive oil
3 onions, minced
1 tablespoon pine nuts
1/2 cup uncooked long-grain rice
2 teaspoons sugar**

1 tablespoon currants
1/2 teaspoon salt
1/4 teaspoon cinnamon
1/8 teaspoon allspice
Pinch cloves
Pinch nutmeg
2 tablespoons fresh mint,
  minced, or 1 tablespoon dry
  mint
2 teaspoons fresh dill, minced,
  or 1 teaspoon dried dill weed
Water

Bell Pepper *Dolmas* in Olive Oil
Zeytinyağlı Biber Dolması

1. Cut off the tops of peppers and save them. Remove the seeds and membranes; wash and drain the peppers. Set aside.

2. In a heavy pan, heat 3/4 cup oil and sauté the onions and pine nuts for 15 to 20 minutes. Add the rice and cook 10 to 15 minutes, stirring frequently. Add the tomatoes and cook 5 minutes longer. Blend in the currants, sugar, mint, dill, spices, 1 teaspoon salt, and 3/4 cup hot water. Simmer, covered, for 15 minutes until all the water is absorbed. Remove from heat and allow to cool.

3. Mix the filling well. Stuff the peppers firmly but not too tightly, leaving a little room for the rice to expand. Place the tops on the peppers. Spread a sheet of wax paper in the bottom of the same heavy pan. Stand the peppers upright, side by side on top of the wax paper. Combine 1 cup hot water with 1/4 teaspoon salt and 2 tablespoons olive oil. Pour over the peppers. Place a plate upside down over them to add some weight. Cover and cook 40 to 50 minutes until the peppers are tender.

Usually there is no need to add more water. If at any time while cooking the liquid in the pan is absorbed, add 2 or 3 tablespoons hot water. When the *dolmas* are cooked, there should be no more than 1 or 2 tablespoons water left in the pan. Serve cold, sprinkled with lemon juice.

6 Servings

6 or more small green bell
  peppers
3/4 cup plus 2 tablespoons
  finest virgin olive oil
5 medium onions,
  finely chopped
2 heaping tablespoons pine
  nuts
1 cup uncooked long-grain rice
2 small tomatoes, mashed
2 heaping tablespoons currants
1 tablespoon sugar
3 tablespoons fresh mint,
  chopped, or 1 tablespoon
  dried mint
3 tablespoons fresh dill,
  chopped, or 1 teaspoon dill
  weed
1/2 teaspoon cinnamon
1/8 teaspoon allspice
Pinch cloves
Pinch nutmeg
Salt
Juice of 1 lemon
Water

"Imam Fainted"
Imam Bayıldı

A celebrated dish. It is delicious and easy to make.

There are two stories—both doubtless apocryphal—about how this dish got its name. According to one, the Imam fainted from pleasure when first served with the dish by its inventor, his wife. According to the other, he fainted when he discovered how much olive oil had been required to produce it.

1. Cut off the stem of each eggplant. Using a vegetable peeler, peel lengthwise, remove a strip of skin; leave the next strip on. Continue to peel in this striped fashion. Fry the eggplants in 3 tablespoons olive oil over medium heat, turning them frequently until they turn golden brown. Place them on a paper towel to drain. Slit the eggplants open along one side, from top to bottom, being careful not to cut all the way through. Use your hands to enlarge the openings as much as possible without tearing so that the eggplants will hold a maximum amount of filling

2. Add the remaining oil into the frying pan you used for frying the eggplants. Sauté the onion and garlic until limp. Add the tomato and sauté 2 minutes longer. Stir in the parsley, salt, and sugar. Remove from heat. Fill the eggplant to heaping with the tomato mixture. Place the stuffed eggplant in a heavy shallow pan. Measure any remaining sauce and add water if necessary to make 1/4 cup. Pour into the pan. Cover it and cook over very low heat for 45 minutes to 1 hour until the eggplants are very tender. Check occasionally and add hot water in very small quantities if the liquid level is too low. At the end of cooking there should be no more than a few tablespoons liquid left in the pan. Serve cold with lemon juice.

2–4 Servings

4 small or 2 large
  Japanese eggplants (1 1/4 lb.)
1/2 cup finest virgin olive oil
2 (2 cups) finely sliced onion
6 large cloves garlic, cut
  lengthwise into 4 to 6 pieces
2 (1 cup) large ripe tomatoes, diced
1/2 cup finely chopped parsley
1/4 teaspoon salt
1-2 teaspoons sugar
Water

Green Beans in Olive Oil
Zeytinyağlı Yeşil Fasulye

1. Trim the beans and cut into 2 or 4 pieces. Wash and drain them.

2. Put the onion and tomatoes in a heavy pan. Sprinkle with salt and rub it in lightly with your fingers. Stir in the beans, olive oil, and sugar; mix well. Cover and cook 15 minutes over medium heat, stirring occasionally, until the beans begin to soften and lose their color and all the moisture has been absorbed. At this point, stir and fry the beans 2 to 3 minutes. Add 1/2 cup water; cover and simmer 40 to 50 minutes or until the beans are tender. Check frequently and add more hot water, 1/2 cup at a time, as necessary. When fully cooked it should be very moist with ample sauce but not watery. Serve cold.

4-6 Servings

1 lb. green beans
1 medium onion, chopped
2 chopped tomatoes
1 teaspoon salt
1/3 cup finest virgin olive oil
3 1/2 teaspoons sugar
1/2–2 cups water

Leeks in Olive Oil
Zeytinyağlı Prasa

1. Trim the leeks. Remove a few of the outer layers. Slice 3/4 inch thick; discard the tough green leaves. Wash several times in plenty of water and drain.

2. In a heavy pan, heat the olive oil. Stir in the leeks and carrots. Cover and cook for 30 minutes over low heat, shaking the pan occasionally. Blend in the rice, sugar, salt, lemon juice, and water. Cover and simmer 30 minutes longer, until the leeks are tender. Check the liquid occasionally and add hot water, a small amount at a time, if necessary. When fully cooked, it should be very moist but not watery. Serve cold with lemon juice.

4 Servings

2 lbs. leeks
1/3 cup finest virgin olive oil
2 small carrots, halved lengthwise, then sliced 1/2 inch thick
2 tablespoons uncooked rice
1 1/2 teaspoons sugar
3/4 teaspoon salt
Juice of 1/2 lemon
1 1/2 cups water

Fresh Fava Beans in Olive Oil
Zeytinyağlı Taze Bakla

This is a very popular summer dish in Turkey. Unfortunately, the fresh fava beans available in

America are usually overgrown and very tough. This recipe calls for fava beans as tender as green beans. When I come across such beans, which usually happens once or twice a year, I feel as if I found gold. With the overgrown ones, one can remove the jackets and use the large fava beans inside them.

String the beans. Wash and drain them. Put them in the bottom of a heavy pan with the chopped onion on top. Sprinkle with the olive oil, dill, sugar, salt, and lemon juice. Pour in 1 cup water. Spread a sheet of wax paper on top. Cover and cook over medium heat for 10 minutes. Reduce the heat to low; as it cooks, gradually add more hot water (up to 3/4 cup). Continue to simmer 1 to 1 3/4 hours until the beans are tender. Transfer to a serving platter and cool. Serve cold with the following sauce.

YOGURT SAUCE:
Blend the garlic and salt into the yogurt and beat until it becomes creamy.

4–6 Servings

**1 lb. very young fresh fava
  beans**
1 chopped onion
1/3 cup finest virgin olive oil
**1/2 cup chopped fresh dill or
  1 tablespoon dill weed**
1 1/2 teaspoons sugar
1 teaspoon salt
Juice of 1/2 lemon
1 3/4 cups water

YOGURT SAUCE:
3/4–1 cup yogurt
1 teaspoon mashed garlic
Salt to taste

Artichokes with Dill and Vegetables

Zeytinyağlı Enginar, Sebzeli

1. Prepare the artichokes (see page 162).

2. Peel the vegetables and wash. Cut the celery root and the potatoes into eighths, and slice the carrot 1/2 inch thick. When all the vegetables have been prepared, remove the artichokes from the lemon-water mixture, dry with a towel, and arrange them in a heavy shallow pan stem side down. Reserve 5 cups of the liquid. Arrange the vegetable chunks around the artichokes in the pan. Pour in the olive oil and 1 1/2 cups of the lemon-water. Sprinkle with the juice of 1/2 lemon, some salt, and the sugar. Spread the dill over all. Put a sheet of wax paper on top. Cover and cook until everything is tender, approximately 1 to 1 1/2 hours. Check occasionally and add more of the liquid, 1 cup at a time, as needed. When it is ready, the liquid should be absorbed. Remove from heat and allow to cool. Serve cold.

4–6 Servings

8 large artichokes
Water
3 lemons
2 tablespoons all-purpose flour
4–5 lemons, cut into halves
Salt
2 chopped onions
1 small celery root
2 small potatoes
2 small carrots
3/4 cup finest virgin olive oil
2 teaspoons sugar
1/2 cup fresh dill, chopped, or
    2 teaspoons dill weed

Celery Root in Olive Oil
Zeytinyağlı Kereviz

1. Peel the dark outer skin of each root until you reach the white part. Wash, drain, and cut in half. Cook in 6 cups boiling, salted water with the juice of 1 lemon. Simmer 10 minutes, drain, and set aside.

2. Heat the olive oil. Sauté the onions, potato, and carrot lightly. Stir in the peas, dill, sugar, and salt. Remove from heat.

3. Scoop the soft pulp out of the celery root halves; discard. Fill the shallow hollows with the vegetable mixture. Put the celery root in a heavy shallow pan. Add 1 1/2 cups water. Spread a sheet of wax paper over the top. Cover and cook 30 to 40 minutes. Check occasionally and add small amounts of hot water as needed. Add the juice of 1 lemon 5 minutes before all the vegetables are fully tender. There should be just a few spoonfuls of liquid left at the end. Transfer the celery root to a platter; pour the sauce over. Serve cold with lemon wedges.

4 Servings

1 1/3 lbs. celery root
Juice of 2 lemons
Water
1/2 cup finest virgin olive oil
10 pearl onions, or 1 1/2 chopped
   onions
1 diced potato
1 diced carrot
1/4 cup fresh peas
1/2 cup chopped fresh dill
1 teaspoon sugar
Salt to taste
Lemon wedges for garnish

Zucchini with Dill and Mint
Zeytinyağlı Kabak

In a heavy pan, heat the olive oil. Sauté the onions and garlic for 5 minutes. Add the zucchini and continue to sauté 7 to 10 minutes. Stir in the tomatoes; cook 2 or 3 minutes. Add the dill, mint, sugar, salt, pepper, and 1/2 cup water. Spread a piece of wax paper on top. Cover and cook over low heat until the zucchini is tender. Check the liquid frequently and add hot water, 1/2 cup at a time, as necessary. Serve hot or cold.

6 Servings

11/2 lbs. zucchini, lightly
   scraped and cubed
1/2 cup finest virgin olive oil
2 finely chopped onions
6–8 cloves garlic, cut
   lengthwise into quarters
2 cubed tomatoes
1/4 cup chopped fresh dill or
   1 tablespoon dill weed
1/4 cup chopped mint leaves or
   1 tablespoon dry mint
1 teaspoon sugar
Salt and pepper to taste
1/2–1 cup water

Sautéed Eggplant with Tomato-Garlic Sauce
Domates Salçalı Patlıcan Kızartması

Everybody's favorite!

1. Cut the stem off the eggplant. Using a vegetable peeler, and peeling lengthwise, remove a strip of skin; leave the next strip on. Continue to peel in this striped fashion. Cut the eggplant lengthwise in half, then crosswise into slices 1/4–1/3 inch thick. Spread the slices in a large tray and sprinkle them with 2 1/2–3 tablespoons salt. Put them in a collander and set aside for 4 hours.

2. Rinse the eggplant well under running water. Squeeze each slice in your hand and then in a clean old towel to get all the water out without tearing. Heat the oil and fry the eggplant slices over high heat on both sides until golden brown. Place them on a paper towel to drain.

3. Pour off all but 1 tablespoon of the oil from the skillet. Mash the tomatoes with a fork and put them in the same skillet. Simmer, stirring often, 5 to 10 minutes until they form a thin sauce. Blend in the tomato paste and water. Cook 1 minute. Stir in the garlic and vinegar and remove from heat.

4. Arrange the eggplant slices in a serving dish and pour the sauce over them. Serve warm or cold.

4 Servings

1 eggplant
Salt
Finest virgin olive oil for frying
1 10-oz. can tomatoes with
   liquid
1 chopped tomato
1 tablespoon tomato paste
2 tablespoons water
2 teaspoons or more mashed
   garlic
2 teaspoons vinegar

Sautéed Zucchini
Kabak Kızartması

Scrape the zucchini lightly and wash them. Cut lengthwise into 1/4-inch-thick slices and dry well. Heat the olive oil over high heat. Dredge the zucchini with flour and fry in hot oil until golden brown on both sides. Arrange on a serving platter; sprinkle with a little salt. Serve hot or cold with Yogurt Sauce.

4 Servings

1 lb. zucchini
1/2–1 cup olive oil for frying
1 cup flour
Salt to taste
Yogurt Sauce, page 178

Sautéed Carrots
Havuç Kızartması

Scrape and wash the carrots. Cook whole in boiling salted water until almost tender. Cool and slice diagonally 1/6-inch thick. Dry well. Dredge with seasoned flour and fry in hot olive oil until golden brown on both sides. Serve warm with the following sauce.

YOGURT SAUCE:
Blend the garlic and salt into the yogurt and beat to a creamy consistency. Allow to reach room temperature.

4–6 Servings

1 lb. carrots
1/2 cup all-purpose flour
Salt to taste
1/2 cup olive oil for frying

YOGURT SAUCE:
2 cups yogurt
1–2 teaspoons or more
   mashed garlic
Salt to taste

Sautéed Cauliflower
Karnıbahar Tavası

1. Wash and trim the cauliflower but leave it whole. Place it in a bowl with 6 cups salted water head down and soak 30 minutes. Put it in a pan with water to cover, salt, and the lemon juice and simmer about 15 to 20 minutes until barely tender. Remove immediately from the water and drain. Separate into florets.

2. Mix the eggs, cheese, salt, and pepper to taste in a bowl. Put the flour in another bowl. Dip each floret into the flour, then into the egg and cheese. Fry in hot oil until golden brown on both sides. Serve hot with Yogurt Sauce.

4–6 Servings

1 medium head cauliflower
Water
Juice of 1 lemon
Salt
4 eggs, lightly beaten
3/4 cup grated kasseri or
   Romano cheese
Pepper
1/2 cup all-purpose flour

1 cup oil for frying
Yogurt Sauce, p. 178

Vegetable Patties
Mücver

1. Scrape, wash, and dry the zucchini. Grate it coarsely into a collander, sprinkle with salt, and let it stand 30 minutes. Squeeze it dry with your hands and put it in a bowl with all the ingredients. Mix well.

2. Heat the oil very hot in a frying pan. Drop the zucchini mixture by tablespoonfuls one at a time into the oil. Fry on both sides until golden brown. Serve hot or cold.

6 Servings

1 lb. zucchini
1 small onion, grated
3 green onions including tops,
   minced
1/2 cup fresh dill, chopped, or
   2 teaspoons dried dill weed
1/2 cup chopped parsley
4 eggs, slightly beaten
2/3 cup all-purpose flour
2/3 cup grated kasseri or
   Romano cheese, or
   crumbled feta cheese
Salt and pepper to taste
1 cup oil for frying

Eggplant Purée
Patlıcan Beğendi

Traditionally prepared for the dish "Sultan's Delight" (page 89), this also makes an interesting, tasty side dish that goes well with many meat entrées.

1. Place the unpeeled eggplant over a charcoal fire or directly on a gas flame. Cook, turning on all sides, until it is thoroughly soft and the skin is black and charred. Allow to cool slightly. Peel the eggplant and carefully remove all the pieces of burnt, black skin, and wipe clean with wet hands. Place in a bowl.

2. Melt the butter in a saucepan. Blend in the flour and stir over medium heat 2 or 3 minutes. Take small pieces of the eggplant and squeeze out all the water. Stir into the butter and flour mixture. Add all the eggplant and beat well with a fork until smooth. Gradually add the hot milk, beating briskly with a wire whisk. When the mixture becomes a smooth paste, stir in the cheese. Correct the seasoning. Remove from heat and serve immediately.

6 Servings

2 medium eggplants
4 tablespoons butter
3 tablespoons flour
1 1/2 cups hot milk
**1/2 cup grated kasseri or
 Romano cheese**
Salt and pepper to taste

Sautéed Spinach with Yogurt
Yoğurtlu Ispanak Kavurması

1. Wash the spinach and cut off the stems (use for another dish). Chop the spinach leaves very finely. Drop them in 2 cups boiling, salted water and boil 3 minutes. Drain and cool; use your hands to squeeze out all the water.

2. Heat the olive oil and sauté the spinach 10 minutes. Add salt, remove from heat, and arrange on a serving dish.

3. Combine the yogurt with a little salt and the mashed garlic. Beat until smooth and creamy; pour over the spinach and mix together. Sprinkle paprika on top to garnish.

6 Servings

1 lb. spinach
2 cups boiling water
Salt
1/4–1/3 cup olive oil
2 cups yogurt
1–11/2 teaspoons or more
  mashed garlic
Paprika

Salads

In Turkey, salads are eaten together with the main dish, not as a prelude to it as in America or after it as in Europe. According to Turkish palates, the taste of a good salad enhances that of the main dish, particularly meat or fish, with which it is eaten.

Salad ingredients range from garden greens to raw or cooked vegetables, including legumes, salted dry fish, and even lamb's brains. But the most frequently used salad ingredients are various varieties of lettuce, cucumbers, tomatoes, onions, green onions, fresh garlic, and long, tender green peppers. Fresh herbs like parsley, dill, basil, and mint are also used. The fact that these vegetables are the best of their kind—tomatoes, for example, being almost as sweet and juicy as fruits—may explain why they are almost never masked with thick, elaborate salad dressings, but dressed only in finest quality, virgin olive oil and a little vinegar or lemon juice. Olive oil, after all, is an abundant commodity in Turkey, and the excellence of a salad depends very much on the quality and the variety of the oil. It is perhaps not surprising then that in Turkey, if a person wishes to comment on the salad, he will praise the olive oil rather than the vegetables used.

Oil and Lemon Dressing

Combine all the ingredients in a small bowl and beat well with a fork.

1/4 **cup finest virgin olive oil**
2–4 tablespoons lemon juice
1/4–1/2 **teaspoon salt**
Freshly ground pepper
   (optional)
1–2 tablespoons fresh parsley,
   dill, or mint, minced

Oil and Vinegar Dressing

Prepare as in the Oil and Lemon dressing, replacing lemon juice with vinegar.

Cucumber Yogurt Salad
Cacık

Very cool and refreshing, this is a summer favorite.

1. Peel the cucumbers and chop very finely, so that they almost look grated. Sprinkle with salt; set aside.

2. Beat the yogurt with a wire whisk until creamy. Gradually stir in 1/2 to 1 cup water, depending on the thickness of the yogurt. Mix in the garlic and the cucumbers. Add salt to taste. You may dribble olive oil over the top. Sprinkle with mint leaves and chill.

4 Servings

2 cucumbers
Salt
2 cups yogurt
1/2 cup water
2 large cloves garlic,
  mashed
2 tablespoons olive oil
  (optional)
1–2 tablespoons chopped mint,
  fresh or dried

Shepherd's Salad
Çoban Salatası

This salad is especially good with broiled meat and fish dishes.

Make sure all the vegetables are very finely chopped. Toss them all together in a bowl. Add the dressing and vinegar and mix well.

8 Servings

3 large ripe tomatoes, diced
2 small cucumbers, diced
1 small onion, diced
3–4 minced green onions,
    including tops
1–2 large green bell peppers,
    diced
1 (or more) hot green chilies,
    minced
1 cup chopped parsley
1 tablespoon vinegar
Salt
Oil and Lemon Dressing,
    page 182

Tomato Salad
Domates Salatası

1. Put the onions in a bowl with 1 tablespoon salt. Rub them with your hands, rinse with cold water several times, and squeeze in the palm of your hand until dry.

2. Arrange the tomatoes and onions on a serving plate. Sprinkle with the diced chili peppers.

Pour the dressing over all just before serving. Serve with meat or fish dishes.

4–6 Servings

1 onion, halved lengthwise,
**   then sliced paper-thin**
Salt
3 large tomatoes, sliced
2 or more small chili peppers,
**   diced**
Oil and Lemon Dressing with
**   mint leaves, page 182**

Spinach Salad
Ispanak Salatası

Very good and interesting.

1. Cut off the stems; wash, drain, and chop the spinach. Put it in a mixing bowl and dry well with a kitchen towel.

2. In a salad bowl combine the spinach, onion rings, tomatoes, and cheese.

3. Toss salad with the dressing. Adjust the salt, if necessary (feta cheese is salty).

6–8 Servings

1 bunch spinach
1 small red onion, sliced in
**   rings**
1 large tomato
1/2 cup crumbled feta cheese
Double batch Oil and Lemon or
**   Oil and Vinegar Dressing,**
**   page 182-83**

Romaine Salad

Marul Salatası

    1. Wash and thoroughly dry the lettuce. Shred it finely.

    2. In a salad bowl, combine the lettuce, tomato, olives, onion, and radishes. Mix in a little salt. Sprinkle the dressing over the salad and toss to moisten. Sprinkle the cheese on top. Serve with meat or meat and vegetable combination dishes.

6 Servings

1 head romaine or red lettuce
1 large tomato, chopped
1 sliced cucumber
10 black Greek olives
4–5 chopped green onions,
    including tops
1 bunch radishes
3 tablespoons crumbled feta
    cheese
Oil and Lemon Dressing,
    page 182

Green Leaf Lettuce Salad

Kıvırcık Marul Salatası

    Wash the lettuce and dry it well. Shred it finely. In a salad bowl, combine the lettuce with the green onions and a little salt. Sprinkle the dressing over the salad and toss well. This salad is good with fish dishes, especially with fried or broiled fish.

6 Servings

1 head green leaf lettuce
4–5 finely chopped green
  onions, including tops
Salt
Oil and Lemon Dressing,
  page 182

Cucumber and Tomato Salad
Domates ve Salatalık Salatası

1. Cut the tomato into 10 or so wedges. Pare the cucumber; cut it in half lengthwise and then in thin slices. Cut the onion in half lengthwise, then slice it paper-thin; put the slices in a bowl, sprinkle with salt, and gently squeeze in the palm of one hand. Rinse and dry the onions.

2. On a platter, arrange in succession rows of tomato wedges, rows of overlapping cucumber slices and rows of overlapping onion pieces. Sprinkle all with the dill or parsley, salt to taste, and the chili pepper, if you are using it.

3. Mix together the dressing and vinegar with a fork. Sprinkle enough dressing over the salad to moisten it well. Serve with meat or meat and vegetable dishes.

6 Servings

1 large tomato
1 cucumber
1 small onion
1 tablespoon chopped fresh dill
  or parsley
Salt
1–2 green chili peppers, finely
  chopped (optional)
1 tablespoon vinegar

Eggplant Salad
Patlıcan Salatası

1. Place the unpeeled eggplant directly on a gas burner over a high flame or over a charcoal fire. Turn frequently to cook on all sides. It is done when the skin is charred and black and the eggplant is thoroughly soft. Cool slightly. Peel the eggplant, carefully removing all the pieces of burnt, black skin. Wipe clean with wet hands. Squeeze out all the water.
2. Place the eggplant in a bowl with the lemon juice and salt; mash well. Add the olive oil, garlic, and vinegar or lemon juice; blend thoroughly. Serve on a plate garnished with tomato and onion slices and olives. Serve as a side dish.

4 Servings

1 large eggplant (1 1/2 lbs.)
Juice of 1/2 lemon
Salt
1/3 cup olive oil
1 1/2–2 teaspoons garlic, mashed
2 1/2 tablespoons or more
   vinegar or lemon juice
Tomato slices, onion slices, and
   black Greek olives for
   garnish

Marinated Roast Peppers
Sirkeli Sarmısaklı Yeşil Biber

1. Place the peppers directly on a gas burner over a high flame or over a charcoal fire. (If you must use an electric stove, cook them in an ungreased cast-iron skillet over medium heat.) Turn frequently to cook on all sides. They are done when the skins are charred and black and the peppers are limp. Remove from heat. To skin, put the peppers immediately into a large plastic bag and seal it closed. Cover with a towel; let stand 30 minutes. Peel off the skin and rinse the peppers in cold water. Pat dry. Cut off the tops and remove the seeds. Cut each lengthwise into 4 or 5 pieces. Arrange in a serving dish.

2. Combine the garlic, vinegar, and salt. Pour over the peppers. Refrigerate several hours. Serve at room temperature.

4 Servings

**6 chilies pascillas, or green bell
  peppers
2–3 cloves garlic, mashed
1/2 cup vinegar
Salt to taste**

Roast Peppers with Yogurt
Yoğurtlu Izgara Yeşil Biber

1. Place the peppers directly on a gas burner over a high flame or over a charcoal fire. (If you must use an electric stove, cook them in an ungreased cast-iron skillet over medium heat.) Turn frequently to cook on all sides. They are done when the skins are charred and black and the peppers are limp. Remove from heat. To skin, put the peppers immediately into a large plastic bag and seal it closed. Cover with a towel; let stand 30 minutes. Peel off the skin and rinse the peppers in cold water. Pat dry. Cut off the tops and remove the seeds. Cut into pieces, put half of them in a mortar with the garlic and salt and pound 2 minutes. Remove from the mortar and pound the remaining peppers. Put all in a bowl and blend. Arrange on a serving dish.

2. Whip together the yogurt, water, garlic and a dash of salt until creamy. Pour over the peppers. Serve at about room temperature.

4 Servings

6 chilies pascillas, or green bell
  peppers
1 cup yogurt
1 tablespoon water
3 cloves garlic, mashed
Salt

Cauliflower Salad
Karnıbahar Salatası

1. Remove the thick stem and the leaves from the cauliflower. Soak it head down in cold, salted water for 10 minutes. Place it in a pan with 3 tablespoons salt, juice of 1/2 lemon, and water to barely cover it. When the water comes to a boil, cook 20 minutes, or until tender. Drain and cool. Separate it into florets and arrange them on a serving platter with the olives.

2. Sprinkle the cauliflower and olives with the chopped parsley and scallions and pour the salad dressing over all. Serve at about room temperature.

DRESSING:
Mix together the olive oil, lemon juice, and a dash of salt.

6 Servings

1 small head cauliflower
Salt

Juice of 1/2 lemon
10 black Greek olives
1/2 cup chopped parsley
4 chopped scallions or green
   onions, including tops

DRESSING:
1/3 cup olive oil
1/3 cup lemon juice
Salt to taste

Cauliflower with Tarator Sauce
Taratorlu Karnıbahar Salatası

1. Remove the thick stem and the leaves from the cauliflower. Soak it head down in cold, salted water, for 10 minutes. Place it in a pan with the lemon rind, salt, and water to barely cover it. Bring to a boil and cook 20 minutes, or until tender. Remove from heat. Drain and cool. Separate it into florets and arrange on a platter. Pour tarator sauce on top.

4–6 Servings

1 large head (2 lbs.) cauliflower
Rind of 1 lemon
Salt
Tarator Sauce, page 58

Beet Salad
Pancar Salatası

1. Bring the beets to a boil in salted water; simmer until tender but not too soft, about 20 to 30 minutes. Drain and cool. Grate coarsely.

2. Combine the yogurt with the garlic and about 1/3 teaspoon salt and beat until smooth and creamy. Mix in the beets and blend well. Transfer to a serving dish. Dribble the olive oil on top to garnish. Serve at about room temperature.

4 Servings

1 bunch (1 lb.) beets
Salt
1 cup yogurt
3 cloves garlic, finely mashed
1 tablespoon olive oil

Turnip Salad
Turp Salatası

1. Pare, wash, and grate the turnips. Mix with a little salt.
2. Combine the olive oil and the lemon juice. Pour dressing over the grated turnip and blend well. Garnish with the olives. Serve at about room temperature.

4 Servings

2 turnips
Salt
Oil and Lemon Dressing,
    page 182
10 black, Greek olives for
    garnish

Cabbage Salad
Lahana Salatası

Toss the shredded cabbage with the dressing. Garnish with parsley.

4 Servings

**1 small head white or red
  cabbage, shredded
Oil and Lemon Dressing,
  page 182
Chopped parsley and 8 black
  olives for garnish**

Shredded Carrot Salad
Havuç Rende Salatası

In a salad bowl, toss the shredded carrots with the dressing to moisten. Adjust the salt. Sprinkle the chopped parsley on top.

4 Servings

**4 large carrots, shredded
Oil and Lemon dressing,
  page 182
1 tablespoon chopped parsley**

Bean Salad
Fasulye Piyazı

1. Soak the beans in plenty of water overnight. Drain.

2. Boil the beans about 2 hours or longer until tender. Let cool in the pan. Drain, mix with the onion, salt, and 1/3 cup vinegar, and let stand 2 or 3 hours. Add the parsley and green pepper; blend.

3. Mound salad onto a salad platter. Decorate with the olives and wedges of egg and tomato.

4. Mix the vinegar with the olive oil and pour over the salad. Serve at about room temperature. It can be served as a side dish or salad for luncheons. In Turkey, it is often prepared in advance and taken for picnics.

6 Servings

1 cup Great Northern beans
1 onion, halved lengthwise,
  then sliced paper-thin
Salt to taste
1/3 cup vinegar
1/2–1 cup chopped parsley
1–2 bell peppers, chopped, or
  2–3 small green Mexican
  chilies, chopped
10 black Greek olives
3 hard-boiled eggs, cut
  lengthwise into eighths
2 tomatoes, cut in wedges
1/4 cup or more vinegar
1/2 cup olive oil

Mashed Bean Salad
Fasulye Ezmesi

1. Soak beans overnight in plenty of water. Drain.

2. Boil the beans 2 hours or longer until thoroughly cooked and tender. Drain and cool slightly. Purée the beans using a meat grinder or a blender.

Mix in the olive oil, vinegar, salt to taste, and lemon juice and blend well. Arrange on a serving plate. Decorate with the onions, parsley, and eggs.

6 Servings

1 cup dried Great Northern
  beans
1/2 cup olive oil
1 tablespoon vinegar
Salt
1/4–1/3 cup lemon juice
1 tablespoon chopped parsley
2–3 chopped green onions,
  including tops
2 hard-boiled eggs, quartered

Tabbouleh

Kısır

1. Pour 2 cups cold water over the bulgur. Cover and let stand 30 minutes.

2. Squeeze dry with your hands and try to extract as much moisture as possible. Add salt and the onions and rub together with your hands 2 to 3 minutes. Add the remaining ingredients and blend well. Adjust the salt.

3. Arrange romaine lettuce leaves on a platter. Mound the salad on top. This is a very good salad for luncheons and buffet dinners.

8 Servings

1 cup fine-grain bulgur
Water
1 tablespoon paprika
Salt

2 cups minced parsley
3 tablespoons minced
  mint
3 ripe tomatoes, sliced
1 cup finely chopped green
  onions, including tops
1/3 cup or more olive oil
1/4 cup or more lemon juice
Romaine lettuce

Potato Salad
Patates Salatası

1. Cook the potatoes in boiling water until tender. Peel and slice very thin into a salad bowl. Stir in the onions, dill, or parsley.

2. Combine the oil with the vinegar, lemon juice, mustard, salt, and pepper to taste; blend well. Pour enough dressing over the salad to moisten; mix thoroughly. Adjust the salt and add more vinegar if necessary. Garnish with black olives. Serve at about room temperature.

6 Servings

1 lb. potatoes
2 onions, halved lengthwise,
  then sliced paper-thin
1/2 cup chopped fresh dill, or
  1/2 cup chopped parsley
1/2 cup or more olive oil
1/4 cup vinegar
2 tablespoons lemon juice
1 teaspoon dry mustard
Salt and coarsely ground pepper
10 black Greek olives for
  garnish

Brain Salad

Beyin Salatası

1. Wash the brains under running water and soak for 1 hour in cold water to which 1 tablespoon vinegar has been added. Remove the membrane and veins under cold running water.

2. Put 4 cups water in a saucepan along with 1 tablespoon vinegar, the onion, and 1 teaspoon salt. Add the brains and simmer 15 minutes. Remove from the pan. Cool, pat dry with a towel, and cut crosswise into 1/2-inch slices.

3. Arrange the brain slices on a serving plate. Garnish with the olives and tomato slices. Sprinkle the green onions and parsley on top. Pour enough dressing over the salad. Serve as a salad for luncheons or buffet dinners.

6 Servings

2 sets lamb's brains
Water
2 tablespoons vinegar
1 small onion
1 teaspoon salt
10 black Greek olives
1 large tomato, sliced
3 chopped green onions
Chopped parsley
Oil and Lemon Dressing
  dressing, page 182

Anchovy Salad

Ançuez Salatası

1. Rub off as much salt as possible from the

anchovies. Place the anchovies in a bowl. Add vinegar to cover. Let stand 1 hour; drain.

2. Divide each anchovy into 2 fillets; remove the bone in the center. Arrange the fillets on a platter with the tomato and egg slices and the olives. Mix the vinegar with the olive oil and pour over the salad.

6 Servings

1/2 **lb. salted, dried anchovies**
1/2 **cup or more vinegar to soak**
   the fish
2 **sliced tomatoes**
2 **hard-boiled eggs, sliced**
10 **black Greek olives**
1/3 **cup vinegar**
3 **tablespoons olive oil**

Mackerel Salad
Çiroz Salatası

1. In a heavy skillet, cook the fish over high heat on both sides until they turn yellow. Wrap them in a clean old kitchen towel and pound until thoroughly crushed. Place in a bowl.

2. Bring 3/4 cup vinegar to a boil. Pour over the fish, cover, and let stand 1 hour. Drain.

3. Mix the fish with the olive oil and 1/4 cup vinegar. Arrange on a serving platter and garnish with the chopped dill and black olives.

6 Servings

10 **thin salted, dried mackerel**
3/4 **cup vinegar to soak the fish**
1/4 **cup olive oil**

1/3 cup vinegar
**1 bunch fresh dill, chopped, and
10 black Greek olives for
garnish**

Stuffed Eggplant Pickles
Patlıcan Dolma Turşusu

Pickles form another distinct specialization in Turkish cookery. Special pickle shops are still to be found beckoning the passers-by inside with colorful rows of pickle jars. Connoisseurs will often stop to sample pickles on the spot as a delicacy in their own right, not necessarily to be taken with a meal. Pickle brine *(turşu suyu)* is also appreciated as a surprisingly tasty drink.

To prepare this, you will need a glass jar that has a tight-fitting lid and is large enough to hold all the eggplants.

1. Boil the unpeeled eggplants about 5 to 10 minutes until tender but not too soft. Drain and cool them. Squeeze out all the moisture. Place a heavy object over the eggplants and let them stand overnight to extract all the moisture.

2. Boil whole ribs of the celery until tender; drain and set aside.

3. Slit the eggplants lengthwise, stopping just short of the end and being careful not to cut through to the other side. Stuff with the cabbage and garlic filling.

4. Tie each eggplant with the celery ribs to keep the filling in. Place the eggplants in a clean large jar with a tightly fitting glass top. Combine vinegar, enough to cover them, with salt and pour over eggplants. Cover the jar tightly. Let stand 2 to 3 weeks at room temperature. When the pickles are ready, keep refrigerated.

STUFFING:

Shred the cabbage; mince the bell pepper, garlic, dill, and the leaves from the celery very finely; mix together.

10 eggplant pickles

10 Japanese eggplants
1 bunch celery
Vinegar
Salt (2 teaspoons salt for each
  cup of vinegar)

STUFFING:

1/2 small head cabbage
1-2 red bell peppers
1 small bulb garlic, separated
  into cloves and peeled
1 bunch fresh dill
Celery leaves

Pickled Beets
Pancar Turşusu

Boil the beets until tender but not too soft. Peel them and slice thinly. Put them in a glass or earthenware bowl or a glass jar with vinegar to cover, garlic, and salt. Set aside 5 to 6 days at room temperature. When they are ready, keep refrigerated.

2-quart jar of pickles

1 bunch beets
Vinegar
4-5 large cloves garlic, finely
  mashed

Salt (2 teaspoons salt for each
  cup of vinegar)

Pickled Cabbage
Lahana Turşusu

1. Break off all the cabbage leaves and chop coarsely. Place in a nonmetal bowl and sprinkle with 2 tablespoons salt. Mix well and let stand 2 to 3 hours.

2. Rinse the leaves in cold water; drain. Arrange them in a large clean glass jar or enamel container, spreading the garlic, ginger, hot chili peppers or flakes, and chick-peas here and there among the leaves. Mix together cold water, enough to cover the cabbage, and salt to taste, and sugar; pour over the leaves. Place a clean, heavy stone or other object on top of the leaves to keep them submerged in the brine. Every day, open the lid and stir briefly with a ladle to let air in and prevent development of an unpleasant odor. It will be ready in 2 weeks. Taste the brine every few days and add more salt as necessary. When the pickle is ready, keep in the refrigerator.

2-quart jar of pickles

1 head cabbage
Salt (2 teaspoons salt for 1 cup
  of water)
1 small bulb garlic, separated
  into cloves and mashed ‚
1–2 tablespoons fresh ginger,
  mashed (optional)
5–10 small red hot chili peppers
  or 1 tablespoon chili pepper
  flakes
1/2 cup chick-peas
1 teaspoon sugar

Mixed Pickles
Karışık Turşu

1. Wash and drain all the vegetables. Mix together the minced cabbage, carrots, garlic, red pepper, and dill in a bowl. Stuff the bell peppers with this mixture. Arrange all the vegetables in a jar. Put the garlic cloves and dill here and there. Decorate with the lemon slices.

2. Mix the water with the vinegar and salt. Pour over the vegetables to cover. Cover the jar tightly. Let stand at room temperature 2 to 3 weeks. When the pickles are ready, keep in the refrigerator.

Note: Adjust the salt content once or twice during the pickling process by simply tasting the brine.

2–3 quarts jar of pickles

2 small, whole pickling
  cucumbers
2 thickly sliced carrots
2–3 cauliflower florets
2 green bell peppers
1 red bell pepper
3–4 raw green beans
2 small green tomatoes
1–2 long green peppers
2 cups minced cabbage
1/2 cup minced carrots
5 cloves minced garlic
1/4 cup minced red pepper
2 tablespoons minced dill
5–8 cloves garlic
A few dried chili pepper pods
A few sprigs fresh dill
A few slices lemon

4 cups water
1 cup white vinegar
Salt (2 teaspoons salt for 1 cup
  of water and vinegar mixture)

Pilav

Turkish pilav is something different from simple boiled rice. The art of cooking it begins with identifying the rice being used and estimating its capacity to absorb water, since the amount of liquid required for cooking the pilav will vary according to the kind of rice used. Even a small miscalculation in the amount of liquid used can adversely affect the quality of the pilav.

Pilav in Turkish cookery—in contrast with Iranian and Indian cuisine—is fundamentally a side dish; it accompanies but is not mixed with meat dishes. But there are, of course, particularly elaborate pilavs that can be served as main courses. By using his or her imagination creatively and incorporating different ingredients, a cook can invent an almost infinite variety of pilav dishes. Some pilavs are made with bulgur instead of rice.

Long-Grain Rice Pilav
Sade Pilav

1. Wash and drain the rice until the water runs clear. In a bowl, cover the rice with hot water mixed with 1 teaspoon salt. Cover the bowl and let the rice soak 1 hour.

2. In a heavy pan, bring the meat stock or water to a boil with the butter and salt. Drain the rice well and stir it into the boiling liquid. Cover and cook over medium-high heat for 5 minutes. Reduce heat to low and cook until all the water is absorbed. Fold up a clean towel and cover the top of the pan with it; put the pan lid over the towel. Move the pan to a heat diffuser over the lowest heat or some other warm surface and leave it there, covered, for 30 minutes. Stir and serve hot.

6 Servings

2 cups long-grain rice (very good quality, such as basmati rice)
Salt
3 cups meat stock or water (standard)
4–6 tablespoons butter

Basic Short-Grain Rice Pilav
Pirinç Pilavı Sade

1. Put the rice in a bowl and cover it with hot (not boiling) water mixed with 1 teaspoon salt. Cover and let stand until the water turns cold. Rinse several times with cold water and drain.

2. Melt the butter in a heavy pan. Stir in the rice and cook 10 minutes, stirring constantly. Stir in the hot stock or water. Add salt. Cover and cook over medium heat 5 to 10 minutes. Reduce the heat to low and cook until all the water is absorbed. Fold up a clean towel and place it firmly over the top of the pan; on top of that, place the pan lid. Move the pan to a heat diffuser over a burner on the lowest heat or some other warm surface and leave it there for 20 minutes. Stir and serve hot.

6 Servings

2 cups short-grain rice
Salt
3 cups hot meat stock or water
4–6 tablespoons butter

Pilav with Peas

Bezelyeli Pirinç Pilavı

Prepare Long-Grain Rice Pilav, page 204, or Short-Grain Rice Pilav, page 205. Add the peas when you combine the rice with the meat stock or water and proceed as directed.

6 Servings

2 cups rice
Salt
3 cups meat stock or water
6–8 tablespoons butter
1 cup peas (frozen)

Pilav with Chick-Peas

Pirinç Pilavı Nohutlu

Prepare Long-Grain Rice Pilav, page 204, or Short-Grain Rice Pilav, page 205, but use 8 tablespoons butter. When the rice has cooked in the stock or water for 10 minutes, stir in the chick-peas and proceed as directed.

6 Servings

2 cups rice
Salt
3 cups meat stock or water
6–8 tablespoons butter
1 cup cooked chick-peas

Chicken Pilav
Tavuklu Pilav

Put the chicken stock, butter, and some salt in a heavy pan; bring to a boil. Stir in the rice and chicken. Cover and cook over medium until the liquid is aborbed. Remove the lid, cover the top of the pan with a folded towel, and replace the lid. Move the pan to a heat diffuser on top of the lowest heat or some other warm surface. Leave it there for 30 minutes. Stir, sprinkle with freshly ground pepper, and serve.

6 Servings

1 cup cooked chicken, cut into bite-sized pieces
3 cups chicken stock
6–8 tablespoons butter
Salt
2 cups long-grain rice
Pepper to taste

Bukhara Pilav
Buhara Pilavı

1. Wash and drain the rice until the water runs clear. Cover the rice with hot water mixed with a little salt. Cover and let stand 1 hour. Drain.
2. Melt 4 tablespoons butter in a heavy pan. Stir in the meat, onion, and carrots and cook 25 to 30 minutes, stirring frequently. Stir in the tomatoes and cook 2 or 3 minutes longer. Add 1/2 cup hot water and some salt and pepper; cover and simmer 30 minutes to 1 hour, or until the meat is tender. Add more hot water, as needed, in small quantities.

3. Melt the rest of the butter in a heavy pan. Stir in the almonds and sauté 2 or 3 minutes until almost golden brown. Add the rice and sauté with the almonds 3 or 4 minutes.

4. Measure the liquid from the cooked meat into a bowl. Add enough hot water to make 3 cups and return it to the pan containing the meat. Bring it to a boil. Stir in the rice. Cover and cook over medium heat 5 to 10 minutes; reduce the heat to low and cook until all the liquid is absorbed. Fold up a clean towel and cover the top of the pan with it; on top of that, place the pan lid. Move the pan to a warm surface and let stand 20 minutes.

4–6 Servings

2 lbs. lamb shoulder or lamb
   neck, cut into 1- or 2-inch
   chunks
2 cups long-grain rice
Salt
8 tablespoons butter
1 large onion, chopped
6 carrots, peeled and cut
   into matchstick-size pieces
2 ripe tomatoes, minced
1/2 cup blanched almonds, whole
Salt and pepper to taste

Lamb Pilav
Kuşbaşı Etli Pirinç Pilavı

In a heavy pan, sauté the onions in 2 table-spoons butter until golden brown. Stir in the lamb and cook, stirring frequently, until it browns. Stir in the tomatoes or tomato paste and cook 5 minutes longer, mashing the tomatoes with a fork and stirring. Add 1/2 cup hot water, salt, and pepper. Cover and simmer 1 to 2 hours until the meat is very tender. Check the liquid occasionally and add a small amount of the hot water or stock if necessary. When the meat is thoroughly cooked and all the moisture has been absorbed, add 3 cups hot water or meat stock and the remaining butter. Bring to a boil. Stir in the rice, cover, and cook until all the water is absorbed. Fold up a clean towel and cover the top of the pan with it; on top of that, place the pan lid. Move the pan to a heat diffuser over the lowest heat or some other warm surface and leave it there for 20 minutes. Mix well and serve.

4–6 Servings

1 lb. lamb, cut into bite-sized
  pieces
2 finely chopped onions
6–8 tablespoons butter
2 ripe tomatoes, diced, or
  1 1/2 tablespoons tomato paste
Salt and pepper to taste
3 cups hot water or meat stock
2 cups long-grain rice,
  washed and drained

Pilav with Currants and Pine Nuts
İç Pilav

The different seasonings of this dish are so flavorful that it is almost as tasty without meat.

1. Wash and drain the rice. Put the rice in a bowl and cover it with hot water mixed with 1 teaspoon salt. Cover and let stand until the water is cool. Drain well.

2. If you are using lamb kidneys, sauté them in 1 tablespoon butter and set aside.

If you are using the chicken parts, put them in boiling, salted water and allow them to simmer until they are tender. Drain them well. Dice them and sauté in 1 tablespoon butter. Set aside.

3. Sauté the onion with the pine nuts in the remaining butter until golden brown. Stir in the rice and cook 5 to 8 minutes, stirring frequently. Stir in the tomatoes and cook 5 minutes. Stir in the currants, then the meat stock, sugar, allspice, salt, pepper and kidneys or chicken parts. Cover and cook until all the liquid is absorbed. Stir in the dill. Fold up a clean towel and cover the top of the pan with it; on top of that, place the pan lid. Move the pan to a heat diffuser over the lowest heat or some other warm surface and leave it there for 30 minutes. Mix well and serve.

6 Servings

2 lamb kidneys, diced, or
   chicken gizzard, liver, and
   hearts (optional)
8 tablespoons butter
1 chopped onion
2 tablespoons pine nuts
2 diced tomatoes

2 cups long-grain rice
2 tablespoons currants
3 cups meat stock or chicken
   stock
1/2 teaspoon sugar
1/2 teaspoon allspice
Salt and pepper to taste
1/2 cup fresh dill, chopped, or
   1 tablespoon dill weed

Tomato Pilav
Domatesli Pilav

Prepare Long-Grain Rice Pilav, page 204, or Short-Grain Rice Pilav, page 205. After you have completed step 1, melt the butter in a heavy pan. If you are using fresh tomatoes, sauté them until they become soft and reach the consistency of a sauce. If you are using tomato paste, blend it into the melted butter and heat it thoroughly. For Long-Grain Rice Pilav, add the meat stock or water and salt to the pan of tomatoes. For Short-Grain Rice Pilav, stir the rice into the pan of tomatoes.
Proceed with the rest of step 2 as directed.

6 Servings

2 cups rice
Salt
3 cups meat stock or water
6 tablespoons butter
2 ripe tomatoes, mashed, or
   1 1/2 tablespoons tomato paste

Vermicelli Pilav
Şehriyeli Pilav

Prepare Long-Grain Rice Pilav, page 204, or Short-Grain Rice Pilav, page 205, but use 8 tablespoons butter in all and chicken broth for the liquid in step 2.

After you have completed step 1, sauté the vermicelli in 2 tablespoons butter until golden brown. Set aside.

Proceed with step 2 and add the sautéed vermicelli when you combine the rice with the broth.

6 Servings

2 cups rice
Salt
3 cups chicken broth
6–8 tablespoons butter
3/4 cup vermicelli, roughly
    broken up

Quail Pilav
Bıldırcınlı Pilav

1. Soak the rice in hot water for 1 hour. Drain and set aside.

2. Clean the quail thoroughly. Pat dry and rub with salt. Heat the oil and butter mixture in a frying pan. Sauté the quail on all sides until golden brown. Remove them from the pan and keep them warm. Stir 3 cups water into the drippings. Keep the pan warm.

3. In another pan, melt the butter and stir in the rice. Cook 10 minutes, stirring constantly. Stir in the tomato and sauté 5 minutes. Add salt to taste and the hot liquid from the quail. Cover and cook 10 minutes over medium heat. Reduce the heat to low; cook until the liquid is absorbed. Fold up a clean towel and cover the top of the pan with it; on top of that, place the pan lid. Move the pan to a heat diffuser over the lowest heat or some other warm surface and leave it there for 20 minutes. Stir the rice. Spoon it onto a serving platter and arrange the quail on top. Serve hot.

6 Servings

6 quail
2 cups rice
Salt
1 tablespoon oil mixed with
  1 tablespoon butter
Water
8 tablespoons butter
1 large tomato, chopped

Azerbaijani Pilav
Azerbaycan Pilavı

1. Wash the rice until water runs clear and drain. Soak in hot water for 1 hour. Drain.

2. Remove the thin green skins from the fava beans. Put the beans in a saucepan with 4 tablespoons butter, 1 1/2 cups water, the lemon juice, flour, and 1 teaspoon salt. Cover and cook over low heat 30 to 40 minutes until most of the liquid is absorbed and the beans are almost tender. Set aside.

3. In a heavy pan, sauté the rice in 6 tablespoons butter for 10 minutes. Stir in the cooked fava beans, hot meat stock, and more salt to taste. Cover and cook, 5 minutes over medium heat; reduce the heat to low and cook until all the liquid

is absorbed. Stir in the dill. Fold up a clean towel and cover the top of the pan with it; on top of that, place the pan lid. Move the pan to a heat diffuser over the lowest heat or some other warm surface and leave it there for 30 minutes. If the rice is not quite tender at that point, add 2 tablespoons hot water and continue to let it stand a while as before.

6 Servings

2 cups long-grain rice
1/2 lb. fresh fava beans, shelled,
  or 1/2 package frozen baby
  lima beans (thawed)
10 tablespoons butter
Water
1 1/2 teaspoons lemon juice
1 teaspoon all-purpose flour
Salt
3 cups meat stock or water
1 cup fresh dill, chopped, or
  1 1/2 tablespoons dill weed

Pilav Wrapped in Phyllo
Perde Pilav

A very interesting and impressive looking pilav dish.

1. Place the chicken in a pan with 1 1/2 cups water, the carrot, onion halves, peppercorns, and some salt. Bring to a boil. Cover and simmer until tender. Cool; remove the bones and skin. Cut the chicken into bite-sized pieces and strain the stock. Set both aside.

2. Allow the rice to soak in hot water with 2 teaspoons salt until the water turns cool. Rinse several times. Drain well and set aside.

3. In a heavy saucepan, sauté the chopped onion with the almonds in 8 tablespoons butter for 8 minutes. Add the rice and cook, stirring constantly, for 5 minutes. Stir in the chicken; cook 2 minutes longer. Stir in the currants, 3 cups of chicken stock, and salt to taste. Cover and bring to a boil. Cook over medium heat 5 minutes. Reduce the heat to low and cook until almost all the liquid is absorbed. Let stand 10 minutes on a heat diffuser over the lowest heat.

4. Melt the remaining butter. Brush a 4-quart casserole well with part of it. Arrange the sheets of phyllo dough in the casserole so that their bottom halves line the bottom and sides of the dish, overlapping each other, and their top halves hang out over the rim. Spoon in the chicken and rice. Fold the phyllo sheets over the rice to seal it in a package. Brush the top with the remaining butter and bake at 350° for 15 to 20 minutes or until golden brown. Serve hot.

6–8 Servings

1 small chicken
Water
1 carrot
1 onion, cut in half
8 peppercorns
Salt to taste
2 cups long-grain rice
1 finely chopped onion
3/4 cups blanched almonds
12 tablespoons butter
2 tablespoons currants
8 sheets phyllo pastry

Eggplant Pilav
Patlıcanlı Pilav

1. Cut the stem off the eggplant. Using a vegetable peeler, and peeling lengthwise, remove a strip of skin; leave the next strip on. Continue to peel in this striped fashion. Cut the eggplant into 1/2-inch cubes. Sprinkle generously with salt and set aside for 3 hours.

2. Turn to Long-Grain Rice Pilav, page 204, or Short-Grain Rice Pilav, page 205, and complete step 1.

3. Rinse the eggplant cubes well under running water. Squeeze each piece in your hand and then in a clean towel to get out as much water as possible without tearing. Sauté the eggplant in hot oil over high heat until golden brown on all sides. Drain on paper towels to remove the excess oil.

4. Return to the recipe for Long- or Short-Grain Rice Pilav. Proceed with step 2 and add the sautéed eggplant when you combine the rice with the meat stock or water.

6 Servings

1 eggplant
Salt
1/4 cup oil
2 cups rice
2 1/2–3 cups meat stock
   or water
4–6 tablespoons butter

Eggplant Pilav in Olive Oil
Zeytinyağlı Patlıcanlı Pilav

1. Cut the stem off the eggplant. Using a vegetable peeler, and peeling lengthwise, remove a strip of skin; leave the next strip on. Continue to peel in this striped fashion. Cut the eggplant into 1-inch cubes. Sprinkle generously with salt and set aside for 3 hours. Rinse well under running water. Squeeze each piece in your hand and then in a clean old towel to get out as much water as possible without tearing.

2. Soak the rice in hot water mixed with 2 teaspoons salt until the water turns cool. Drain well and set aside.

3. Heat the olive oil in a heavy pan and cook the eggplant cubes, stirring frequently, until tender and golden brown on all sides. Drain on paper towels to remove the excess oil.

4. Add the onions and pine nuts to the same pan. Sauté 15 to 20 minutes. Stir in the rice; cook, stirring frequently, 8 to 10 minutes. Stir in the tomatoes and cook a few minutes longer. Stir in the eggplant, currants, sugar, cinnamon, allspice, salt, pepper, and 3 cups hot water; bring to a boil. Cover and cook over medium heat 5 minutes. Reduce the heat to low and cook until all the water is absorbed. Stir in the dill. Fold up a clean towel and cover the top of the pan with it; on top of that, place the pan lid. Set the pan on a heat diffuser over the lowest heat or some other warm surface and leave it there for 30 minutes. Stir. Serve cold.

8–10 Servings

1 medium (1 lb.) eggplant
Salt
2 cups long-grain rice
Water

3/4 cup olive oil
3 chopped onions
2 tablespoons pine nuts
1 large ripe tomato, diced
2 tablespoons currants
1 tablespoon sugar
2 teaspoons cinnamon
2 teaspoons allspice
Salt and pepper to taste
1 cup fresh dill, chopped

Pilav with Mussels
Midyeli Pilav

1. Soak the rice in hot water mixed with 2 teaspoons salt until the water turns cool. Rinse several times. Drain well and set aside.

2. Wash the mussels thoroughly, scrubbing them and rinsing under cold water several times. Cut off the beards. Soak them in warm salted water to cover for 5 minutes. Open them, using a sharp paring knife, and holding them over a bowl to catch all the mussel liquid. Remove the meat and discard the shells. Place the mussels on a clean kitchen towel. Cover them with another towel and pat gently dry. Set them aside. Reserve the liquid.

3. Sauté the onions and pine nuts in olive oil for 20 minutes. Stir in the rice; cook, stirring frequently, for 8 minutes. Stir in the tomato and cook a few minutes longer. Strain the mussel liquid; measure and add water, if necessary, to make 1 1/2 cups. Bring it to a boil and stir into the rice mixture. Stir in the mussels, currants, sugar, cinnamon, allspice, salt, and pepper. Cover and cook 5 minutes over medium heat. Reduce the heat to low and cook until all the water is absorbed. Fold up a clean towel and cover the top of the pan with it; on top of that, place the pan lid. Set on a heat diffuser over the lowest heat or some

other warm surface and leave it there for 30 minutes. Stir. Serve cold.

6 Servings

40 mussels
1 cup long-grain rice
Water
Salt
1 medium onion, finely
   chopped
1 1/2 tablespoons pine nuts
1/2 cup olive oil
1 tomato, finely chopped
1 1/2 tablespoons currants
1 tablespoon sugar
1 teaspoon cinnamon
1 teaspoon allspice
Salt and pepper to taste
3/4 cup fresh dill, chopped, or
   1 tablespoon dried dill weed

Bulgur Pilav with Tomato and Green Pepper
Bulgur Pilavı

In a heavy pan, sauté the onion in the butter for 20 minutes. Add the green pepper and tomato; sauté 10 minutes or until the tomato becomes soft. Stir in the broth and salt; bring to a boil. Stir in the bulgur. Cover and cook 5 minutes over high heat. Reduce the heat to low and cook until all the water is absorbed. Fold up a clean towel and cover the top of the pan with it; on top of that, place the pan lid. Set the pan on a heat diffuser over the lowest heat or some other warm surface and leave it there 30 minutes. Stir and serve.

4 Servings

1 large onion, diced
5 tablespoons butter
1 large green pepper, diced
1 large tomato, diced, or
   1 tablespoon tomato paste
1 1/2 cups chicken or beef broth
Salt to taste
1 cup coarse-grain bulgur

Bulgur Pilav with Lentils
Mercimekli Bulgur Pilavı

1. Wash and soak lentils overnight; drain. Cook until tender in 2 cups water. Check occasionally and add more water if necessary. Drain the lentils and set aside. Measure the cooking liquid and add meat broth to make 1 cup.

2. Sauté 1 onion in 4 tablespoons butter for 15 to 20 minutes. Stir in the bulgur and sauté 10 minutes. Stir in the lentils, salt, pepper, and the broth and cooking liquid mixture. Cover and cook until all the liquid is absorbed. Fold up a clean towel and cover the top of the pan with it; place the pan lid on top of that. Put the pan on a heat diffuser over the lowest heat or some other warm surface and leave it there for 30 minutes.

3. Sauté 1 onion in the remaining butter until golden brown. Transfer the bulgur to a serving dish and top with the sautéed onion.

8–10 Servings

1/2 cup lentils
Water
2 large onions, finely chopped
8–10 tablespoons butter
2 cups coarse-grain bulgur
Salt and pepper to taste

**3 cups beef or chicken broth
and cooking liquid from
lentils**

Bulgur Pilav with Lamb
Etli Bulgur Pilavı

1. In a heavy pan, sauté the onions in 2 table-spoons butter for 10 minutes. Stir in the meat. Cover and cook until the meat releases its moisture, reabsorbs it, and browns. Add the tomatoes or tomato paste; sauté 5 minutes. Stir in 1/2 cup hot water and some salt and pepper. Cover and cook until the meat is tender, about 1 1/2 to 2 hours. Stir it occasionally and add more hot water, a small amount at a time, if the liquid gets too low. When the meat is tender, uncover the pan and continue cooking until all the liquid has been absorbed.

2. In a second pan, melt 6 tablespoons butter and sauté the bulgur for 10 minutes. Stir in the broth and the cooked meat and onions. Cover and cook until all the liquid is absorbed. Fold up a clean towel and cover the top of the pan with it; on top of that, place the pan lid. Place the pan on a heat diffuser over the lowest heat or some other warm surface and leave it there for 30 minutes. Stir and serve.

6 Servings

**1 lb. lamb, cut into 1/2-inch
cubes
2 large onions, diced
8 tablespoons butter
2 large tomatoes, diced, or
2 tablespoons tomato paste
Hot water
Salt and pepper to taste
2 cups coarse-grain bulgur
3 cups beef or chicken broth**

Pasta Dishes

Homemade Noodles
Erişte

EQUIPMENT:
A large, wooden work surface or a table top; a regular rolling pin; a special rolling pin 25 inches long and 3/4 inch in diameter (a wooden curtain rod or dowel rod may be used).

1. Place the all-purpose flour and the cake flour in a mixing bowl and blend. Make a hollow in the middle and put the eggs and salt there. Mix these ingredients with your fingertips. Gradually combine the flour with the mixture in the hollow. Work the dough with your hands to form a cohesive dough. Place the dough on the lightly floured work surface and knead until smooth and elastic The dough should not stick to your hands and should be fairly stiff. If it is too soft, place some flour on the work surface a tablespoon at a time and knead it into the dough. Divide the dough into 2 portions; shape each into a ball; cover with wax paper; and let it rest 1 or 2 hours. The longer it stands, the easier it will be to roll out the pastry.

2. Place 1 piece of the dough on the work surface. Using a regular rolling pin, roll it into a circle as large as a dinner plate. Dust the work surface and the surface of the pastry with some flour. Take the special rolling pin; wrap one edge of the pastry around the center of the pin. With a slight back-and-forth motion, press gently and continuously toward the ends of the pastry and of the rolling pin, gradually moving the rolling pin forward, so that the whole piece of pastry is wrapped around it. At the same time, repeatedly move your hands toward the ends of the rolling pin and quickly bring them back to the center. As your hands move toward the ends, let the heels of your hands gently pull and stretch the pastry outward. After the pastry is entirely wrapped around the rolling pin, gently flip the pastry open and loose. Now move the pastry slightly clockwise and start with a different edge. At every other rolling, dust the work surface and the pastry with some flour. Repeat this rolling process several times until the pastry is approximately 1/13 inch thick. Roll out the other half of the dough in the same manner. Let the sheets of pastry dry very slightly on a table top.

3. Using a sharp knife, cut the sheets into 2-inch-wide strips. Stack 5 or 10 strips on top of each other. Place one stack in front of you. Place the 3 middle fingertips of one hand gently over one end of the stack, 1/4 inch away from the edge. Using your fingertips as a guide, cut 1/4-inch-wide noodles. As you cut the noodles, move your fingertips 1/4 inch back to make room for the next 1/4-inch-wide cut. Continue cutting the noodles until all the pastry has been cut. These noodles can be cooked right away or may be left out to dry for later use.

4. To cook the noodles, take a pan that will hold at least 8 quarts of water. Bring the water and 4 tablespoons salt to a boil. Drop the noodles into the rapidly boiling water. Cover and bring to a boil. Uncover and cook 1 minute or so for fresh noodles and 3 or 4 minutes for dry noodles. Test frequently. Do not overcook. Drain, place in a serving dish, and toss with butter and salt. Serve immediately.

1 pound noodles

2 cups unbleached all-purpose*
  flour (Scoop measuring cup
  into flour and level off with
  a knife)
1/2 cup plain, bleached cake*
  flour
3 eggs
1/4 cup water
3/4 teaspoon salt
1/3 cup all-purpose flour for
  rolling out the pastry

  *In Britain, use strong
white flour

Noodles with Kasseri Cheese
Kaşar Peynirli Makarna

  1. Cook the pasta according to the directions
and drain.
  2. Melt the butter in a pan, stir in the pasta,
and sauté 1 minute. Stir in the cheese with a fork
and cook until the cheese is melted (a few minutes).

  4–6 Servings

8 oz. Homemade Noodles; page
  222, or 8 oz. egg noodles or
  macaroni
4 tablespoons butter
2/3 cup kasseri cheese, grated

Noodles with Tomatoes
Domatesli Erişte veya Makarna

  1. Cook the pasta according to directions;
drain well.

2. Melt the butter in a pan; stir in the tomatoes and salt. Cook until the tomatoes are soft and reach the consistency of a sauce. If using tomato paste, cook it only a few minutes, stirring constantly. Stir in the pasta; cover the pan and cook 3 or 4 minutes over very low heat. Toss well and serve hot.

4–6 Servings

**8 oz. Homemade Noodles, page
   222, or 8 oz. egg noodles or
   spaghetti
4 tablespoons butter
2 ripe tomatoes, minced, or 1–2
   tablespoons tomato paste
Salt**

Noodles with Feta Cheese
Beyaz Peynirli Makarna

1. Cook the pasta according to directions; drain well.

2. Melt the butter in a pan, stir in the pasta, and cook 1 minute. Stir in the cheese; cook, stirring constantly, until the pasta is thoroughly heated.

4–6 Servings

**8 oz. Homemade Noodles, page
   222, or 1 package (8 oz.)
   macaroni
4 tablespoons butter
1/3 lb. feta cheese, crumbled
Salt**

Macaroni with Ground Beef
Kıymalı Makarna

1. Cook the pasta according to directions; drain.

2. Melt 2 tablespoons butter in a pan and sauté the onions until soft. Add the meat and cook until it has released its moisture, reabsorbed it, and browned in its own juice and fat. Stir in the tomatoes; sauté 2 to 3 minutes. Mix in the tomato paste and water and cook until all the moisture is absorbed, about 30 minutes.

3. Heat 2 tablespoons butter in a pan; stir in the pasta and heat through, stirring constantly. Combine with the meat sauce; mix well. Serve hot.

4–6 Servings

1/2 **lb. lean ground beef**
1 **package (8 oz.) spaghetti or noodles, or 8 oz. Homemade Noodles, p. 222**
4 **tablespoons butter**
1 **chopped onion**
2 **minced tomatoes**
1 **tablespoon tomato paste**
1/2 **cup water**
Salt and pepper to taste

Pasta Pie
Makarna Fırında

1. Cook the spaghetti according to the directions on the package; drain.

2. Melt the butter in a pan, stir in the pasta, and sauté 1 or 2 minutes. Set aside.

3. Beat the eggs in a mixing bowl; stir in the milk and 3/4 cup cheese; mix well. Add 2/3 of this mixture to the pasta in the pan; blend well.

4. Butter a casserole; place the pasta in the casserole; pour the remaining egg-and-milk mixture over it. Sprinkle the remaining cheese on top. Bake at 350° for 30 to 35 minutes. Remove from the oven and cut into squares. Serve hot.

6 Servings

8 oz. spaghetti
1/2 cup butter
7 eggs
1 cup milk
1 cup kasseri or Romano
 cheese, grated

Noodles with Chicken and Mushrooms
Tavuklu Mantarlı Kesme Makarna

1. Cook the pasta according to directions; drain.

2. Melt 2 tablespoons butter in a pan and sauté the mushrooms. Set aside.

3. Melt 1 tablespoon butter in the same pan and lightly sauté the chicken. Set aside.

4. Melt 5 tablespoons butter in the same pan, stir in the flour, and cook 2 to 3 minutes, stirring constantly. Gradually stir in the hot chicken stock, stirring constantly with a wire whisk or a wooden spoon. Cook until the sauce is thick and smooth. Add the half-and-half and stir until well blended. Season with salt and set aside.

5. In a bowl, mix the pasta with 2/3 of the white sauce, 2/3 of the cheese, and all of the mushrooms and chicken; blend well.

6. Butter a casserole; arrange the pasta mixture in the casserole; pour the remaining sauce over it; top with the remaining cheese. Bake at 350° for 15 minutes or until golden brown on top. Serve immediately.

6 Servings

2 cups cooked chicken, cut into
  bite-sized pieces
1 lb. Homemade Noodles,
  page 222, or 1 lb. fettucini
  or egg noodles
1/2 cup butter
1/2 lb. mushrooms, chopped
6 tablespoons all-purpose flour
21/2 cups hot chicken stock
1/2 cup half-and-half
Salt
1 cup kasseri or Romano
  cheese, grated

Noodles with Chicken in Béchamel Sauce
Beyaz Salçalı Tavuklu Makarna

1. Cook the noodles according to directions; drain.

2. Place the tomatoes in a saucepan; cook over low heat, mashing them with a fork until they are soft and have the consistency of a sauce. Set aside.

3. Melt 1 tablespoon butter in a pan and lightly sauté the chicken. Set aside.

4. Melt 5 tablespoons butter in the same pan; blend in the flour and stir 2 to 3 minutes over medium heat. Gradually add the hot milk. Stirring briskly with a wire whisk, cook until the sauce is thick and smooth. Season with salt. Set aside.

5. Toss the pasta in a bowl with 2 tablespoons

butter; stir in the chicken, 2/3 of the tomato sauce, 2/3 of the white sauce, and 2/3 of the cheese; toss well.

6. Butter a casserole; arrange the pasta in the casserole. Pour the remaining white sauce over the pasta, top with the remaining cheese, and bake at 350° for 15 to 20 minutes. Remove from the oven. Heat the remaining tomato sauce and pour over the pasta. Serve immediately.

4–6 Servings

2 cups cooked chicken, cut into
   bite-sized pieces
1 lb. Homemade Noodles,
   page 222, or 1 lb. fettucini
   or egg noodles
5 minced tomatoes
1/2 cup butter
5 tablespoons all-purpose flour
21/2 cups milk
1 cup kasseri or Romano
   cheese, grated
Salt to taste

Böreks

Börek constitutes one of the most significant parts of traditional Turkish cuisine. It is also, in fact, one of its most ancient elements, having been developed by the Turks of Central Asia before their westward migration to Anatolia. Although concoctions vaguely similar to *börek* can be found in other cuisines, the *böreks* of Turkey are unique because of the care and imagination that have gone into developing them in such great variety.

Börek is a general term that applies to a family of pastries with about fifty different members. What they have in common is that they are all made out of thin layers of dough and butter and have different kinds of cheese or meat filling as their core. They are the favorites of everyone and are served frequently as appetizers, side dishes, breakfast treats or delightful snacks. There are few things more enjoyable than a buttery, delicate, golden brown *börek* freshly out of the oven accompanied by a cup of tea.

The variety comes from the different methods employed in creating and arranging these delicate, precious layers. There are two basic methods for making *börek* layers. The first is similar to that used in making *pâte feuilletée*: a process of buttering, folding, and rolling out, repeated several times until thin flaky layers have been produced. The other method, a far more sophisticated one calling for more skillful handling, involves rolling out each individual layer of pastry until it is very thin, sometimes only 1/25 inch thick, using a 3/4-inch-thick long rolling pin similar to a wooden curtain rod (known as an *oklava*).

One method of arranging the *börek* layers is to stack them in as many as fifteen or twenty layers and, after inserting the filling, to bake them in large round trays. Another method is to cut them into strips and squares and fold them, with the filling inside, into many different shapes.

Today, ready-made *börek* pastry is available in Turkey, as is phyllo pastry (which may be used for both *börek* and *baklava*). These are widely used, particularly by busy people living in large cities. In fact, some years ago, during one of my lengthier stays in Turkey, I sent my little boy next door to borrow an *oklava*. He returned empty-handed, and I was told that no one owns such an item any more. But the traditional methods described below have not yet been entirely displaced.

The social context of traditional *börek* making has an almost dramatic aspect. I remember that on certain days my grandmother would announce her intention to make *börek*. An old friend of the family would then be invited to the house, a lady who had somehow fallen on hard times but was nonetheless always a welcome guest, in part because of her skill in the art of making *börek*. She always accepted the invitation with great pleasure, both because she liked my grandmother and appreciated the help she had given her and also because *börek* making gave her the chance to enjoy the atmosphere of a grand house again. Although my grandmother was a masterly cook herself, she made only the simpler and less time-consuming varieties of *börek*; for more complex varieties, she called on the services of her friend. This lady came early in the day and took her breakfast and tea with my grandmother, who waited for her so that she would not be faced with the indignity of taking breakfast alone. Then with great authority my grandmother's friend took charge of the *börek* making, an operation that filled a good four to five hours. It was universally understood in the house that everyone's duty that day was to assist in the operation and to await the commander's softly delivered orders, such as "would you please bring me more flour?" and "could you please wipe the sweat off my brow?" We offered her tea or coffee many times during the day, but once she had begun her task, she would not be interrupted.

The beginning of the operation, and its easiest part, was making the dough. Once that had been done, the dough was left to stand for fifty minutes, and then she could afford to light a cigarette and watch the other ingredients being prepared. A sun-bleached white sheet would then be spread on the floor and a low, round wooden table placed in the middle of it. A big sack of flour and an *oklava* were brought in, a large floor cushion was placed next to the table, and everything was ready for her to begin rolling out sheet after sheet of pastry. She started by dividing the dough into several small pieces, shaping them into perfect little rounds with quick and skillful movements of her hands. As soon as they were ready, they were removed from the table to leave it empty for the rolling of the pastry. The first ball of dough was placed on the table and flattened, and then the *börek* expert took up the *oklava* and began to demonstrate her skill. At first she rolled the small, flat piece of dough until it was as big as a dinner plate. My eyes followed the rhythmical motion of her arms wrapping the pastry around the rolling pin; three short back-and-forth motions that gradually moved the rolling pin forward were followed by one grand sweep forward, with the arms fully extended, and a large, thin sheet of pastry was quickly released from the rolling pin. This sequence of motions was repeated time and again until the sheet of pastry attained its maximum length and delicacy. To draw an analogy with music, the process encompassed three soft, short notes of a single tone, followed by a high, long note expressive of accumulated emotion.

Many hours later, when the pastry was finally finished, my grandmother's friend relaxed with a look of satisfaction on her face. A few select neighbors were hastily summoned to four o'clock tea to share the freshly baked treasure, and the house was filled with the mingled aromas of freshly brewed tea and pastry hot from the oven. Now grandmother's friend was not allowed to lift a finger, for she had just completed a long, tiring, and important task destined to give joy to many people. Making two large trays of *börek* was indeed no small accomplishment. Everyone sat around the table, enjoying tea and *börek* and conversing, and whoever happened by —my aunts on their way home from school, their piano teacher — was invited to the table. Tradespeople and the postman were at least offered a piece before they went on their way.

Then gradually everyone dispersed. The visiting *börek* expert generally stayed the night. While she retired into a corner to begin her crocheting, my grandmother began preparations for dinner, and my aunts played the piano, accompanied by their friends. Then it was time for the lady to retreat upstairs for the silence needed to perform her afternoon prayers, because downstairs was bursting with the sound of Italian operas from the gramophone.

Such were the contrasts that marked life in my grandmother's house, and these are the memories that the preparation and eating of *börek* evoke for me even now.

IMPORTANT NOTE ON FLOUR

Börek pastry, which is made by rolling out a piece of dough into a very thin sheet of pastry, requires a great deal of handling. This pastry should therefore be made with a kind of flour that is made of hard wheat and is strong and high in glutin. Such flour will yield strong and resilient pastry.

In Britain, strong white flour (or strong plain flour), which is high in glutin, should be used in place of all-purpose flour in the following recipes in this section. In some of the recipes, all-purpose flour is combined with a smaller quantity of cake flour to decrease the elasticity and to make rolling easier. In such recipes, use only strong white flour (for example, replace 2 cups all-purpose flour and 1/2 cup cake flour with 2 1/2 cups strong white flour).

Another important point is that types of flour vary in the amount of liquid they absorb. For this reason, it may sometimes be necessary to increase slightly the amount of flour or the liquid given in the recipes in order to achieve the desired consistency of a given pastry. In fact, strong white flour does absorb a little more liquid than all-purpose flour or plain flour (approximately 1 tablespoon more water for 2 1/2 cups of flour). In all cases, the important thing to remember is that once kneaded the dough must always be smooth, bouncy and elastic, and it should never stick to one's hands. A little experience usually enables one to recognise the proper consistency of a pastry by its look and its feel.

Börek with Golden Crust
Su Böreği

To my mind, this justly celebrated *börek* is the most cherished and distinctive of the entire family, as well as being the most traditional. Through the years I have come across a certain variety of *börek* in the form of the Greek *tiropites* or *spanakopita*; I have been pleasantly surprised when I discovered Chinese egg rolls and wonton, both similar to some kinds of Turkish *börek*; and I have recognized the similarities between certain Turkish *böreks* and various pastries made with the French *pâte feuilletée*. However, I have never tasted anything in the least resembling this particular *börek*: *su böreği*. It is made with many thin, buttery layers of pastry. The taste is unique. It is delicate yet, at the same time, very wholesome. However, it is a form of *börek* that requires much time to prepare, and one has to be willing to make an effort to master the method of rolling thin pastry sheets in order to make this worthwhile delicacy.

Börek with Golden Crust with Cheese Filling
Peynirli Su Böreği

The following recipe is given for 11 layers, which is not too many for a beginner to handle. However, I would like to mention that this *börek* can be made in many more layers, sometimes as many as 20.

EQUIPMENT:
A large wooden work surface or a table top to roll out the pastry; a regular rolling pin; a special rolling pin 25 inches long and 3/4 inch in diameter (an old wooden curtain rod or a dowel rod, 24 inches long and 3/4 inch in diameter can also be used). A 12-inch round baking pan, 2 inches deep (a 12-inch cast iron frying pan works very well) or a 12-inch cake pan.

1. Place the all-purpose flour and the cake flour in a mixing bowl and blend. Make a hollow in the middle. Put the eggs, salt, and water there. Mix these with your fingertips. Gradually combine the flour with the mixture in the hollow. Work the dough with your hands to form a cohesive dough. Place the dough on a lightly floured work surface and knead 5 minutes or until the dough is smooth and elastic. The dough should not stick to your hands. If necessary, add a few teaspoons of flour to make the dough relatively stiff. Wrap it in wax paper and let it rest 1 hour.

2. In a later step you will need one large pan filled with boiling water and another filled with cold water, placed adjacent to one another. Have these ready and keep the boiling water at a simmer over low heat. Add some salt to this pan as if you were preparing to cook pasta. Also have ready 2 large clean towels.

3. Place the dough on the work surface, roll it back and forth under the palms of your hands, and shape it into a long roll. Divide the roll into 6 equal pieces. Divide 5 of these in half. Roll each of the 11 pieces into a ball. Place them on a baking pan; cover with a sheet of wax paper and let rest for 30 minutes.

4. Sprinkle a little corn starch on the work surface, place on it one of the equal-sized pieces of dough and flatten it with your hand. Sprinkle some cornstarch on the dough and roll it out as large as a dessert plate using a regular rolling pin. Dust the work surface and the surface of the pastry with a little corn starch. Wrap one edge of the pastry around the center of the special rolling pin. Place the heels of both hands at the center of the pin. With a slight back-and-forth rolling motion, press down gently and continuously toward the ends of the pin, gradually moving the pin forward so that the whole piece of dough is wrapped around it. At the same time, repeatedly move your hands toward the ends of the pin and then bring them quickly back to the center. As your hands move toward the ends, let the heels of your hands gently pull and stretch the pastry outward. After the pastry is entirely wrapped around the rolling pin, gently flip the dough open and loose. Now move the pastry slightly clockwise and roll again in the same way, starting with a different edge. Repeat this process several times, until the pastry is 12-13 inches in diameter and very thin, about 1/25 inch thick. At every other rolling, dust the work surface and the pastry with corn starch. You may speed up this process by stretching the dough with your hands as if making strudel pastry. Place slightly clenched hands, palms down, under the pastry sheet; very gently stretch it from the center outward, using the flat plane of your knuckles. Place the sheets of pastry on a large, clean surface, gently brush off all the excess cornstarch, and cover. Roll out all 10 pieces of equal size to 12 to 13 inches in diameter. Roll out the eleventh and largest piece almost twice as large.

5. Bring the hot water in one of the large pans to a boil. Brush the baking pan with butter. Preheat the oven to 350°.

6. Take the largest sheet of pastry and place it in the baking pan. The sides of this sheet will extend up and over the sides of the pan. Spread 1 1/2 to 2 tablespoons butter over the sheet. Ease one of the pastry sheets gently into the rapidly boiling water, submerging it completely. Leave it in the boiling water for only 40 to 50 seconds. Take it out carefully with a slotted spoon and drop it into the pan containing cold water. Take it out and place it on a clean, dry towel, pat it gently with another towel to remove the excess water, and place it on the first sheet in the baking pan. It will not lie flat in the pan, for it is larger than the pan. It is meant to be so. Even out the wrinkles. Again spread 1 or 2 tablespoons butter over the sheet. Repeat this until 5 out of the 11 sheets have been used up. Some sheets will tear, but this does not matter. Now spread the filling evenly over the pastry.

Repeat the process with the 6 remaining sheets. Bring the edges of the first sheet up over the sides of the other sheets to seal the edges. Spread the remaining butter on top. Bake 45 minutes or until golden brown. Cut into wedges. Best when served hot.

CHEESE FILLING:
Combine all ingredients and blend well.

6–8 wedges

2 cups unbleached all-purpose
  flour (scoop measuring cup
  into flour and level off with
  a knife)
1/2 cup plus 2 tablespoons cake
  flour
3 eggs
1 teaspoon salt
1/4 cup water
3/4 cup butter, melted
1 cup cornstarch

CHEESE FILLING:
1/2 lb. feta cheese, crumbled
1 egg, lightly beaten
1 egg yolk, lightly beaten
1/4 cup cream
3/4 cup chopped parsley

Börek with Golden Crust with Meat Filling
Kıymalı Su Böreği

1. Sauté the onion in the butter for 1 to 2 minutes. Stir in the meat and cook until it releases its moisture, reabsorbs it, and browns in its own juice and fat. Remove from heat; stir in the parsley, salt, and pepper; mix well.

2. Follow the recipe for the *Börek* with Golden Crust with Cheese filling, replacing the cheese filling with the meat filling.

4–6 Servings

1/2 lb. lean ground beef or lamb
1 large onion, chopped
3 tablespoons butter
1 cup chopped parsley
Salt and pepper to taste
Pastry as for *Börek* with
 Golden Crust, p. 234

Palace *Börek* (Cheese Filling)
Saray Böreği, Peynirli

This is one of the most delicious of all Turkish *böreks*. The interesting and celebrated method of layering *(katmerlemek)* the dough results in a beautiful pastry made of many thin layers of pastry interspersed with sweet butter.

1. Place the flour in a mixing bowl. Make a hollow in the middle. Put the margarine, lemon juice, salt, and water in the hollow; mix with your fingertips. Gradually combine small portions of the flour with the mixture in the hollow. Work with your hands to form a cohesive dough. Place the dough on a lightly floured work surface and knead until smooth and elastic. The dough should not stick to your hands. It should be a soft dough. If necessary, add a few teaspoons of water. Wrap the dough in a sheet of wax paper and let it rest 1 hour in a cool place.

2. Place the dough on a lightly floured work surface and, rolling it back and forth under the palms of your hands, shape it into a long roll. Divide the roll into 10 equal pieces. Working with 1 piece at a time, roll and shape each piece into a round ball. Spread the olive oil in a baking pan. Place the 10 balls of dough on the tray; cover with a sheet of wax paper. Let stand in a cool place 1 hour.

3. The butter should be at room temperature and soft enough to be pliable but still firm enough to hold its shape.

4. A marble work surface is best for rolling out the pastry layers, but a Formica surface also works very well. If neither is available, a wooden surface will work if the room is kept very cool. Coat the work surface lightly with oil. Place a piece of dough on the surface; flatten it slightly with your hands. Using a rolling pin, roll the dough into a circle by pressing down on the rolling pin and moving it outward in different directions. Turn the dough over frequently to prevent it from sticking to the work surface. When all 10 pieces of dough have been rolled out in this manner into circles 5 inches in diameter, spread butter evenly in equal amounts to cover each pastry circle, using up all the butter.

5. Working with one pastry at a time on the work surface, fold it into thirds. Fold it into thirds again in the opposite direction. Now you will have a cubical shape. Repeat this procedure with each circle of pastry. Put them back on the tray spread with oil; cover them with a sheet of wax paper; and let them rest 1/2 hour in a cool place. (It is very important to keep them in a cool place because otherwise the dough might sag and become impossible to roll. However, the butter in the dough should not harden because that might cause tearing. Therefore, do not place the dough in the refrigerator.

6. Coat the work surface with a little oil once again. One at a time, place each cubical piece of folded dough on the work surface and roll it out into a circle 5 inches in diameter. Do not butter it this time. Again fold it into thirds in one direction, and again into thirds in the opposite direction in the same manner described above. Put them back on the tray; cover them with a sheet of wax paper; and let them rest 1 hour in a cool place.

7. Coat the work surface lightly with oil. Place each piece of dough on the work surface and roll it out into a circle 6 1/2 inches in diameter. Place 1/10 of the filling in the middle. Fold one edge over the filling to cover; fold the opposite edge over the already folded one. Repeat with the remaining two edges. Glaze the tops with a lightly beaten egg. Place the pastries on a cold baking sheet that has been sprinkled lightly with very cold water.

8. Preheat the oven to 450° for 20 minutes. Bake the pastries at this temperature for 12 to 15 minutes or until they have puffed up. Reduce to 350° and bake 20 to 30 minutes longer. If the pastries brown too quickly, place a sheet of foil loosely over them.

CHEESE FILLING:
Mix all the ingredients until well blended.

10 böreks

2 1/2 **cups unbleached, all-purpose flour (scoop measuring cup into flour and level off with a knife)**
2 **tablespoons melted butter**
1 **teaspoon lemon juice**
3/4 **teaspoon salt**
1/2 **cup plus 2 tablespoons water**
1/3 **cup olive oil**
12 **tablespoons sweet butter, at room temperature**
1 **egg for glaze**
1/4 **cup oil to coat the work surface**

CHEESE FILLING:

2/3 **lb. feta cheese (if too salty,
soak 1 hour in warm water
and drain)**
2 **egg yolks**
2/3 **cup chopped parsley**

Palace *Börek* (Chicken Filling)
Saray Böreği, Tavuklu

1. Place the chicken in a pot with the onion, carrot, water, bay leaves, salt, and peppercorns. Simmer until cooked. Remove from the pot; discard the skin and bones. Put the chicken through the coarse blade of a meat grinder or coarsely chop in a blender.

2. Melt the butter in a saucepan; add the flour and cook 3 minutes over medium heat, stirring to blend. Gradually stir in the hot chicken stock and half-and-half, mixing constantly with a wire whisk or a wooden spoon until the sauce is thick and smooth. Remove from heat.

3. Beat the egg yolk with a few tablespoons of the hot sauce, then stir this mixture into the sauce. Cook a few minutes. Remove from heat and cool. Add the chicken to the sauce. Mix in the coconut, chervil, salt, and pepper.

4. Follow the recipe for Palace *Börek* (Cheese Filling), replacing the cheese filling with the chicken filling.

10 böreks

1 **whole chicken breast or 2 legs
(2/3 lb. chicken meat)**
1 **onion**

1 carrot
3 cups water
2 bay leaves
Salt
1/2 teaspoon peppercorns
2 tablespoons butter
2 tablespoons all-purpose flour
1/2 cup chicken stock
1/2 cup half-and-half
1 egg yolk
2 teaspoons shredded
  unsweetened coconut
1 teaspoon chervil
Salt and pepper to taste
Pastry as for Palace Börek, p. 238

Palace *Börek* with Spinach
Ispanaklı Saray Böreği

Follow the recipe for Palace *Börek* (Cheese Filling) replacing the cheese filling with spinach filling.

Pastry as for Palace Börek, p. 238
Spinach Filling, p. 256

Nemse *Börek*
Nemse Böreği

Nemse *Börek*, unlike the other traditional Turkish *böreks*, such as *Börek* with Golden Crust or Palace *Börek*, is made with *pâté feuilletée*. As with all sorts of pastries made from this dough, Nemse *böreks*, filled with various fillings, puff up into hundreds of light, buttery, paper-thin, golden layers in the oven. If followed carefully, this recipe always gives excellent results.

I would like to take this opportunity to make a few statements about this celebrated pastry, hoping that it will help dispel some of the misconceptions concerning it and encourage the reader to try making it. This pastry has come to be known as an extremely difficult one that must be left to a few experts and that takes an entire day to prepare. In reality, it is not all that difficult, and the time spent handling the pastry is minimal. It seems to take a very long time because the dough is left to rest in the refrigerator for periods of time. Moreover, by comparison with the other more traditional *böreks*, such as the *Börek* with Golden Crust *(Su Böreği)*, in which the layers are created as a result of more time-consuming and sophisticated rolling activity, **Nemse** *börek* or *pâté feuilletée* is simpler to make and far less time-consuming; it also requires less skill. However, this pastry is a delicate one, and it is governed by certain rather rigid rules that must be followed carefully. If the recipe is faithfully followed, the result of making this delightful *börek* will be a feeling of pride and satisfaction.

Nemse *Börek* (Cheese Filling)
Peynirli Nemse Böreği

PRELIMINARY PREPARATIONS:
Because of the high butter content of the dough, it is very important to work in a cool place and to keep the ingredients, utensils, and work surface, and even the hands very cool. The butter and water must be chilled for several hours. The room you are working in must be cool. The most preferable work surface is a marble one. However, a wooden surface also works well if the work area is kept cool.

1. Combine the all-purpose flour and cake flour in a mixing bowl. Make a hollow in the middle. Mix the chilled water with the lemon juice and salt. Put the soft butter and the chilled water, salt, and lemon juice mixture in the hollow and mix with your fingertips. Gradually combine the flour with the mixture in the middle. Work with your hands 1 minute or just long enough to form a relatively firm, smooth and cohesive dough. Do not overwork the dough. Wrap it in a sheet of wax paper and refrigerate 30 minutes.

2. Place the 1/2 cup all-purpose flour on the work surface. Using a sharp knife, cut the chilled butter sticks lengthwise into thin squares. Put the squares of butter over the flour and knead with your hands until the butter becomes soft, pliable, and well incorporated with the flour. Work fast; cool hands with water if necessary and dry them thoroughly. It is important that the butter be softened through kneading rather than through melting. The aim is to have relatively soft but thoroughly chilled butter. Shape the butter into a flat, 5-inch square, wrap it in a sheet of wax paper, and refrigerate 20 minutes.

3. Place the dough on the generously floured work surface and roll out into a 14-inch square. Place the 5-inch square butter in the center of the dough. Fold one side over the butter to cover it. Fold the opposite side over the already folded portion. Do the same with the remaining sides. Gently roll out the pastry into an approximately 7-inch-by-14-inch rectangle, with the short end facing you. Take care not to press the very ends of the dough. Roll the pastry in opposite directions at the ends to achieve the same thickness all over the pastry. Adjust corners to keep them square. (If at any time the butter gets soft and the pastry becomes very soft and sticky, refrigerate it until well chilled again.) Fold the pastry into thirds, as if folding a business letter. Press down the open edges gently to seal in the butter. Rotate the pastry so that the open flap will be to your right. Again roll out this pouch into an approximately 1/2-inch thick rectangle and fold into thirds. Wrap the pastry in a sheet of wax paper and refrigerate 1 hour.

4. Repeat the rolling and folding 2 more times. Correct the position of the pastry before each rolling so that the open flap will be to your right. Refrigerate 1 hour.

5. Repeat the rolling and folding again 2 times and refrigerate 2 hours or overnight. The pastry will keep a few days if tightly covered and stored in the refrigerator. It can also be kept frozen for about 6 months.

6. Place the chilled pastry on the clean, lightly floured work surface, open flap to your right. Dust the pastry surface lightly with flour and roll it out into a 1/5- to 1/4-inch thick rectangle. The rectangle will measure about 10 inches by 20 inches. Using a very sharp knife, cut the pastry rectangle into 3 approximately 3-inch-wide strips. Then cut each strip into 6 squares. You will have 18 3-inch squares of pastry. Mentally divide each square into 2 triangles. Place 1/18 of the filling in the middle of one of each pair of triangles and fold the other triangle over the filling. Press the edges to seal. If you wish, you can shape the squares into rectangles instead of triangular shapes. Place the *böreks* on a baking sheet and refrigerate 30 minutes.

7. Preheat the oven to 425°. Beat the egg with the milk to blend and glaze the tops of the *böreks*, taking care not to let the glaze run down the edges. Bake at this temperature until the *böreks* are well puffed, about 10 to 15 minutes. Reduce the temperature to 350° and bake about 20 minutes or until light and golden brown.

CHEESE FILLING:
Mix all the ingredients.

18 böreks

2 cups unbleached, all-purpose
  flour (scoop measuring cup
  into flour and level off with
  a knife)
1/2 cup bleached, plain cake flour
1/4 cup soft butter
1 tablespoon lemon juice
1/2 teaspoon salt
1/2 cup plus 3 tablespoons
  chilled water
1 1/4 cups (2 1/2 sticks) chilled
  unsalted butter
1/2 cup all-purpose flour to mix
  with butter
Flour to dust work surface
1 egg and 1 tablespoon milk for
  glaze

CHEESE FILLING:
3/4 lb. feta cheese, crumbled
1 egg
1 egg yolk
1/2 cup chopped parsley

Nemse Pastry with Yeast
Çarşı Böreği

This pastry makes the flakiest, spongiest, most
delicious *böreks*. In Turkey, they are bought ready-
made from the pastry shops. The pastry is identical
to that used for croissants.

Because of the high butter content of the
dough, it is important to work in a cool place. The
preferable work surface is marble. If the work surface is wood, the room must be kept quite cool.

1. Combine the flour and salt in a mixing
bowl and blend well.

2. Dissolve the yeast and sugar in the tepid
milk and let stand 5 minutes.

3. Combine the flour and the dissolved yeast and work with your hands until all the ingredients are thoroughly blended. Do not overwork the mixture. The dough will be loose and sticky. Cover with a plastic wrap and let it rise slowly, about 7 to 8 hours or overnight in a cool place or refrigerator.

4. When the dough is ready to use, place the 1/2 cup flour on the work surface. Using a sharp knife, cut the butter sticks lengthwise into thin squares. Put the butter squares over the flour and knead with your hands until the butter is soft, pliable, and well incorporated into the flour. Work fast; cool hands with water if necessary and dry them thoroughly. It is important that the butter be softened through kneading rather than through melting. The aim is to have soft but thoroughly chilled butter.

5. Scrape and clean the work surface. Dust it lightly with flour. Place the dough on the surface, and flatten it into an approximately 7-inch-by-14-inch rectangle, short end facing you. Do not use a rolling pin at this time. Taking small pieces of butter (1 1/2 inches in diameter) spread the pieces evenly over the lower 2/3 of the rectangle. Some pieces of butter will overlap each other. Do not spread the butter all the way to the edges, but leave a 1/2 inch area around the edges unbuttered. Fold the unbuttered upper 1/3 of the dough to the middle as if folding a business letter. Fold the buttered remainder over it. Press down the open edges gently to seal in the butter. Dust the work surface with flour; place the folded pastry on the work surface, short end facing you and the open flap to your right. Gently roll it out into an 8-inch-by-16-inch rectangle. Take care not to press the very ends of the rectangle. Roll the pastry in opposite directions at the ends to achieve the same thickness all over the pastry. Adjust the corners to keep them square. (If at any time the butter gets soft or the dough becomes too soft and sticky to handle, wrap it and place it in the refrigerator to chill.) Fold the pastry into thirds. Rotate the dough so that the open flap will be to your right. Roll again on the lightly floured work surface lengthwise until the rectangle measures about 10 inches by 18 inches. Fold the pastry into thirds and wrap in a sheet of wax paper and a plastic wrap and refrigerate at least 2 hours.

6. Place the dough on the lightly floured work surface, the open flap to your right, and dust it lightly and evenly with flour. Roll it out again first lengthwise then widthwise into an approximately 10-inch-by-20-inch rectangle. Fold it into thirds and roll it out again following the same procedure. Wrap it in wax paper and plastic wrap and refrigerate again at least 2 hours or overnight.

7. Place the chilled pastry on a clean, floured work surface, short end facing you and the open flap to your right. Dust the surface lightly with flour and gently roll lengthwise. Make sure not to roll over the very ends. Roll the pastry in opposite directions at the ends to roll them into the same thickness as the rest of the pastry. Lift portions of the pastry frequently and dust underneath to prevent it from sticking to the work surface. Adjust the corners to keep them square. When the pastry rectangle measures roughly 10 inches by 18 inches, start rolling the pastry widthwise. Finally the rectangle should measure approximately 16 inches by 21 inches. The pastry should be approximately 1/5 to 1/4 inch thick.

8. Using a very sharp knife, cut the pastry into 4 strips, each about 4 inches wide. Then cut each strip into 5 pieces. You will have 20, 5 inch squares. Mentally divide each square of pastry into 2 triangles. Place 1 teaspoon filling in the middle of one triangle and fold the other triangle over the filling to seal it. Now you will have a triangular-shaped *börek*. Press the edges to seal the filling. Repeat this with the remaining pieces. Place the *böreks* in a baking pan. Glaze the tops. Make sure the glaze

does not run down the sides. Let the *böreks* rise at room temperature until doubled in size. This will take 1 or 2 hours.

9. Preheat the oven to 375°. Bake the *böreks* 20 to 25 minutes until golden brown.

20 böreks

3 1/2 **cups unbleached,**
  all-purpose flour
1 **teaspoon salt**
3 1/2 **teaspoons dry-active yeast**
2 **teaspoons sugar**
1 1/2 **cups plus 3 tablespoons**
  tepid milk
1 1/4 **cups (2 1/2 sticks) chilled**
  unsalted butter
1/2 **cup all-purpose flour to mix**
  with butter
Flour to dust work surface
1 **egg mixed with 2 tablespoons**
   milk for glaze
Cheese, Chicken, or Spinach
  filling, pp. 246, 241, 256

Nemse *Börek* with Kasseri or Roquefort Cheese
Kaşar Peynirli Nemse Böreği

Follow the recipe for Nemse *Börek* (Cheese Filling), replacing the feta cheese filling with the kasseri or roquefort cheese filling.

CHEESE FILLING:
Combine all the ingredients and blend well.

10–12 böreks

Nemse *Börek*, p. 242

CHEESE FILLING:

3/4 cup kasseri or roquefort
    cheese, crumbled
1 egg yolk, lightly beaten
2 tablespoons sour cream
1/4 cup fresh dill, chopped, or
    1 teaspoon dried dill weed

Nemse *Börek* (Chicken Filling)
Tavuklu Nemse Böreği

Follow the recipe for Nemse *Börek* (Cheese Filling),
replacing the cheese filling with the chicken filling.

10-12 böreks

Nemse *Börek* pastry, p. 242
1/2 batch Chicken Filling, p. 241

Puff *Börek* (Cheese Filling)
Puf Böreği

These plump little pastries puff up delightfully in
hot oil. They can be served either hot or cold as
appetizers. They are especially good served hot
with tea.

   1. Place the flour in a mixing bowl. Make a
hollow in the middle. Put the yogurt, egg, vinegar,
olive oil, water, salt, and baking powder in the
hollow; mix with your fingertips. Gradually combine small portions of the flour with the mixture
in the hollow. Work with your hands to form a cohesive dough. Place the dough on a lightly floured
work surface and knead at least 5 minutes or until
smooth and elastic. It should be a relatively soft

dough and should not stick to your hands. If necessary, you may add a few teaspoons of flour. Wrap the dough in a sheet of wax paper; let it rest 1 hour at room temperature.

2. Place the dough on the work surface; divide it into halves. Roll out each piece of dough into a circle 16 or 17 inches in diameter. Spread 2 tablespoons melted margarine or butter on the pastry; roll into a long, narrow log, as if rolling a jelly roll. Then cut the roll into 20 or 22 equal pieces. Roll and cut the other piece of dough in the same way. Place these small pieces of dough on a tray; cover with wax paper; let them rest 30 minutes.

3. Place one piece of dough smooth side—not cut side—down on the lightly floured work surface; press down and flatten into a small circle with your hands or with a rolling pin. Sprinkle some flour on the work surface and on the circle of pastry. Using a rolling pin, roll it out into a circle 5 to 6 inches in diameter. After rolling out all the pieces, spread 1 tablespoon filling over half of each circle; fold the other half over the filling to form a half-moon. Crimp the edges to seal.

4. Shortly before serving, heat the oil in a frying pan or, preferably, in a wok. When the oil is hot, drop the pastries into the oil, a few at a time. Ladle oil over them to make them puff up. When they are golden brown on both sides, place them on a piece of paper towel to drain. Transfer to the serving platter.

CHEESE FILLING:
Mix all the ingredients and blend well.

About 4 dozen böreks

Note: If you would like to make only 2 dozen *böreks*, cut the recipe in half.

3 cups all-purpose flour (scoop
  measuring cup into flour and
  level off with a knife)
1 tablespoon yogurt
1 egg
1 tablespoon vinegar
2 tablespoons olive oil
1/2 cup plus 2 tablespoons water
1/2 teaspoon salt
1/2 teaspoon baking powder
4 tablespoons melted butter or
  margarine
1 1/2 cups oil for frying

CHEESE FILLING:
1/2 lb. feta cheese
1 egg, lightly beaten
1/2 cup chopped parsley

Puff *Börek* (Meat Filling)
Kıymalı Puf Böreği

1. Sauté the meat and the onion in the butter.
Cook until the meat absorbs all its natural juices
and browns. Remove from heat; add parsley and
seasonings; mix well.

2. Follow the recipe for Puff *Börek*, replacing
the cheese filling with the meat filling.

4 dozen böreks

1/2 lb. lean ground beef
1 large onion, finely chopped
3 tablespoons butter
1 cup chopped parsley
Salt and freshly ground pepper
  to taste
Pastry as for Puff Börek, p. 250
1 1/2 cups oil for frying

Tatar *Börek (Manti)*

Tatar Böreği (Manti)

These small squares of pasta filled with meat resemble wontons. They are cooked and served with
a yogurt-garlic sauce and sizzling butter and red
pepper topping. Unlike the other *böreks*, Tatar *Börek*
is served as a main dish.

EQUIPMENT:
A large, wooden work surface or a table top; a
special rolling pin 25 inches long and approximately
3/4 inch in diameter (a wooden curtain rod or a
dowel rod may be used).

   1. Combine the meat with the onion, salt,
and pepper. Blend well and set aside.
   2. Place the all-purpose flour and the cake
flour in a mixing bowl and blend. Make a hollow
in the middle. Put the eggs, water, and salt in the
hollow and mix with your fingertips. Gradually
combine small portions of flour with the mixture.
Work the dough with your hands to form a cohesive dough. Place the dough on a lightly floured
work surface and knead at least 5 minutes or until
the dough is smooth and elastic. The dough should
not stick to your hands. It should be a fairly stiff
dough. If necessary, add a few teaspoons of flour.
Cover with a piece of wax paper and let it rest
1 hour at room temperature.
   3. Place the dough on the lightly floured work
surface and divide into halves. Take each piece,
knead well, and shape into a round ball. Cover
one piece with wax paper and set aside. Place the
other on the work surface. Using a regular rolling
pin, roll it into a circle as large as a dinner plate.
Dust the work surface and the surface of the
pastry with flour. Wrap one edge of the pastry
around the center of the special rolling pin. Place
the heels of both hands at the center of the pin.

With a slight back-and-forth motion, press gently and continuously toward the ends of the pastry and the rolling pin, gradually moving the rolling pin forward so that the whole piece of pastry is wrapped around it. At the same time, repeatedly move your hands away from each other toward the ends of the pin and then quickly bring them back to the center. As your hands move toward the end, let the heels of your hands gently pull and stretch the pastry outward. After the pastry is entirely wrapped around the rolling pin, gently flip the pastry open and loose. Now, move the pastry slightly clockwise and start with a different edge. Repeat this process several times until the pastry measures 19 to 20 inches in diameter. Dusting the work surface and the pastry with flour at each rolling. Repeat this process with the other half of the dough.

4. Place each pastry sheet on the work surface and using a very sharp knife cut into strips 1 1/4 inches wide. Then cut the strips into squares measuring 1 1/4 inches on a side. Place 1/4 to 1/2 teaspoon meat filling in the middle of each square. Bring the four corners together and pinch firmly, creating small packages.

5. Fill a large pan with cold water, add some salt, and bring to a boil. Drop all or part of the pastries into the rapidly boiling water, but do not crowd them. Reduce the heat a little to prevent them from boiling too rapidly and possibly tearing. Cook 8 to 10 minutes, stirring occasionally, until the pasta is cooked. Do not overcook. Transfer the cooked pasta into a serving bowl; pour 1/2 to 1 cup of the cooking liquid over the pasta; keep it hot.

6. Pour the yogurt sauce over the pasta in the serving bowl. Top with the butter and red pepper mixture. Serve very hot.

YOGURT SAUCE:
Beat all ingredients together until smooth and creamy.

254

BUTTER AND RED PEPPER TOPPING:
Melt the butter in a saucepan and stir in the cayenne or paprika. Heat until bubbly. Keep it warm until ready to serve.

4–6 Servings

1/2 **lb. lean ground beef**
1 large onion, chopped
Salt and freshly ground pepper
   to taste
2 cups unbleached all-purpose
   flour (scoop measuring cup
   into flour and level off with
   a knife)
1/2 **cup plain bleached cake**
   flour
2 eggs
6 tablespoons water
3/4 **teaspoon salt**
1 cup all-purpose flour for
   rolling out the pastry

YOGURT SAUCE:
2 pints yogurt at room
   temperature
1 teaspoon salt
1–2 tablespoons or more
   mashed garlic

BUTTER AND RED PEPPER
TOPPING:
6-8 tablespoons butter
1/2-**1 teaspoon cayenne or 1-2**
   teaspoons paprika

BÖREKS MADE WITH PHYLLO PASTRY

Spinach *Börek* with Phyllo
Ispanaklı Börek

Made with phyllo pastry, this recipe is very easy and is everyone's favorite.

1. Cook spinach with 1 1/2 cups water 5 minutes or until wilted. Drain and press out as much water as possible. Sauté the onion in the oil for 5 minutes; add the spinach and 4 tablespoons butter and cook 8 to 10 minutes, stirring frequently. Remove from heat; stir in 4 lightly beaten eggs, cheese, salt, and pepper. Blend well and remove from heat.

2. Melt the remaining butter in a saucepan; cool to tepid. Stir in the milk and 2 lightly beaten eggs and mix well. Have a pastry brush ready.

3. Preheat the oven to 350°. Brush an approximately 10-inch-by-14-inch baking pan with butter. Unfold the phyllo pastry and cover with wax paper. Take only one sheet at a time and keep the remaining sheets covered at all times to prevent them from drying. The size of the phyllo sheet (approximately 14 inches by 18 inches) will not correspond exactly to the area of the pan. It is therefore necessary to fold the sheets in a certain way to adjust them to the size of the pan. Place the shorter edge of the pastry sheet against the longer side of the pan, brush lightly with the butter, egg, and milk mixture, and then fold the area of the sheet left hanging over the edge of the pan inwards to form part of a second layer. Brush with the butter, egg, and milk mixture. Using the edge of this layer as your point of departure, place a second pastry sheet in the pan, folding it inwards to cover the second layer. Continue this procedure until about 1/3 of all the pastry sheets have been used. Spread the filling evenly over the pastry sheets. Continue adding the remaining sheets of phyllo, brushing each with the butter, egg, and milk mixture. Tuck the edges under. Brush the top with the remaining mixture. Using a sharp knife, cut into squares and bake 30 to 40 minutes. Serve warm. This *börek* can also be served cold, but it is much better warm.

8–10 Servings

2 lbs. spinach washed, drained,
   and finely chopped, or 3
   packages frozen, chopped
   spinach
1 large onion, chopped
2 tablespoons oil
1 cup plus 2 tablespoons
   butter
4 eggs, lightly beaten
1/2 cup Romano cheese, grated
Salt and pepper, freshly
   ground, to taste
2 tablespoons milk
2 eggs, lightly beaten
1 lb. thin phyllo pastry

Spinach Roll
Baklava Yufkasıyla Burma Börek

1. Prepare the filling.

2. Melt the butter; cool to warm and mix with the milk. Have pastry brush ready.

3. Unroll the pastry and take out 8 sheets. Rewrap the rest of the pastry and store in the refrigerator or freezer for another use. Work with 1 pair of sheets at a time and keep the rest well covered at all times to prevent them from drying. Put 1 pair of sheets, one directly on top of the other, on the work surface. Brush lightly with the butter. Place 1/4 of the filling along the long edge of the pastry rectangle nearer you, 1 inch away from 3 edges. Shape the filling into an approximately 1-inch-thick roll. Fold left and right side in to seal. Fold the long edge nearer you over the filling. Roll the whole thing into an approximately 15- or 16-inch-long log, as if rolling a jelly roll. Twist this log into a coil in the middle of a lightly greased 9-inch-by-13-inch baking pan. Fill and roll a second log in the same way. Align one end of this log with the free end of the first log in the baking pan, and continue twisting it around the first coil, enlarging the coil as you twist it around (see illustrations, page 000). Preheat oven to 375°. Continue with the remaining ingredients, forming 2 more logs, twisting them in the pan and ending with a large coil almost filling the baking pan. Brush the top of the whole pastry with the remaining butter. Bake 25 minutes or until golden brown. Remove from the oven and let cool 5 or 10 minutes. Transfer to a serving platter. Cut the logs into 3- or 4-inch-long slices as you serve. Serve hot or cold. It is best when served hot.

8–10 Servings

Spinach filling (see p. 256)
8 sheets thin phyllo pastry
1/2 cup butter
2 tablespoons milk

Cheese *Börek* with Phyllo
Peynirli Tepsi Böreği

1. Combine the feta cheese, ricotta or cottage

cheese, parsley, dill, and egg yolks and mix until well blended.

2. Follow the recipe for Spinach *Börek* with Phyllo, replacing the spinach filling with cheese filling.

10 Servings

2/3 **lb. feta cheese, crumbled**
1 **cup ricotta or cottage cheese**
2/3 **cup parsley, chopped**
1/2 **cup fresh dill, chopped**
4 **egg yolks, lightly beaten**
14 **tablespoons butter**
2 **tablespoons milk**
2 **eggs, lightly beaten**
1 **lb. thin phyllo pastry**

Chicken *Börek* with Phyllo
Baklava Yufkası ile Tavuklu Börek

1. Prepare chicken filling (page 241).

2. Preheat the oven to 400°. Unfold the phyllo pastry and take out 8 sheets. Rewrap the remaining sheets to save for another use. Work with only one sheet at a time, keeping the rest covered to prevent them from drying out. Spread one sheet on a flat surface. Fold it in half by bringing the two longer sides together, thus forming a long rectangle. Brush with butter, fold it in half again, bringing the short sides of the rectangle together to form an approximate square. Brush lightly with butter. Place 1/8 of the filling in the middle, spreading it to cover an area much smaller than the pastry. Fold the slightly longer side over the filling; brush lightly with butter. Fold the opposite side over and butter again. Fold over one end and brush with butter; then fold the other end over and but-

ter it too. Repeat this process with the remaining sheets of phyllo. Placing the *böreks* seam side down on a baking sheet; brush the tops with butter. Bake 15 minutes or until golden brown.

8 böreks

Chicken Filling, p. 241
8 thin phyllo sheets
6 tablespoons melted butter

PIDES

Pide
Ramazan Pidesi

This is a delicious leavened flat bread, very much like the Indian *nan*. In some parts of Anatolia, it is made in special ovens, called *tandır*. In Istanbul, they are especially made during the month of Ramadan. In the evening, people rush to the bakeries to buy some of this bread, fresh from the oven and still hot, to bring home for *iftar* (breaking the fast).

The dough is a very simple one to make. However, to be successful, this bread must be carefully shaped in the baking pan and baked in the hottest oven possible.

1. Dissolve the yeast in 1/2 cup tepid water mixed with the sugar. Let stand 10 minutes.

2. Place the flour in a mixing bowl. Make a hollow in the middle. Put the salt, dissolved yeast, and water here and mix with your fingertips. Gradually combine the flour with this mixture. Work the dough with your hands to form a cohesive dough. Place the dough on a floured work surface and knead 5 minutes or until smooth and elastic. Cover and let it rise in a warm place 1 hour.

Punch the dough down and let it rise again for 1 hour.

3. Place the dough on a floured work surface. Rolling it back and forth under the palms of your hands, shape it into a long roll. Divide the roll into 4 to 6 equal pieces. Take each piece and roll it under the palm of one hand into a ball. Then, with swift up and down jabs of fingertips flatten and enlarge each round to 7 inches in diameter. Place it on a very generously floured surface. Repeat this process with all the pieces. Hold one hand under cold running water and then brush the tops of the pides with this wet hand. Let the dough rest for 20 minutes.

4. Preheat the oven to 550° for at least 20 minutes. Place a large earthenware baking sheet in the lower-middle section of the oven to preheat. (An aluminum baking pan may be used if earthenware is not available, but the earthenware will produce a better bread.)

5. Remove the baking sheet from the oven and sprinkle it lightly with water. Pick up one piece of dough with two hands, gently stretch it into an oval, and place it on the baking sheet. Wet your fingertips and with swift up and down jabs, distributed all across the dough, flatten and enlarge it further in the pan.

The end result will be a thin, oval 9-inch-long piece of dough marked with craterlike hollows left by the imprints of your fingertips. These hollows should be as deep as possible without actually creating a hole, and the mounds with which they alternate should not be higher than 1/5 inch.

If there is room on the baking sheet, add more pides. Lightly glaze the tops with water and sprinkle with nigella or sesame seeds, if desired. Bake for 3 to 4 minutes. The pides should come out fairly soft and pale. These pides can also be glazed with an egg yolk. Continue to bake pides in the same way until all the dough is used. They are best when served hot.

1 1/4-oz. package dry-active
   yeast
1/2 cup tepid water
1 teaspoon sugar
4 cups plus 2 tablespoons
   unbleached, all-purpose flour
   (scoop measuring cup into
   flour and level off with a
   knife)
1 teaspoon salt
1 cup warm water
Nigella (known as kalonji in Indian
   cookery, sometimes called black
   caraway seeds) or sesame seeds
   (optional)

Cheese Pide
Peynirli Pide

Simple to make, surprisingly rewarding.

1. Dissolve the yeast in 1/2 cup tepid water, mixed with the sugar. Let stand.

2. Place the flour in a mixing bowl. Make a hollow in the middle. Put the remaining water, salt, and dissolved yeast in the middle and mix with your fingertips. Gradually combine the flour with the ingredients in the hollow. Work the dough with your hands to form a cohesive dough. Place the dough on a floured work surface and knead 5 minutes or until smooth and elastic. Put it back in the mixing bowl, cover, and let it rise 1 hour. Punch the dough down and let it rise again for 1 hour.

3. Place the dough on a lightly floured work surface. Rolling it back and forth under the palms of your hands, shape it into a long roll. Divide the roll into 10 equal pieces. Take each piece and roll it under the palm of one hand into a round bun. Place the buns on a generously floured surface. Cover and let them rest 20 minutes.

4. Place each bun on a lightly floured work surface. Using a rolling pin, roll it into a 1/8-inch-thick disc, 6 inches in diameter.

5. Place 1 to 1 1/2 tablespoons filling in the middle of the 1/8-inch-thick disc. Shape it into a small canoe by folding the opposite edges of the dough over the filling to meet in the middle and pinching the ends to seal. The filling should be visible on top. Fill each bun. Glaze the tops with a mixture of the egg yolk and the milk. Preheat the oven to 550° for 20 minutes. Place a large earthenware baking sheet (or aluminum baking pan) in the lower-middle section of the oven to preheat. Transfer the pides to the baking sheet, pulling each end of the dough very slightly longer and thinner or flatter. At this point the canoes will measure approximately 7 inches long. Bake 4 to 6 minutes. They should come out fairly soft. Serve hot.

CHEESE FILLING:
Combine all the ingredients and blend well.

10 small pides

1 1/4-oz. package dry-active
   yeast
1/2 cup tepid water
1/2 teaspoon sugar
4 cups plus 2 tablespoons
   unbleached all-purpose flour
   (scoop measuring cup into
   flour and level off with a
   knife)
1 cup warm water

1 teaspoon salt
1 egg yolk for glaze
1 tablespoon milk for glaze

CHEESE FILLING:
3/4 lb. feta cheese, crumbled
3/4 stick butter at room
    temperature
4 egg yolks, lightly beaten
3/4 cup fresh dill, chopped, or
    1/2–1 tablespoon dried dill
    weed

Meat Pide
Kıymalı Pide

1. Mix the meat, onions, tomatoes, bell peppers, green chilies, parsley, salt, paprika, and pepper flakes and blend well.

2. Follow the recipe for Cheese Pide, p. 262, replacing the cheese filling with the meat filling.

10 small pides

3/4 lb. ground lamb
2 onions, finely chopped
3 tomatoes, finely chopped
1 bell pepper, chopped
1 or 2 green chilies, chopped
1 cup chopped parsley
Salt
2 teaspoons paprika
2 teaspoons red pepper flakes
Pide Dough, p. 260
1 egg yolk for glaze

Turko-Arab Pizza

Lahmacun

This is a Middle Eastern specialty, sometimes called Middle Eastern pizza in the United States. In Turkey, it is found in kebab shops and is not made at home. However, after several trials, I finally succeeded in making it just as if it had been ordered from a regular kebab shop, an event that would greatly surprise my friends in Turkey. *Lahmacun* is excellent for parties or lunches.

1. Dissolve the yeast in 1/2 cup tepid water mixed with the sugar. Let stand.

2. Place the flour in a mixing bowl. Make a hollow in the middle. Put the dissolved yeast, salt, and warm water in the hollow and mix with your fingertips. Gradually combine the flour with the mixture in the hollow. Work the dough with your hands until it forms a cohesive dough. Place the dough on the work surface dusted with 1 tablespoon flour. Knead five minutes or until smooth and elastic. Place it back in the bowl, cover with a piece of cloth, and let it rise in a warm place 60 minutes.

3. Place the dough on a lightly floured work surface. Rolling it back and forth under the palms of your hands, shape it into a long roll. Divide the roll into 6 to 8 equal pieces. Take each piece and roll it under the palm of one hand into a ball. Cover and let rise on a floured surface 20 to 30 minutes.

4. Dust a large surface, like a table top or large kitchen counter, with generous amounts of flour. Place each bun on the work surface and, using a rolling pin, roll it into a circle 1/8 inch thick. Place the circles on a large, well-floured surface after they have been rolled out.

5. Preheat the oven to 550° for at least 20 minutes. Place a very large earthenware baking sheet in the lower-middle section of the oven to preheat. (An aluminum baking pan may be used if earthenware is not available, but earthenware will produce a better pizza.)

6. Spread 2 teaspoons tomato paste evenly on each circle of dough. Then spread an equal amount of the filling on each circle. Remove the baking sheet from the oven and quickly transfer one of the pizzas to the sheet, pulling each end of the dough gently and very slightly in opposite directions. This will give it an oval shape and it will flatten the dough, which will have risen again while standing. Add more pizzas if there is room on the sheet. Bake 4 to 5 minutes. They should still be fairly soft. Place them in a large pot on top of one another as they come out of the oven. Set the cover of the pan slightly ajar, leaving an opening to allow the steam to escape. This will keep them soft and warm. Serve hot.

LAHMACUN FILLING:
Mix all the ingredients and knead well to blend.

4–6 Servings

1 1/4-oz. package dry-active
    yeast
1/2 cup tepid water
1/2 teaspoon sugar
4 cups plus 2 tablespoons
    unbleached, all-purpose flour
    (scoop measuring cup into
    flour and level off with
    a knife)
1 cup warm water
1 teaspoon salt
5–6 tablespoons tomato paste
Extra amount of flour for
    handling the dough

LAHMACUN FILLING:

1/2 **lb. ground lamb**

2 **ripe tomatoes, very finely chopped**

1 **large onion, very finely chopped**

1 **large bell pepper, very finely chopped**

1 **or more hot green chili peppers, finely chopped**

1 **cup parsley, finely chopped**

1–11/2 **teaspoons red pepper flakes**

1 **teaspoon paprika**

Salt to taste

Middle Eastern Bread
Arap Pidesi

These pides will have pockets in them.

1. Dissolve the yeast in 1/2 cup tepid water and sugar; let stand 5 minutes.

2. Place the flour in a large mixing bowl. Make a hollow in the middle. Put the thoroughly dissolved yeast, the warm water, and salt in the middle and mix these ingredients with your fingertips. Gradually combine the flour with this mixture and work with your hands to form a cohesive dough. Place the dough on a well-floured work surface and knead 5 minutes or until the dough is smooth and elastic. It should not stick to your hands. Put the dough back in the bowl, cover with a piece of cloth, and let rise in a warm place for 2 hours. Punch the dough down and let it rise again for 1 hour.

3. Place the dough on a lightly floured work

surface. Rolling it back and forth under the palms of your hands, shape it into a long roll. Divide the roll into 12 equal pieces. Take each piece of dough and roll it under the palm of one hand into a ball. Then, using a rolling pin, roll out each ball into a 1/4-inch-thick disc. When all the pieces of dough have been rolled out into pancake-like circles, preheat the oven to 550°.

4. Preheat an earthenware baking sheet in the lower-middle section of the oven. (A large aluminum baking pan may be used if earthenware is not available.) Place the pitas on the baking sheet and bake only 2 minutes. Because they have pockets, they are good for making interesting sandwiches.

12 small pita breads

1 1/4-oz. package dry-active
  yeast
1/2 cup tepid water
1 teaspoon sugar
4 cups plus 2 tablespoons
  unbleached all-purpose flour
  (scoop measuring cup into
  flour and level off with
  a knife)
11/2 teaspoons salt
1 cup warm water

Traditional Sweets

Turkish cuisine is distinguished by its wide variety of desserts. A foreign friend once remarked that two kinds of establishment are particularly common in Turkish cities, pastry shops and drugstores, and jokingly suggested that the former necessitated the latter. Whether this is true or not, there can be no doubt about the importance of pastries and sweets in Turkey. Rich, sweet pastries such as *baklava* are relatively well known in the West. But almost completely unknown are the dairy desserts, which are specially delightful and refreshing and more easily digested than items like *baklava* that use butter, nuts, and syrup liberally. These two main categories of dessert are sold in different shops: *pastahaneler* offer pastries (both Turkish and European) for sale; *muhallebiciler*, dairy desserts. The making of some pastries, notably *baklava*, is so complex that it requires a further degree of specialization; separate shops are devoted to these desserts alone. Such specialization is often cultivated within a family and handed down from one generation to the next.

Many Turkish desserts, in fact, have interesting historical backgrounds. *Baklava*, as mentioned in the introduction, was prepared in the Topkapı Palace during Ramadan in several different varieties; some for consumption within the palace, others for distribution to the soldiers and the public at large. The origins of *aşure*—if the legend is to be believed—are even more ancient, going back to the last days of Noah's Ark. Anxious to avoid wasting anything, Noah concocted a mixture of the remaining foodstuffs, the same mixture that now goes to make up *aşure*. It is also associated with the tenth day of the month of Muharram (hence its name) and is eaten in mourning commemoration of the tragic event that took place on that day: the martyrdom of Imam Husayn, the grandson of the Prophet. Now served by *muhallebici* shops, *aşure* used to be cooked in dervish convents, as a distinct kind of ritual, and, to a lesser extent, in well-to-do homes. As for *helva*, it too was eaten on occasions of religious significance, a custom that has persisted more vigorously, perhaps, than the eating of *aşure* during Muharram.

Even now, most of the heavy pastry and syrup desserts such as *baklava*, *tulumba* dessert, and *lokma* are prepared chiefly on festive days and holidays; they are not an essential part of the everyday diet. They are occasionally eaten in tea houses or bought at pastry shops and brought home as treats. However, lighter sweets such as dairy desserts or *helvas* or fruit desserts are often prepared at home and enjoyed as snacks.

They are not usually served immediately after dinner, for fruit is considered a more fitting conclusion to the meal. And as any visitor to Turkey can testify, Turkish fruit is exceptionally good, varied, and abundant. Colorful and artistic displays of fruit are one of the unforgettable features of Turkish markets. Each fruit, moreover, comes in different varieties; it is not enough to ask simply for peaches, for example, one has to specify whether it is a Bursa or an Izmir peach one is after.

The lightly sweetened yeast cakes, pound cakes or sponge cakes, and rolls and cookies (see section of Tea Time Favorites, p. 307), are more frequently enjoyed during the day and in the evenings with tea.

In the case of desserts containing syrup, the amount of sugar used may be adjusted according to taste.

DESSERTS OF PASTRY AND SYRUP

"Lady's Navel"
Kadın Göbeği

This is a very traditional dessert that was prepared in the kitchens of the Topkapı Palace. These small golden rounds with a hole in the middle, indeed resembling ladies' navels, are made from an egg-base paste.

1. Dissolve the sugar with 3 cups water in a saucepan; bring it to a boil. Turn the heat to low and simmer the syrup 10 minutes. Add lemon juice; simmer 5 minutes longer. Remove from heat and cool.

2. Place 2 cups water and butter in a heavy pan. Bring to a boil, and add the flour all at once, stirring quickly with a wooden spoon. At first, the dough will look rough, but in a minute or two it will become very smooth. When the mixture is smooth and no longer sticks to the spoon and the sides of the pan, remove the pan from the heat. If overcooked, the dough will not puff as it is supposed to. Cool to lukewarm.

3. Add the eggs one at a time, beating with an electric mixer after each addition or beating vigorously by hand. The dough will look slippery. Put a little oil on your hands and take walnut-sized pieces, shape them into a ball, flatten them, and make a hole in the middle by putting your finger through the dough. Put a little more oil on your hands from time to time as you continue shaping the dough.

4. Heat the oil in a deep pot, preferably a wok, until lukewarm or a little warmer but not more than 250°F. The temperature of the oil is very important because if the oil is too hot, the pastries will not puff as they should. Because they expand in the oil, do not crowd the cooking pot. As they swell and rise to the top, gradually increase the temperature. It should not exceed 300°, or the exterior will cook too fast and the inside will remain uncooked. Fry each side to a golden brown. After each batch is fried, cool the oil by turning off the heat for a little while. Briefly drain the pastries on a paper towel, then drop them in the cool syrup. Leave them in the syrup for 5 to 10 minutes or for a shorter or longer period of time, depending on the level of sweetness you desire. Place them on a serving platter. Serve plain or with whipped cream.

About 4 dozen pastries

SYRUP:
3 cups sugar
3 cups water
1 teaspoon lemon juice

2 cups water
7 tablespoons unsalted butter
2 1/2 cups all-purpose flour
4 large eggs at room
   temperature
1 1/2 cups oil for frying

Tulumba Dessert
Tulumba Tatlısı

This is another traditional dessert, very similar to *kadın göbegi,* "Lady's Navel."

1. Dissolve the sugar with 3 cups water; bring to a boil and simmer 10 minutes. Add lemon juice and simmer 5 minutes longer. Cool.

2. Mix flour, semolina, and wheat starch or corn starch in a bowl.

3. Place 2 1/2 cups water and butter in a heavy pan. Bring the mixture to a boil and add the flour mixture all at once, stirring quickly with a wooden spoon. At first the dough will look rough, but in a minute or so it will become very smooth. When the mixture is smooth and does not stick to the spoon or the sides of the pan, remove the pan from the heat. Do not overcook or the dough will not puff as it is supposed to. Cool to lukewarm.

4. Add the eggs one at a time, beating with an electric mixer after each addition or beating vigorously by hand. The dough will be slippery. Put the dough in a pastry bag with a zig-zag-shaped nozzle.

5. Heat the oil in a deep pot, preferably a wok, until a little warmer than lukewarm. It is very important that the temperature of the oil not exceed 250°F because the dough will not puff as it is supposed to in hot oil. When the oil is warm, drop 1 1/2-inch-long pieces of dough from the pastry bag. (Or shape them into finger-thick, 1 1/2-inch-long pieces using a little oil on your hands to prevent the dough from sticking.) Do not crowd the pot, because the pastries expand. As they puff up and rise to the surface, gradually increase the temperature of the oil but do not exceed 300°. If the oil gets too hot, the insides will remain raw. You need to be able to regulate the temperature when making this dessert. It is very important to cool the oil after each batch by turning the heat off until the oil cools down. Briefly drain the pastries on a piece of paper towel. Then drop them into the cool syrup. Leave them in the syrup for 5 to 10 minutes or for a longer or shorter period of time, depending on the level of sweetness you desire. Place on a serving platter. Serve plain or with whipped cream.

About 4 dozen pastries

SYRUP:
3 cups sugar
3 cups water
1 teaspoon lemon juice

2 1/2 cups unbleached all-purpose flour
1 tablespoon fine semolina or cream of wheat
1 tablespoon wheat starch (cornstarch may be used instead)
2 1/2 cups water
7 tablespoons unsalted butter
5 large eggs at room temperature

Sweet Almond Cakes
Badempare

SYRUP:

Dissolve the sugar in the water and bring to a boil; simmer 5 minutes. Add the lemon juice; simmer 5 minutes longer. Remove from heat and cool.

1. Cream the butter, powdered sugar, and baking power together until smooth and fluffy. Add the egg and egg yolk and mix well.

2. Toss the flour with the ground almonds in a bowl. Stir this into the butter and egg mixture. Work the dough with your hands to form a cohesive dough. Cover it with a sheet of wax paper and let it rest 15 minutes.

3. Preheat the oven to 350°. Shape walnut-sized pieces of dough into round balls. Flatten them between your palms slightly and place on a lightly buttered baking sheet. Press an almond into the middle of each cake. Bake 20 minutes. Remove from the oven. Place them side by side, in a deep dish. Pour the syrup over them and let them soak several hours.

About 1 dozen

SYRUP:
3 cups water
21/2 cups sugar
1 teaspoon lemon juice

1/2 cup unsalted butter or
   margarine
1/2 cup powdered sugar
1/2 teaspoon baking powder
1 egg, lightly beaten
1 egg yolk, lightly beaten
2 cups all-purpose flour
1 cup ground blanched
   almonds
10 or 12 blanched almonds,
   whole

Little Sweet Cakes
Şekerpare

1. Prepare Syrup.

2. Cream the butter, powdered sugar, and baking powder together until light and fluffy.

3. Stir in the egg, egg yolk, lemon rind, and vanilla; mix well. Gradually stir in the flour. The dough will be crumbly. Stir in the milk and work with your hands rapidly to form a cohesive dough. Cover with a sheet of wax paper and let it rest 15 minutes.

4. Preheat the oven to 350°. Shape walnut-sized pieces into balls. Flatten them between your palms and place on a lightly buttered baking sheet. Gently press down an almond into the middle of each piece. Bake 20 minutes. Remove from the oven and place them side by side in a dish deep enough to hold the syrup. Pour the syrup over them and let them soak several hours.

About 1 dozen

Syrup, p. 274
1/2 **cup unsalted butter, at room**
    temperature
1/2 **cup powdered sugar**
1/2 **teaspoon baking powder**
1 **egg, lightly beaten**
1 **egg yolk, lightly beaten**
1 **teaspoon grated lemon rind**
1 **teaspoon vanilla**
2 **cups unbleached all-purpose**
    flour
1 **teaspoon milk**
10 **or 12 blanched almonds**

Revani Dessert
Revani

SYRUP:

Heat the 4 cups sugar and the water in a saucepan,

stirring until the sugar is dissolved. Bring to a boil and simmer 15 minutes. Add the lemon juice and simmer 5 minutes longer. Remove from heat and cool.

1. Beat the egg yolks with 3/4 cup sugar and the lemon rind until pale yellow in color (about 7 minutes). When the beater is lifted from the egg mixture, it should form thick ribbons.

2. Beat the egg whites into soft peaks.

3. Preheat the oven to 350°. Mix the semolina and the flour in a bowl to blend; fold into the egg-yolk mixture.

4. Fold in the egg whites and the butter alternately into the batter. Folding should be done gently taking care not to disturb the volume of the batter and the air beaten into it.

5. Pour the batter into a greased pan (8 inches by 12 inches by 2 inches). Bake 45 minutes or until done. Remove from the oven and pour the cool syrup over the hot cake. Let it stand several hours to absorb the syrup. Cut into squares or diamonds. Serve cold with whipped cream.

8–12 Servings

SYRUP:
4 cups sugar
5 cups water
1 teaspoon lemon juice

9 eggs, separated
3/4 cup sugar
Grated rind of 1 lemon
2 cups fine-grain semolina or
    cream of wheat
1/4 cup flour
1/4 cup unsalted butter, melted

Almond Cake
Badem Tatlısı

A light, spongy almond cake moistened with syrup.

SYRUP:
Dissolve the 3 cups sugar in the water and bring
to a boil. Simmer 10 minutes. Add the lemon juice
and simmer 5 minutes longer. Remove from heat
and cool.

1. Preheat the oven to 375°. Toss the ground
almonds and flour together in a bowl.

2. Beat the eggs with 1/2 cup sugar into a thick
mayonnaise-like cream; mix in the vanilla. Fold
in the flour and almond mixture.

3. Butter a round cake-pan 10 ins. in diameter and sprinkle 1/4 cup chopped almonds in the
bottom. Pour in the batter; sprinkle the remaining
almonds on top. Bake 30 to 35 minutes. Remove
from the oven. Pour the syrup over the hot cake.
Let it stand until the syrup is absorbed. Serve
plain or with whipped cream.

8–12 Servings

SYRUP:
3 cups sugar
21/2 cups water
1 teaspoon lemon juice

**11/4 cups almonds, blanched
and ground**
**1 cup plus 1 tablespoon
all-purpose flour (scoop
measuring cup into flour and
level off with a knife)**
10 eggs, at room temperature
1/2 cup sugar

1 teaspoon vanilla
1/2 cup chopped almonds

Palace *Lokma*
Saray Lokması

Crisp outside, spongy inside, these golden balls
are made with a yeast dough, puffed in hot oil,
and served with syrup.

SYRUP:
Mix 2 cups sugar and 2 cups water and bring to
a boil. Simmer 10 minutes. Add the lemon juice and
simmer 5 minutes longer. Remove from heat and
cool.

1. Dissolve the yeast in a small bowl with
1/2 cup plus 3 tablespoons tepid water and 1/2 teaspoon sugar. Let stand 10 minutes in a warm
place. Add 3/4 cup flour and beat with a wooden
spoon 3 to 4 minutes into a smooth batter. Cover
with plastic wrap and let stand 30 minutes in a
warm place.

2. In a large mixing bowl, mix the yeast batter
with the remaining flour, 1/2 cup tepid water, salt,
and egg into a smooth batter. Beat it repeatedly
with the striking, slapping, circular motion of one
hand 2 to 3 minutes. Cover the bowl with plastic
wrap and let it rise in a warm place 30 minutes or
so. The batter will not rise much, but there will
be bubbles on top.

3. Heat the oil in a deep pot, preferably a wok,
to about 350°F (deep fat frying temperature). Do
not let the oil get any hotter than this, or the
lokmas will cook too fast to cook inside.

Take a handful of dough, squeeze your hand
into a fist, and squeeze out as much as a rounded
teaspoonful of batter through the hole formed
by your thumb and your first finger. Drop the

batter into the oil. You may use a knife or spoon to separate the batter from your hand. This is the traditional or professional way of doing it. If this does not work for you, take a metal teaspoon, scoop up a rounded teaspoonful of batter, and drop it into the oil. As soon as the batter hits the hot oil, it will expand, puff up, and rise to the surface. In 20 to 30 seconds, gently touch the top of the *lokma* to flip it over. Sometimes they will do this by themselves, but if they are not turned within the first 20 or 30 seconds, they will not easily turn over and will tend to stay on one side, causing one side to brown and the other to remain pale. Drop 5 or 6 *lokmas* into the oil at one time depending on the size of the pot. Do not crowd the pot. Cook the *lokmas* 6, 7, or 8 minutes depending on the degree of crispness desired. Those cooked longer will have crispier outsides and hollower insides. Throughout the cooking, continue to flip the *lokmas* over to achieve even browning.

4. Place the *lokmas* on a platter lined with paper towels to drain. If you wish very little sweetening, put a few *lokmas* on individual dessert plates and sprinkle 1 or 2 tablespoons of syrup on top of them. Or you can drop them into the syrup and leave them in syrup only briefly, then serve. Usually they are left in the syrup for at least 10 minutes or so.

10 Servings

SYRUP:
2 cups sugar
2 cups water
1 teaspoon lemon juice

1 teaspoon dry yeast
**1 cup plus 3 tablespoons tepid
   water**
1/2 teaspoon sugar

1 3/4 cups unbleached all-
     purpose flour (Scoop measuring
     cup into flour and level off
     with a knife
1 teaspoon salt
1 egg
Oil for frying

DAIRY DESSERTS

"Chicken Breast"
Tavuk Göğsü

To make this celebrated delicacy, you must shred
a cooked chicken breast into stringlike fibers. In
Turkey, one simply goes to a *muhallebici* shop, which
specializes in and serves only dairy desserts, and
enjoys this dessert. Housewives hardly ever go
to the trouble of making it. I was told by professional *muhallebici* that the breast must be taken
from a freshly slaughtered chicken or the fibers
cannot be properly separated from each other.
Nonetheless, I have made the effort many times,
and even though the stringy fibers may not have
been as thin as I desired, the end result was still
a delicious *tavuk göğsü*. Since there are no *muhallebicis*
outside Turkey, the temptation is very strong to
make *tavuk göğsü* for anyone who is fond of it.
Shredding the fibers takes time, but once this is
done, the rest is very easy.

1. Place the chicken breast in a pan with 2 cups
water. Bring to boil and simmer approximately 15
minutes or until it is almost, but not quite, done.
If cooked too long, the fibers will disintegrate and
not separate into strings. While the chicken is still
warm, cut it into pieces 1/2 inch wide and 1 1/2 inches
long. Using the thumb and the first finger of both
hands, shred each piece string by string. The strings

should be thin; the thinner, the better. Do not be concerned if you cannot get them all equally thin. Some will be thin, others not so thin. (Despite all my efforts, I have never gotten all the fibers to be string-thin.) You will need 1 1/2 cup loosely packed, shredded chicken. Once you have this amount, you can stop shredding. Place these strings in a sieve and wash with cold water many times in order to remove the smell of chicken. Press out as much moisture as you can. Now they are ready to use.

2. Boil the milk with the sugar.

3. Dissolve the cornstarch and the rice flour in 1 1/2 cups water and slowly add this mixture to the boiling milk, stirring constantly. Cook 15 to 20 minutes over low heat until it thickens a little. (To test whether it is ready, put a teaspoon on a saucer and cool it in the refrigerator. When completely cool, turn the saucer upside down and lift the drop of pudding off the saucer with your finger. If it leaves the saucer without sticking and leaving a mark, the pudding has cooked long enough.)

4. Take a cupful of the pudding and mix it with the chicken, beating with the back of a large wooden spoon. Now add the chicken and pudding mixture to the pudding in the pan. Let it simmer over very low heat for 30 minutes. Put it in a 9 inch by 13 inch baking pan and chill in the refrigerator. Cut into squares and serve.

10 Servings

1 chicken breast
Water
7 cups milk
1 1/2 cups sugar
1/4 cup cornstarch
1/2 cup plus 2 tablespoons
rice flour

Pudding with Rose Water
Su Muhallebisi

Delicate, chilled squares of milk dessert topped with powdered sugar and rose water. It has a very interesting, delicate, and refreshing taste.

1. Mix the milk and sugar in a large and heavy pan and bring it to a boil.

2. Dissolve the rice flour and cornstarch in the cold water. Gradually add this mixture to the gently simmering milk, stirring constantly. Cook it for 30 to 40 minutes, stirring frequently. At one point the mixture will start to bubble. Cook it until it thickens. (To test whether it is ready, place a teaspoonful on a saucer and cool it in the refrigerator. When completely cool, turn the saucer upside down and lift the drop of pudding off the saucer. If it leaves the saucer without sticking and leaving a mark, the pudding is done. If it is not done, cook it longer, and test again.)

3. Empty the pudding into a baking pan (9 inches by 13 inches). The pudding should be at least between 1/2 and 1 inch deep. Chill for at least 6 hours or overnight. Cut into squares. Place the squares on individual dessert plates. Sprinkle powdered sugar on top. Sprinkle rose water over the sugar and serve.

10 Servings

7 cups milk
1/4 cup sugar
1/4 cup plus 2 tablespoons cornstarch
1/2 cup plus 2 tablespoons rice flour
1 cup cold water
Powdered sugar
Rose water

Almond Cream
Keşkülü Fukara

1. Bring the milk to a boil in a heavy pan.
2. Put 3 to 4 cups of the hot milk in a bowl with the almonds and blend in the blender in batches, until the almonds are pulverized.
3. Dissolve the rice flour in the water in a bowl and gradually stir this mixture into the simmering milk. Cook 10 minutes, stirring constantly.
4. Stir the sugar and the almond milk into the simmering mixture of milk and rice flour in the pan. Cook over low heat 20 to 30 minutes, stirring almost constantly. Remove from heat and pour into individual bowls. Decorate with grated coconut or pistachios. Chill several hours.

10 Servings

7 cups milk
1 1/2 cups blanched almonds
7 tablespoons rice flour
1 cup water
1 1/2 cups sugar
**Grated coconut, or ground
  pistachios, for garnish**

Pudding with Mastic
Sakizlı Muhallebı

Mastic is a gumlike substance obtained from the resin of certain trees, and it gives a subtle, distinct, and pleasant fragrance and taste to this pudding.

1. Mix the sugar with the milk in a heavy pan and bring to a boil.

2. Place the mastic or Greek gum in the middle of a piece of cheesecloth. Tie it in a small bundle with a piece of string. Submerge this bundle in the simmering milk, draping the cheesecloth over the side of the pan. Let it stay there throughout the cooking period.

3. Mix the rice flour and cornstarch in a bowl with the water. Gradually add this to the simmering milk, stirring constantly. Cook 30 to 40 minutes, stirring almost constantly. Remove from heat. Remove the bag of mastic, squeezing the liquid into the pudding. If there are lumps in the pudding, pour the mixture through a sieve. Pour into individual bowls. Cool for several hours. Decorate with ground almonds and pistachios.

10 Servings

7 cups milk
1 1/4–1 1/2 cups sugar
**2 teaspoons mastic or Greek
  gum**
7 tablespoons rice flour
1/4 cup cornstarch
1 cup water
**Ground almonds and pistachios
  for garnish**

Pistachio Cream
Fıstıklı Muhallebi

1. Boil the pistachios for 2 to 3 minutes. Drain and cover with cold water. Remove the skins. Dry and set aside.

2. Bring the milk to a boil in a heavy pan.

3. Put 4 cups of the hot milk in a bowl with the pistachio nuts; blend in the blender in batches, until the nuts are pulverized.

4. Mix the rice flour with the water in a bowl and gradually stir into the simmering milk. Cook 10 minutes, stirring constantly.

5. Stir in the sugar and pistachio milk into the simmering mixture of milk and rice flour in the pan. Cook over low heat 20 to 30 minutes, stirring almost constantly. Remove from heat. Pour into individual bowls. Chill.

10 Servings

7 cups milk
1 1/2 cups pistachio nuts
7 tablespoons rice flour
1 cup water
1 1/2 cups sugar

Rice Pudding

Sütlaç

1. Place the rice and 2 cups water in a small pan. Bring to a boil; reduce heat and simmer covered, until the rice is done and the water is absorbed, 15 to 20 minutes.

2. Place the milk and rice in a large pan with a heavy bottom and bring to a boil.

3. Mix the cornstarch with 3/4 cup water in a bowl and gradually add this to the simmering mixture of milk and rice, stirring constantly. Cook for 10 minutes. Add the sugar and continue cooking until the mixture thickens slightly. Remove from heat, pour into individual bowls, and chill in the refrigerator. Sprinkle cinnamon on top.

12 Servings

1/2 cup rice
2 cups water
8 cups milk
5 tablespoons cornstarch
3/4 cup water
1 1/2 cups sugar
Cinnamon

HELVA DESSERTS

Flour Helva
Un Helvası

1. Heat the sugar and water until the sugar is dissolved, stirring frequently. Bring to a boil and simmer 15 minutes. Remove from heat.

2. Place the butter in a heavy pan over very low heat. Stir in the flour and almonds; cook for 30 minutes, stirring constantly. Gradually add the syrup, stirring briskly. Remove from heat. Cover and let stand in a warm place for 20 minutes. Stir and empty on to a serving platter and shape into a mound. Serve warm or cold.

4–6 Servings

SYRUP:
1 cup sugar
2 1/4 cups water

1/2 cup unsalted butter
1 cup all-purpose flour
1/2 cup whole or slivered
   blanched almonds

Spoon Helva
Kaşık Helvası

1. Mix the water, milk, and sugar; bring to a boil. Simmer for 15 minutes. Cool.
2. Place the butter in a heavy pan over very low heat. Stir in the semolina or cream of wheat and almonds; cook for 30 minutes, stirring constantly. Gradually add the syrup, stirring briskly. Cover and let stand over very low heat until all the syrup is absorbed. Remove from heat and let stand, covered, in a warm place for 20 minutes. Serve warm in individual dessert bowls.

4–6 Servings

SYRUP:
2 cups water
1 1/4 cups milk
1 cup sugar

1/2 cup unsalted butter
**1 cup coarse grain semolina
   or cream of wheat**
**3/4 cup whole or slivered
   blanched almonds**

Semolina Helva
İrmik Helvası

1. Heat the milk, sugar, and water until sugar is dissolved, stirring constantly. Bring it to a boil and simmer 15 minutes. Remove from heat.
2. Place the butter in a heavy pan over low heat. Stir in the semolina or cream of wheat, and almonds; cook for 30 minutes, stirring constantly with a wooden spoon. Gradually add the syrup, stirring briskly. Cover and let stand over very

low heat until the syrup is absorbed. Remove from heat and let stand, covered, in a warm place for 20 minutes. Stir and empty into a serving plate. Serve warm or cold.

4–6 Servings

SYRUP:
1 1/4 cups milk
1 cup sugar
1 cup water
6 tablespoons unsalted butter
1 cup semolina or cream
of wheat
1 cup whole or slivered
blanched almonds

Saffron Rice Dessert
Zerde

A very interesting, traditional dessert.

1. Cook the rice in 6 cups water for 20 to 25 minutes or until thoroughly cooked.

2. Soak the saffron in 1/4 cup hot water for 10 minutes. Mash the saffron with a teaspoon in its water to get as much color from it as possible.

3. Dissolve the cornstarch in 1/2 cup water. Stir the saffron, sugar, cornstarch, and rose water into the rice mixture and simmer 20 to 30 minutes until it reaches the consistency of a soft pudding. Remove from heat and pour into individual bowls. Decorate with the currants, nuts, and pomegranate seeds. Serve cold.

8–10 Servings

1/2 cup rice
6 cups water

1 teaspoon saffron threads
1/4 cup hot water
1/4 cup cornstarch
1/2 cup water
1 1/2–2 cups sugar
3 tablespoons rose water
1/3 cup currants
1/3 cup finely chopped or
ground almonds or
pistachios
Pomegranate seeds, if available

FRUIT DESSERTS

Pumpkin Dessert with Walnuts
Kabak Tatlısı

1. Peel the pumpkin and cut into strips 2 inches by 4 inches.

2. Layer the pieces in a large, heavy pan, sprinkling the sugar between the layers. Add the water and cook until the pumpkin is tender and almost all the water is absorbed. Add more water in small amounts if needed during cooking. If there is too much liquid left in the pan, cook it uncovered for a while to reduce the amount. Place on a serving platter; sprinkle the walnuts and the pan liquid over the pumpkin pieces. Serve cold.

6 Servings

6 lbs. pumpkin
2 cups sugar
3/4 cup water
1 1/2 cups ground walnuts

Noah's Pudding
Aşure

1. Soak wheat and rice together overnight.
2. Soak chick-peas, white beans, and walnuts separately in water to cover overnight.
3. Next morning, remove the skins from the chick-peas, beans, and walnuts by rubbing them between your fingertips. They come off easily. Rinse the walnuts; drain, chop coarsely, and set aside.
4. Cook the chick-peas and beans in separate pans; they require different cooking times. Cook until almost tender. Drain and set aside.
5. Drain the wheat and rice and put them in a very large, heavy pot with 15 cups water and the orange peel cut into slices. Cook until tender. If the water is reduced by cooking, gradually add more. When the wheat and rice are tender, add the chick-peas and the northern beans and cook 30 minutes more. At this point, there should be approximately 14 cups of liquid in the pan. The pudding thickens as it stands. Add the sugar; mix and cook 10 minutes. Dissolve the rice flour in 3/4 cup water, stir into the pudding, and simmer 2 or 3 minutes. Add the nuts, raisins, apricots, figs, and rose water; remove from heat. Pour into individual bowls, cool for several hours. Decorate with pomegranate seeds. This dessert should have the consistency of a pudding.

16 Servings

1 1/2 cups hulled wheat
1/2 cup uncooked rice
1/4 cup chick-peas
1/4 cup white northern beans
3/4 cup blanched walnuts
**15 cups water and more as
    needed**

Peel of 1/2 **orange**
3 cups sugar
1 cup blanched almonds, whole
1/2 cup rice flour
1 cup golden raisins
10–15 filberts
1/2 cup dried apricots
1/4 cup chopped figs
1/3 cup rose water
1 cup pomegranate seeds, if
    available

Orange Dessert
Portakallı Pelte

A light dessert, very easy to make.

   1. Mix the orange juice with 1/2 cup water and the sugar in a pan and bring to a boil.
   2. Dissolve the cornstarch in 1/2 cup water and gradually add it to the boiling orange-juice mixture. Simmer a few minutes and pour into individual dessert bowls. Sprinkle the nuts on top.

   2 Servings

1 cup fresh orange juice
1 cup water
1/4 cup plus 1 tablespoon sugar
2 1/2 tablespoons cornstarch
2 tablespoons ground toasted
    almonds, filberts or
    pistachios for garnish

Lemon Dessert
Limonlu Pelte

A very light and refreshing dessert.

1. Grate the rind of 2 lemons. Rub the lemon rind with 2 tablespoons of the sugar in a bowl. Squeeze the lemons. Pour the lemon juice and 1 cup water over the lemon rind and sugar. Strain; mix the liquid with the cornstarch; set aside. Discard the lemon rind.

2. Place the remaining sugar and water in a pan; bring to a boil. Stir in the lemon juice and cornstarch mixture. Bring to a boil and simmer 1 minute. Pour into individual bowls. Sprinkle the nuts on top. Chill.

4–6 Servings

2 lemons
3/4 cup sugar
3 1/2 cups water
5 tablespoons cornstarch
2 tablespoons ground toasted almonds, filberts or pistachios for garnish

Rose Petal Jam
Gül Reçeli

Rose jam is a delicacy that remains faithful to the beauty of its origin. It has a delicate color, fragrance, and texture, and its taste is exquisite. In Turkey, the fragrant, pink roses used to make this jam are readily found. Unfortunately, I have not yet been able to find in America a variety of rose suitable for this purpose. But with all the different varieties available, I still believe I will be able to find it one day.

1. Separate the petals from the flowers. Snip off the pointed ends and the white parts of the petals. Put alternating layers of rose petals and 2 cups sugar in a large pan. Cover with a sheet of wax paper and the lid of the pan and let stand overnight.

2. Remove the wax paper. Bring 3 cups water to a boil and pour this over the rose petals; cover and let stand 2 days. Stir well; cover and let stand 1 more day.

3. Put the pan with the rose petals over low heat. Stir in 5 cups sugar and bring to a boil. Remove the scum that forms on the surface. Add the lemon juice and simmer 10 minutes. Remove from heat and pour into an enamel bowl. Pour into hot, sterilized jars. Seal when cold.

5–6 lbs. jam

**1 lb. rose petals (old fashioned
  pink roses)
7 cups sugar
3 cups water
3 tablespoons lemon juice**

Morello Cherry Jam
Vişne Reçeli

This is probably one of the most popular of jams in Turkey. Its dark red color is brilliant and rich. The tartness of cherries gives it its surprising and distinctive flavor. I was informed by the National Red Cherry Institute in Michigan that the sour cherries (Montmorency cherries) found in America come close to the morello cherries the recipe calls for.

Remove the pits from the cherries and arrange them in a pan in layers with alternate layers of sugar. Let stand overnight. Bring the mixture to a boil; add the lemon juice; remove the scum. Simmer over low heat until mixture is the consistency of jam. Cool and pour into hot, sterilized jars. Seal when cold.

Approximately 3 lbs. jam

2 lbs. morello cherries
5 cups sugar
2 tablespoons lemon juice

Quince Marmalade
Ayva Reçeli

1. Peel the quinces, remove the cores and seeds, and grate them. Put the grated quinces in a bowl, cover them with the water, and let them stand overnight. Strain the liquid, but save both the fruit and the liquid.
2. Place the liquid in a pan with the sugar; bring to a boil. Add the lemon juice; simmer 10 minutes. Stir in the grated quince and simmer over low heat about 1 hour. Put a drop of it on a saucer and cool. Tilt the saucer; if the drop does not flow and appears firm, the marmalade is done. If the drop is not firm, cook a little longer. When it is done, bring it to a boil once again, remove from heat, and pour into hot sterilized jars. Seal when the marmalade is cold.

Approximately 6 lbs. marmalade

3 lbs. quince
41/4 cups water
6 cups sugar
2 tablespoons lemon juice

Quince Compote
Ayva Kompostosu

Peel the quinces, cut them into halves, and remove the cores and seeds. Arrange the halves, hollow sides up in a pan. Insert 1 clove in the middle of the hollow of each quince. Sprinkle the sugar over the quinces; add the water and 10 to 15 quince seeds to add a beautiful color. Bring to a boil, cover, and simmer over very low heat until the quinces are soft, about 1 hour. Chill.

4–6 Servings

2 lbs. quinces
12 whole cloves
1 3/4 cups sugar
3 1/2 cups water

Dried Apricot Compote
Kuru Kaysı Kompostosu

Put the apricots in a bowl with the water and soak overnight. Transfer to a pan; add the sugar; cover and simmer over low heat until the apricots are tender. Chill.

4–6 Servings

1/2 lb. dried apricots
4 cups water
1 1/4 cups sugar

DESSERTS WITH PHYLLO PASTRY

Baklava with Nuts
Baklava

1. Make the syrup by mixing the water with the 1 1/2 cups sugar and bringing it to a boil; simmer 5 minutes. (The amount of sugar can be adjusted according to taste). Add the lemon juice and simmer 5 minutes more. Cool and add the rose water or orange flower water if desired.

2. Preheat the oven to 350°. Brush a baking pan 9 by 13 inches with butter.

3. Grind the nuts in a blender in parts, by pressing the "chop" button repeatedly about 10 to 15 times. Then run the blender for a few seconds so that the nuts will be ground but not pulverized. Place the nuts in a mixing bowl; toss with the 3 tablespoons sugar until well blended. Melt the butter.

4. Unfold the phyllo pastry. Take only one sheet at a time and keep the remaining sheets well covered at all times in order to prevent them from drying out. Place half of one sheet on the bottom of the baking pan and leave the other half draped over the side of the pan. Using a pastry brush, brush the half of the sheet on the pan with butter. Fold the other half of the pastry sheet over the first half; brush it with butter. Repeat this process of layering and buttering the pastry sheets until 7 seven pastry sheets have been used. Now, spread 1/3 of the nut mixture evenly over the sheets in the pan. Add another half sheet of phyllo, brush it with butter, and spread another 1/3 of the nut mixture on top. Fold the other half of the sheet, brush it with butter, and spread the remaining nuts over it. Continue layering and buttering the sheets until all the phyllo has been used up. Pour the remaining butter over the top. Press the sheets down gently with your hands or a flat surface. Using a very sharp knife, cut the *baklava* into diagonal strips 2 inches wide across the pan and cut intersecting diagonal lines to form diamond shapes.

5. Bake 30 minutes at 350°. Reduce the temperature to 300°, place a piece of aluminum foil loosely over the *baklava*, and bake 25 minutes longer. Remove from the oven. Tilt the pan and drain off the excess butter if there is any. Pour the cold syrup over the hot *baklava*. Let stand several hours. Recut the pieces before serving.

About 2½ dozen pastries

SYRUP:
1 3/4 **cups sugar**
1 1/2 **cups water**
1 **teaspoon lemon juice**
2–3 **tablespoons rose water or orange flower water (optional)**

1 lb. **blanched almonds, walnuts, or pistachios**
3 **tablespoons sugar**
1 **cup (2 sticks) sweet, unsalted butter**
1 lb. **thin phyllo pastry**

Baklava with *Crème Pâtissière*
Kremalı Baklava

Follow the recipe for Baklava with Nuts, page 296, replacing the nut filling with the *crème pâtissière* and spreading the filling in 1 layer instead of 3 layers.

CRÈME PÂTISSIÈRE FILLING:

Beat the egg yolks and sugar together in a pan with a heavy bottom until thick and pale yellow. Mix in the flour and blend well. Gradually stir in the hot milk and cook over medium heat, stirring briskly with a wire whisk until the mixture becomes very thick. Reduce the heat to low and cook 2 or 3 minutes longer, still stirring constantly. Remove from heat and blend in the vanilla.

2½ dozen pastries

SYRUP:
1 1/2 cups sugar
1 cup water
1 teaspoon lemon juice

CRÈME PATISSIÈRE FILLING:
6 egg yolks
1/4 cup sugar
2 cups hot milk
1/2 cup flour
1/2 teaspoon vanilla
1 cup butter
1 lb. thin phyllo pastry

Almond Cream–Filled Triangles
Badem Kremalı Tatlı

1. In a saucepan, mix the 2 cups sugar and the water, stirring constantly until the sugar is dissolved. (The amount of sugar and the ratio of sugar and to water can be adjusted). Bring this mixture to a boil and simmer 15 minutes. Add the lemon juice and simmer 5 minutes longer. Remove from heat.

2. Preheat the oven to 400°. Place the almonds in a bowl and toss with the powdered sugar. Stir in the eggs one at a time, rubbing the mixture between the palms of both hands after each addition. Mix in the 4 tablespoons soft butter and blend to a paste. Set aside.

3. Take 10 sheets of phyllo out of the box and rewrap the remaining sheets carefully. Refrigerate or freeze for another use. Work with only one sheet at a time and keep the rest covered at all times to prevent them from drying out. Cut each sheet into strips approximately 4 or 4 1/2 inches wide. One sheet will yield three such strips. Using a pastry brush, brush each strip with butter. Place 1 rounded tablespoon almond cream at one end of the strip. Fold one corner over and across the filling to form a triangle. Continue folding (as though folding a flag) until the entire strip is folded. The bottom edge of the triangle should be perpendicular to the side edge. Repeat this with all the strips. Place them on a lightly buttered baking sheet. Brush the tops with butter. Bake 10 or 15 minutes or until golden brown. Remove from the oven and cool.

4. Reheat the syrup. Pour the hot syrup over the cool pastries and let stand 1 hour.

30 triangles

SYRUP:
2 cups sugar
3 cups water
1 teaspoon lemon juice

ALMOND CREAM FILLING
1 cup blanched almonds,
   ground
1 cup plus 3 tablespoons
   powdered sugar
2 eggs
4 tablespoons unsalted butter,
   softened
10 sheets thin phyllo pastry
12 tablespoons unsalted butter,
   melted

DESSERTS WITH *KATAIFI*

Kataifi with Nuts
Tel Kadayıfı

1. In a saucepan, mix the 2 cups sugar and the water, stirring constantly until the sugar is dissolved. Bring this mixture to a boil and simmer 15 minutes. Add the lemon juice and simmer 5 minutes longer. Remove from heat.

2. Preheat the oven to 350°. Mix the walnuts with the 2 tablespoons sugar and set aside.

3. Melt the butter.

4. Place the *kataifi* in a large bowl and loosen with your hands by pulling in opposite directions, gently separating the stringlike strands without breaking them. Work until no lumps are left and the *kataifi* becomes light and fluffy. Toss the *kataifi* with 1/4 of the melted butter.

5. Spread half of the *kataifi* evenly in a greased baking pan (9 inches by 12 inches); press down gently. Spread the nuts evenly over the *kataifi*. Spread the remaining *kataifi* over the nuts; press down gently. Pour the remaining butter over the *kataifi* and bake 40 to 45 minutes until golden brown. Remove from the oven. Heat the syrup and pour it over the hot *kataifi*. Cover and let stand several hours to absorb the syrup. Serve with whipped cream.

12 Servings

SYRUP:
2 cups sugar
2 cups water
1 teaspoon lemon juice

3 cups ground walnuts

2 tablespoons sugar
1 cup unsalted butter
1 lb. *kataifi* (shredded pastry)

Kataifi with Pistachios
Fıstıklı Kadayıf

Follow the recipe for *Kataifi* with Nuts, page 300 replacing the walnuts with the pistachios.

Boil the pistachios 2 to 3 minutes. Drain and cover with cold water. Remove the skins. Dry and grind. Mix with 2 tablespoons sugar.

12 Servings

SYRUP:
2 cups sugar
2 cups water
1 teaspoon lemon juice

3 cups pistachios
2 tablespoons sugar
1 cup unsalted butter, melted
1 lb. *kataifi* (shredded pastry)

Kataifi with *Crème Pâtissière*
Kremalı Kadayıf

Follow the recipe for *Kataifi* with Nuts, replacing the nut filling with the *crème pâtissière*.

12 Servings

SYRUP
2 cups sugar
2 cups water
1 teaspoon lemon juice

1 lb. *kataifi* **(shredded pastry)**

Kataifi with Ricotta
Peynirli Kadayıf

Follow the recipe for *Kataifi* with Nuts, page 300, replacing the nuts with the ricotta cheese.

Beat the ricotta cheese with the 1/4 cup sugar until fluffy.

12 Servings

SYRUP:
2 cups sugar
2 cups water
1 teaspoon lemon juice

1 1/2–2 lbs. ricotta cheese
1/4 cup sugar
1 cup unsalted butter
1 lb. *kataifi* **(shredded pastry)**

Turkish Delight
Lokum

1. Dissolve the sugar in 4 1/2 cups water with the lemon juice in a heavy pan, bring to a boil, and keep at a gentle simmer for about 10 minutes.

2. Mix 1 cup cornstarch with the remaining water and blend in the cream of tartar.

3. Gradually blend the cornstarch mixture into the simmering syrup, stirring briskly with a wire whisk. Stirring frequently, cook this mixture to soft ball stage (234° to 235°F) on a candy thermometer, for about 1 1/2 to 2 hours. Do not let the bulb of the thermometer touch the bottom of the pan. At this stage, if you drop a little of the syrup into ice water, it forms a ball and flattens out when picked up with the fingers. If you are using mastic, stir it in, blending thoroughly. Remove from heat and stir in the nuts and mix well. Pour into a lightly greased 8-inch-square cake pan and spread evenly. Sift 2 tablespoons cornstarch over the top and let it stand at room temperature overnight or several hours

4. Mix 3/4 cup cornstarch with 1/4 cup confectioner's sugar. Using a sharp knife coated with butter, cut the *lokum* into 3/4-inch squares. Dot each piece with the cornstarch and sugar mixture and place on a cake rack. Let it stand 12 hours. Redust with the cornstarch-sugar mixture and pack in box.

About 5 dozen pieces of lokum

5 cups sugar
5 1/2 cups water
1 teaspoon lemon juice
1 3/4 cups cornstarch
1/4 cup confectioner's sugar
1 teaspoon cream of tartar
1/2 teaspoon pulverized mastic (optional)
1 cup toasted pistachios or filberts (filberts should be roughly broken)

FROZEN DESSERTS

Milk Ice Cream
Kaymaklı Dondurma

This is a deliciously different Turkish version of milk ice cream. It is made with milk, cream, and *sahleb*. It also calls for mastic, which gives it a subtle, distinct taste, fragrance, and a chewy texture. An ice cream maker gives the best results, but it can also be made in the freezer.

1. Blend the mastic with 1/2 cup milk and 1 tablespoon sugar in the blender until it is pulverized.

2. Dissolve the *sahleb* in 1/2 cup cold milk. Mix the remaining milk with the cream and heat over medium heat. Stir in the sugar and dissolved *sahleb*, and bring the mixture to a boil, stirring constantly. Blend in the mastic and simmer over low heat 20 minutes, stirring frequently. Remove from heat and beat until smooth.

3. Churn freeze this mixture if you have an ice cream maker. To still freeze, pour the mixture into a 9 inch by 13 inch pyrex or glass baking pan, cover with aluminium foil, and put in the freezer. When it is partly set, stir well to reduce the size of the crystals. Beat with a spoon every 30 minutes to give it a smooth consistency. It should be removed from the freezer and kept in the refrigerator about 15 to 20 minutes before serving.

8 Servings

1/2 **teaspoon mastic**
1 **tablespoon sugar**
2 **teaspoons** *sahleb*
2 **cups milk**
2 **cups cream**
3/4 **cup sugar**

Lemon Ice
Limonlu Dondurma

Dissolve the sugar in the water. Stir in the lemon rind and boil 5 minutes. Remove from heat and chill. Stir in the lemon juice. Churn freeze if you have an ice cream maker. To still freeze, pour the mixture into a freezer tray, cover with aluminum foil, and place in the freezer. When it becomes slushy, beat by hand and return to the freezer. Beat well every 30 minutes to break the crystals and give a churn-frozen consistency. Place in the refrigerator about 15 or 20 minutes before serving.

6 Servings

3/4 **cup sugar**
2 **cups water**
2 **teaspoons grated lemon rind**
2/3 **cup lemon juice**

Melon Ice
Kavunlu Dondurma

1. Soak the gelatin in the cold water.
2. Blend the·cantelope or melon in the blender.
3. Boil the water and sugar 5 minutes. Add the lemon juice. Dissolve the gelatin in the hot syrup and chill the mixture. Stir in the melon, pour into a shallow tray, cover with aluminum foil, and place in the freezer. When it becomes slushy, beat by hand to reduce the size of the crystals. Return to the freezer. Stir well every 30 minutes. Transfer to a refrigerator about 15 to 20 minutes before serving.

8 Servings

1 teaspoon gelatin
2 tablespoons cold water
1 cup water
1 cup sugar
1 tablespoon lemon juice
4 cups crushed cantelope or
   melon

Teatime Specialities or Favorites

Unlike the other sections of this book, this category of Turkish food is defined more by the time it is consumed than by the nature of its ingredients. According to taste, some people take savory things with their afternoon tea, and others prefer lightly sweetened cakes or cookies. More often savory and sweet items are served together. The range of these specialities is wide; here I present a few of my own favorites.

Turkish Pasties
Poğaça

These are small, delicate, flaky, golden half-moon-shaped pastries filled with savory cheese or meat. They are very much like the traditional Cornish pasties and can be served hot or cold. They are especially good eaten with tea as a snack or for breakfast.

1. Place the flour in a mixing bowl and mix it with the salt. Take the butter out of the refrigerator, using a knife, cut it quickly into small cubes. Place the butter in the mixing bowl. Using the tips of your finger and thumb, lift up a small amount of butter and flour; rub together and let the mixture fall into the bowl. Cool your hands frequently in cold water and dry. Continue rubbing the mixture in this manner until the mixture resembles coarse cornmeal. Sprinkle ice water, 1 tablespoon at a time, mixing quickly with a knife. Press together with your fingers until it forms a cohesive dough. Wrap the dough in a piece of wax paper. Chill at least 1/2 hour. Do not knead the dough.

2. Preheat the oven to 425°. Divide the dough into 12 equal pieces. Shape each piece into a round ball. Flatten it with your hands or with a rolling pin into a circle 1/8 inch thick. Spread 1/12 of the filling on half of each circle, leaving a border 1/4 inch wide. Fold the other half of the circle over the filling, creating a half-moon. Crimp edges firmly to seal. Glaze top with a lightly beaten egg. Place the pastries on an ungreased baking sheet. Bake in a preheated oven for 10 minutes. Reduce the temperature to 350° and bake 40 to 45 minutes or until golden brown.

CHEESE FILLING:
Mix all ingredients and blend well.

MEAT FILLING:
Sauté the meat and onion. Combine with the other ingredients and blend well.

1 dozen

1 cup plus 2 tablespoons chilled butter
2 1/2 cups unbleached all-purpose flour
1/2 teaspoon salt
5–6 tablespoons ice water
1 egg for glaze

CHEESE FILLING:

1/2 lb. feta cheese, crumbled
1/2 cup parsley, finely chopped
1 egg, lightly beaten

MEAT FILLING:

1/2 lb. lean ground beef
1 onion, finely chopped
2 medium potatoes, boiled and
   mashed
1 teaspoon salt
2 tablespoons fresh dill or
   1 teaspoon dried dill weed
Freshly ground pepper to taste
1 egg, lightly beaten

Cheese Rolls

Kaşar Peynirli Çörek

1. Place the butter or margarine in a mixing bowl with the egg and beat it with a wooden spoon until smooth. Stir in the cheese and blend well. Add enough flour to make a cohesive dough. Knead the dough until smooth. Cover and let it rest 1 hourr in a cool place.

2. Preheat the oven to 375°. Divide the dough into about 20 pieces. Shape each piece into a round biscuit; flatten them to a thickness of 1/3 inch. Place them on an ungreased baking sheet. Brush the tops with egg yolk. Sprinkle with black caraway seeds. Bake 15 to 20 minutes or until golden brown. Serve warm.

15 rolls

1 cup unsalted butter
   or margarine, softened

1 egg
1/2 lb. grated kasseri or sharp
  cheddar cheese
About 2 cups unbleached all-
  purpose flour (scoop
  measuring cup into flour
  and level off with a knife)
1 egg yolk
Kalonji

Sesame and Caraway Sticks
Susamlı Çörekotlu Çubuk

1. Place the flour in a mixing bowl. Make a hollow in the middle. Place the butter or margarine, water, salt, and 1 egg yolk here. Mix all the ingredients to make a cohesive dough. Knead 5 minutes or until the dough is smooth and elastic. Cover and let it rest 1 or 2 hours.

2. Preheat the oven to 375°. Divide the dough into walnut-sized portions. Roll each one between the palms of your hands into rolls less than 1/3 inch in diameter. Dip them into the lightly beaten egg yolks first. Then dip some of them into the sesame seeds and some into nigella. Place them on a damp baking sheet and bake 15 to 20 minutes or until golden brown.

Yields approximately 1 1/2–2 dozen sticks

1 3/4 cups all-purpose flour
  (scoop measuring cup into
  flour and level off with
  a knife)
1/2 cup unsalted butter or
  margarine, softened

3 tablespoons water
1/3 teaspoon salt
1 egg yolk
1–2 egg yolk(s), lightly beaten
  for glaze
Sesame seeds
 Nigella (known as *kalonji* **in**
  Indian cookery, and sometimes
  called black caraway seeds).

Anise Rounds
Anasonlu Simit

1. Crush the anise seeds slightly between sheets of wax paper with a rolling pin.

2. Preheat the oven to 375°. Place the flour in a mixing bowl. Make a hollow in the middle. Place 4 tablespoons water, butter or margarine, egg yolk, powdered sugar, baking powder, anise seeds, and salt here and mix with your fingertips. Combine the flour with this mixture and make a cohesive dough; knead until smooth.

3. Divide the dough into 20 equal portions. Roll each piece in between your palms into a 5-inch-long roll. Join the ends of these rolls to form circles. Dip the circles first into the lightly beaten egg white then into a bowl of sesame seeds. Place them on a baking sheet and bake 20 minutes or until golden brown.

20 rounds

2 tablespoons anise seeds
1 3/4 cups unbleached all-
  purpose flour (scoop
  measuring cup into flour,
  level off with a knife)
4 tablespoons water

1/2 **cup unsalted butter or**
   margarine, softened
1 **egg yolk**
2 1/2 **tablespoons powdered**
   sugar
1 **teaspoon baking powder**
Pinch salt
1 **egg white, lightly beaten, for**
   glaze
Sesame seeds

Caraway Rolls with Mahleb
Yağlı Simit Veya Çörek

1. Place the yeast in a bowl with 3 tablespoons tepid water and a pinch of sugar. Let stand 10 minutes.

2. Grind the mahleb in a coffee grinder or blender, then put it through a sieve to make sure it is a fine powder.

3. Place the flour in a mixing bowl. Make a hollow in the middle. Place the dissolved yeast, butter or margarine, mahleb, egg, and salt here; mix with your fingertips. Combine the flour with this mixture and form a cohesive dough. Add more water by droplets if necessary. Knead 2 to 3 minutes until the dough is smooth. Place it in a bowl; cover and let rise 1 hour.

4. Preheat the oven to 375°. Divide the dough into 15 equal portions. Shape each piece into a round biscuit 1/4 inch thick and place on a greased baking sheet. Brush with egg yolk and sprinkle with nigella. Let them rest 5 minutes. Bake 20 to 30 minutes or until golden brown.

10–15 rolls

1 **teaspoon dry yeast**
3 **tablespoons tepid water**
Pinch sugar

1 3/4 **cups unbleached all-**
   purpose flour (scoop
   measuring cup into flour,
   level off with a knife)
1/2 **cup plus 2 tablespoons**
   unsalted butter or margarine,
   partly softened
1 **rounded teaspoon mahleb,**
   pulverized
1 **egg**
1/4 **teaspoon salt**
1 **egg yolk, lightly beaten for**
   glaze
Nigella (known as *kalonji* **in**
   Indian cookery and sometimes
   called black caraway seeds).

Easter Braid
Paskalya Çöreği

Although this lightly sweetened and delightful yeast cake originated as an Easter specialty among the Christian minorities in Turkey (as is apparent from its name), it is now eaten by everyone throughout the year.

1. Put the mastic in a piece of clean cheesecloth; tie the cheesecloth with a piece of string to form a small bundle. Pound it with a mortar to break the mastic into small pieces. Put this tiny bundle in a saucepan with 1/2 cup milk and simmer over very low heat for 20 minutes. The aim is to capture the distinct and very interesting taste of mastic in the milk in order to add it to the dough. As the milk evaporates, add more. Remove from heat and cool. Squeeze the liquid from the little bag containing the mastic into the milk and remove the bag. The milk should measure 1/4 cup; if it is less than that, add enough milk to make 1/4 cup.
   2. Grind the mahleb in a coffee grinder or

blender, then put it through a sieve to make sure it is a fine powder.

3. Warm the remaining milk to tepid (105°-110°). Dissolve the yeast in the milk with 1 teaspoon sugar and let stand 10 minutes. Stir in the warm butter and sugar, and blend well until the sugar is dissolved. Mix in the eggs.

4. Sift the flour with the salt into a mixing bowl. Make a well in the middle. Pour in the liquid mixture here. Stir in the mahleb. Add the warm milk simmered with mastic. Mix all these ingredients together and beat with a slapping, circular motion of one hand until the dough loosens from your hands, about 5 to 10 minutes. The dough will be very soft and sticky. Let rise to double in size.

5. Preheat the oven to 300°. Divide the dough into 6 equal pieces. Working on a floured work surface, shape each piece into a ball. Cover and let the pieces of dough rest 30 minutes. Roll each piece of round dough into a 14-inch-long roll that is slightly thicker in the middle and thinner at each end. Take 3 rolls and twist them into a braid. Press ends to seal. Do the same with the remaining 3 rolls. Place them on greased baking pans, allowing room for rising. Let them rise again until double for about 2 hours. Glaze the tops with a lightly beaten egg. Sprinkle with chopped almonds or hazelnuts. Bake 25 to 30 minutes until nicely brown. Do not bake too long or they will dry. Cool on racks.

2 braided loaves

1 teaspoon mastic (optional but recommended)
3/4 cup milk
2 teaspoons mahleb
2 teaspoons dry-active yeast
1 teaspoon sugar
1/2 cup unsalted butter, melted

1/2 **cup sugar**
2 egg yolks, lightly beaten
1 egg, lightly beaten
2 3/4 **cups unbleached all-purpose flour***
1/4 **teaspoon salt**
1 egg for glaze
Chopped almonds or hazelnuts

*In Britain, use strong white flour

Yogurt Cake with Hazelnut
Fındıklı Kek

This is a delicious, rich cake to which toasted filberts give a distinct taste. It is the type of cake that is baked very frequently for afternoon tea in Turkish homes, because it is very simple to make and can be made without a mixer.

1. Spread the hazelnuts on baking pan and place in hot oven for about 10 minutes. When they are properly toasted, they become golden brown and crunchy and their skin can be removed easily. Take them out of the oven and cool slightly. Rub the nuts between your hands to remove the skins. It does not matter if all the skin cannot be removed. Chop 1/4 cup of the nuts coarsely and reserve. Grind the remaining nuts coarsely in a blender. Set aside.

2. Preheat the oven to 350°. Sift together the flour, soda and baking powder. Set aside.

3. In a large mixing bowl, beat the eggs and sugar together with a wire whisk until well blended. Add the yogurt, butter (make sure the butter is not hot), and oil, mixing well with a spoon. Add the ground nuts and flour mixture, and mix until smooth. Pour the batter into a well-greased loaf pan; sprinkle the chopped hazelnuts over the batter, and bake 60 to 70 minutes or until done.

1 1/4 cups shelled hazelnuts
2 cups unbleached all-purpose flour
1/2 teaspoon baking soda
1 1/2 teaspoons double-active baking powder
4 eggs (at room temperature)
1 1/2 cups sugar
3/4 cup yogurt (at room temperature)
1/2 cup butter, melted
1/4 cup vegetable oil

Anise Sponge
Anasonlu Kek

1. Combine; the flour, salt, and anise seeds, and set aside.
2. Preheat the oven to 350°.
3. Beat the egg yolks, water and 1/4 cup sugar . until the mixture falls in a thick ribbon. Beat the egg whites and cream of tartar until foamy. Gradually add 1/2 cup sugar and continue beating until soft peaks form. Fold the flour and egg whites alternately into egg yolk mixture taking care not to disturb the air beaten into the batter. Pour the batter into a greased 10-inch tube pan and bake about 40 minutes.

1 10-inch cake

1 cup all-purpose flour
2-3 tablespoons anise seeds
5 eggs, separated (at room temperature)
1 teaspoon cream of tartar
3/4 cup sugar
3 tablespoons water

Apricot Cookies
Marmelatlı Mecidiye

1. Cream the butter and sugar together until fluffy. Stir in the lemon rind and vanilla and blend. Mix in the flour and work with your hands to form a cohesive dough but do not overmix. Divide the dough into 2 equal portions. Roll each portion into a log 1 inch in diameter. Wrap in wax paper and refrigerate 1 hour.

2. Preheat the oven to 350°. Place the dough on the working surface. Cut into 1/2-inch-thick discs. Place the discs on a lightly greased baking sheet at 1-inch intervals. Make a slight hollow in the middle of each cookie with your finger. Place 1/4 teaspoon or more marmalade in each hollow. Bake 15 minutes.

2 dozen cookies

3/4 **cup unsalted butter**
3/4 **cup powdered sugar**
1/2 **teaspoon grated lemon rind**
1/2 **teaspoon vanilla**
13/4 **cups unbleached**
   all-purpose flour
1/4 **cup apricot or cherry jam**

Almond Crescents
Bademli Kurabiye

These dainty white crescents melt in the mouth.

1. Grind the almonds in a blender. Cream the butter or margarine with the sugar until fluffy. Mix in the flour, almonds, and vanilla and work with your hands to form a cohesive dough. Chill the dough for 45 minutes.

2. Preheat the oven to 350°. Divide the dough into 12 to 18 pieces. Shape each piece into a 1/4-inch thick crescent. Bake on a lightly greased baking sheet for 15 minutes. Coat them with a generous amount of powdered sugar while they are still warm.

12-18 cookies

1/2-3/4 **cup blanched almonds (finely ground)**
1/2 **cup unsalted butter or margarine**
1/2 **cup sugar**
1 **cup unbleached all-purpose flour**
1/2 **teaspoon vanilla**
Powdered sugar for topping

Turkish Sugar Cookies
Kurabiye

1. Cream margarine and sugar until fluffy. Gradually stir in the flour and work with your hands to form a cohesive dough. Wrap in a sheet of wax paper and let rest 1/2 hour.

2. Preheat the oven to 300°. Form walnut-sized pieces into oval, egglike shapes. Flatten them slightly. Line a baking sheet with a piece of wax paper, and place the *kurabiyes* on the pan. Bake 30 to 40 minutes (they will still be white). Coat them with powdered sugar.

1 dozen

1/2 cup clarified butter or
   unsalted margarine
1/2 cup sugar
1 cup all-purpose flour
Powdered sugar to coat

Almond Chews
Acibadem Kurabiyesi

Preheat the oven to 300°. Put the almonds, sugar, and butter or margarine in a mixing bowl and knead with one hand until the dough forms a smooth cohesive paste. Add the egg white and knead 2 or 3 minutes until very smooth. Drop by tablespoons onto a greased baking sheet. Press a blanched almond in the middle of each mound. Bake 15 minutes.

10-12 large cookies

1 1/2 cups almond meal
1 1/2 cups powdered sugar
1/4 cup (1/2 stick) butter or
   margarine
1 egg white
10-12 whole almonds, blanched

Crescents with Hazelnut
Fındikli Ay

1. Cream the butter, sugar, lemon rind, and vanilla together until smooth and fluffy. Mix in the egg and the egg yolk and beat until smooth. Add the nuts and flour and blend well. Chill the dough 45 minutes.

2. Preheat the oven to 375°. Divide the dough into 36 equal pieces. Shape each piece into a crescent. Place the crescents on a lightly greased baking sheet 1/2 inch apart. Bake 8 to 12 minutes.

3 dozen

3/4 **cup unsalted butter**
11/4 **cup powdered sugar**
1/2 **teaspoon grated lemon rind**
1/2 **teaspoon vanilla**
1 **egg**
1 **egg yolk**
11/4 **cups coarsely ground hazelnuts (toasted and blanched)**
13/4 **cup unbleached all-purpose flour**

Yogurt

Yogurt is a distinctive part of Turkish cuisine; it is not only used in cooking but also enjoyed by itself. This dairy product originated in Central Asia, and the word *yogurt* is, of course, of Turkish origin. Long a favorite in southeastern Europe, yogurt has recently become popular in Western Europe, and the United States, too.

Yogurt

1. Place the milk in a heavy saucepan; bring to a boil and simmer 2 or 3 minutes. Remove from heat; set aside until it cools to 115°. The traditional method of determining the correct temperature is to insert your little finger into the milk for about 2 or 3 seconds before you feel the sting of the heat.

2. Pour 1/2 cup of the warm milk into a mixing bowl, add the yogurt, and blend well. Pour this mixture into the milk; stir well.

3. Warm a large bowl (preferably an earthenware container) with hot water and then dry it. Pour the milk and yogurt into the bowl. Cover with a lid or paper. Place 1 or 2 folded blankets or towels in a warm place near a heater or over the pilot light of a gas stove. Put the bowl in the middle of the blankets; wrap it well. Do not uncover or move for at least 6 to 8 hours. Unwrap the yogurt when it is firm and chill it in the refrigerator. To get a sweeter yogurt, unwrap within 6 to 7 hours; the longer it is left wrapped, the sourer it becomes. The next time you make yogurt you can use your own yogurt as a starter. The bacillus will continue reproducing.

1 quart milk
2 tablespoons yogurt

Yogurt Paste
Süzme Yoğurt

Yogurt paste is obtained by draining yogurt of its moisture in a cheesecloth sack. Depending on the yogurt used, it may be low in fat. When it is made with a mild yogurt and drained in the refrigerator, it has a mild, sweet taste and makes a good spread for bread or crackers. It can be used like cream cheese. If, on the other hand, it is made from a relatively sour yogurt and drained at room temperature, it has a strong, tangy flavor.

MILD YOGURT PASTE: If you are making your own yogurt, make a mild yogurt (see page 321). Place fresh yogurt in a cheesecloth sack in a colander; place the colander in a bowl in the refrigerator for several hours or overnight to drain all the moisture out.

SOUR OR TANGY YOGURT PASTE: If you are making your own yogurt, make a sour yogurt (see page 321). Let yogurt stand several hours at room temperature. Place this yogurt in a cheesecloth sack in a colander; place the colander in a bowl and let stand at room temperature for several hours. In Turkey, they tie the sack with a string and hang it from a nail above the sink. The liquid drips into the sink. Yogurt paste made this way becomes very sharp and tangy. It is very good for yogurt drink (see page 326), Cacık (see page 183), yogurt soup (see page 17), or peasant soup (see page 20).

Fresh White Cheese
Taze Beyaz Peynir

This is the type of cheese peasants bring to the cities and sell in open-air markets in the springtime. It is fresh, unsalted cheese. It can, however, be salted and preserved in a salty brine. Making this cheese at home is very simple. It is good to eat, like any other cheese, and can be used for cheese fillings; it is much less expensive than feta cheese.

The primary ingredient is milk; low-fat milk, whole milk, or whole milk and half-and-half can be used at your discretion. Needless to say, the more cream you use, the better the cheese will taste. It is made in two stages. The first stage involves making the yogurt, draining it, and reserving the liquid, which contains the yogurt bacteria, to use in making the cheese. In the second stage, you combine thin liquid with milk or a combination of milk and cream and the liquid from the drained yogurt to make the cheese. You will need a sack to drain first the yogurt and then the cheese. This can be an empty rice sack, a sack sewn from cheesecloth, or an old pillowcase.

YOGURT LIQUID:
Make the yogurt following the directions on page 321). Make the sour or tangy yogurt paste, following the directions on page 322. Remove the sack of yogurt paste from the bowl and use the yogurt for other purposes. Cover the bowl of liquid with a sheet of wax paper and let stand 2 days at room temperature. The ratio between the yogurt liquid and the milk (or the milk and cream) is 1 to 2. For 2 cups of milk product, use no less than 1 cup yogurt liquid.

1. Place the yogurt liquid and the milk (or the

milk and cream) in separate pans and bring them to a boil. Boil rapidly, 2 to 3 minutes. Stir the boiling yogurt liquid into the boiling milk. Turn off the heat. You will observe the rapid cheese formation on the surface of the milk.

2. Place the cheesecloth sack in a colander in the sink and pour this hot mixture into the sack. Let it drain several hours or overnight. Shape the sack with the cheese inside into a roughly round cake. Place some sort of weight on it to keep it firm and flat. (A pan full of water works quite nicely.) Let the weight sit on the cheese several hours. Open the sack; remove the cheese; cut it into slices, and sprinkle the slices with salt. Some people prefer it without any salt.If you want to make it in a large quantity and preserve it for a longer period of time, you can do so by keeping the cheese slices in a jar containing a brine made with water and salt. This brine should be saltier than pickling brine. If the cheese preserved in this way tastes too salty, soaking it 1 or 2 hours in warm water will remove the excess salt.

YOGURT LIQUID:
2 quarts milk
1/3 cup yogurt

3 cups liquid from the yogurt
**2 cups milk and 4 cups half-
  and-half or 6 cups milk**

Some Traditional Turkish Drinks

Turkish Coffee
Türk Kahvesi

Coffee was introduced into Turkey from the Arab world in the sixteenth century. After a long period of controversy regarding the permissibility of coffee under religious law, it became a staple of everyday life. Numerous coffeehouses offered not only coffee but also various forms of entertainment. From Istanbul coffee drinking and the café spread northwest to Vienna and thence to Paris. Always fond of picturesque locales for eating and drinking, the Turks have a particular claim to fame as the originators of the café, one of the most widespread social institutions of modern times.

The amount of sugar used in Turkish coffee varies widely. There are three accepted degrees of sweetness: *sade* (no sugar at all), *şekerli* (some sugar), *çok şekerli* (a lot of sugar). Preferably the coffee used should be freshly ground or even roasted immediately before use. The beans are roasted in a heavy frying pan, being constantly stirred over medium heat until they gradually turn successively darker shades of brown. The darkness to which coffee is roasted is also a matter of taste. After roasting, the husks are blown away, and the beans are ground in a special brass coffeemill (*kahve değirmeni*).

Put the cold water in the *cezve* and stir in the coffee and sugar, mixing well. Put over low heat and cook until the froth on the surface rises to its maximum height. Remove from the heat before it boils. Stir once. Pour into the demitasse. If more than 1 demitasse is made, pour a little froth into each cup, then pour the remaining coffee into the cups. In a good cup of coffee, the surface of the coffee is completely covered with rich froth. If more than 1 demitasse of coffee is made an extra teaspoon of coffee should be used "for the pot."

1 demitasse cold water
1 heaping teaspoon pulverized Turkish coffee
1 teaspoon sugar (standard)
cezve **(a cylindrical pot with a long handle, used to make coffee; it is made of brass, copper, or enamel)**

Yogurt Drink
Ayran

A refreshingly cool drink that is taken with meals, *ayran* is made simply by diluting yogurt with water to a consistency ranging from that of milk to that of buttermilk.

Place the yogurt in a pitcher and beat into a paste. Gradually add the water, stirring constantly. Add salt, mix well. Chill.

Ayran can also be made in the blender.

2–4 Servings

1 cup yogurt
1–3 cups ice water or mineral
  water
Salt to taste

Sahlep

Sahlep is an interesting hot drink made from the powdered root of sahlep *(orchis mascula)*. In winter months, it is prepared and served in all cafés and pastry shops. It is also sold from impressive, shiny copper containers on the streets. On a cold snowy day, it is a welcome drink.

In a saucepan, mix the sugar and sahlep. Gradually add the cold milk. Bring to a boil, stirring constantly; boil 1 to 2 minutes and remove from heat. Pour into individual cups; sprinkle some cinnamon on top. Serve hot.

4 Servings

1 cup sugar
2 tablespoons sahlep
1 quart cold milk
Cinnamon

Rose Syrup Drink
Gül Şurubu

This syrup is preserved in bottles. Mixed with

sugar and ice water, it makes a delightful cold drink in summer. As is the case with the rose jam, I am not sure that I or my readers will be able to track down the variety of rose suitable for this syrup. However, I include the recipe to preserve the memory of those delicate, traditional syrups which even in Turkey are progressively displaced by the bottled soft drinks familiar to everyone.

1. Separate the flowers into petals. Snip off the white parts of the rose petals and the black parts of the poppies.

2. Place the petals and the citric acid in a clean 1 quart bottle. Fill the bottle with cold water. Close it tightly and let it stand in a cool place 1 or 2 months.

3. Dissolve 1 1/2 or 2 tablespoons sugar in 1 cup of ice water. Add some rose syrup to taste. Mix and serve with ice cubes.

20 fragrant, old fashioned
   pink roses
6 red poppies
1 teaspoon citric acid
Water
Sugar

Boza

Boza is a fermented drink made of bulgur or millet. In the colloquial Arabic of Egypt, the same word is used for beer, and, according to some sources, British soldiers occupying Egypt earlier this century distorted the word *boza* into "booze," which then became a widely used slang term for all sorts of alcoholic beverages.

Whatever the destiny of the word in other parts of the world, in Turkey, *boza* has always been a popular fermented drink, particularly in winter. In Istanbul, there are a number of areas celebrated for their *boza* shops, above all Vefa, not far from the covered bazaar. There are also many *boza* vendors who sell the beverage on the streets on cold, snowy evenings, crying out *"boza!"* every now and then as they make their rounds.

Boza is hardly ever made at home. Nonetheless, I developed the following recipe and have found that it works. The only problem is that the *boza* tends to thicken very rapidly; one must be alert to prevent this from happening.

1. Cook the bulgur in plenty of water until mushy. Put through a sieve. It should have the consistency of buttermilk. Add water if necessary. Mix it with 4 to 5 tablespoons sugar in a pan and simmer 2 to 3 minutes. Set aside and let it cool until it is just warm, stirring occasionally.

2. Mix the yeast with a little warm water. Add the dissolved yeast to the warm bulgur. Mix and let it stand 2 to 3 days in a warm place to let it ferment. During fermentation, it is very important to stir it frequently. When it is ready, it will have bubbles on the surface. Add the remaining sugar. Mix and refrigerate. Serve in large glasses. Sprinkle a little cinnamon on top.

Yields ½–1 gallon

2 cups bulgur
Water
2 cups sugar
1 package yeast

Tea
Çay

Although the distinctive variety of coffee that

Turks love to drink has become world renowned, it is not generally realized that Turks are at least as addicted to the drinking of tea. Recently, when Turkey was suffering from an acute shortage of foreign exchange, the importation of coffee was temporarily stopped. This was a severe blow for many people, but if tea disappeared from the market in Turkey, it would be something on the scale of a national disaster.

Most people take tea with their breakfast; there is a distinct tea hour in the afternoon; tea is almost always served to a guest; every shop, office, and workplace has its constant supply of tea; and even religious gatherings often conclude with the drinking of tea. Every city, town, and locality —even the most impoverished village in Anatolia— has at least one coffeehouse, where more tea is drunk than coffee, despite the name, and the menfolk spend hours in conversation.

It follows that Turks should be particular about the way their tea is prepared. It would be an unthinkable sacrilege for them to make use of tea bags or to drink tea that had been made with water not properly boiled. The color of the tea is also important; for most people, the ideal is what is called *tavşan kanı* (rabbit's blood), by which is meant a transparent, rich red.

There is also a pervasive conviction that the container in which tea is drunk affects the taste. In Turkey, therefore, it is inconceivable that tea should be drunk in styrofoam cups; what is usually preferred is a small glass (similar to those used in Russia and Iran) or, occasionally, porcelain cups. My late grandmother was so passionately attached to her own tea glass, one smaller than those usually used, that she would even take it with her on journeys and refuse to drink tea out of anything else.

There are, of course, regional differences in tea consumption. Most of the tea drunk in Turkey grows along the Black Sea coast, so the inhabitants of that region have a particularly intimate relationship with tea. Also those who live in the colder parts of the country, such as the city of Erzurum in the east, drink exceptionally large amounts of tea. The people of Erzurum are said to drink as many as ten or fifteen glasses of tea at a single sitting! It should be remembered, of course, that a glass holds about half as much as a cup. Moreover, in order to avoid an excessive intake of sugar (for almost all Turks like their tea sweet) the people of Erzurum place a cube of sugar beneath their tongue which serves to sweeten the tea as they drink it. This custom, known as *kıtlama*, is also very common in Iran, of course.

PREPARING TEA:
Two utensils are needed to prepare the tea: a teapot, preferably porcelain, and a teakettle with an opening large enough to hold the teapot when the lid is removed. Fill the kettle with cold water; bring it to a full boil, but do not let the water boil too long. Rinse the teapot with hot water. For a teapot that will hold two cups of water, put two to three tablespoons of tea in the teapot and then pour in the boiling water. Put the teapot on top of the kettle opening; turn the heat as low as possible; place a clean folded towel over the teapot to cover the spout and keep the tea as warm as possible. Let the tea brew roughly seven minutes. What is crucial is to avoid the extremes of letting the tea boil on the one hand or grow cold on the other. When pouring the tea, individual taste should be taken into account. Those who like their tea strong should have their glasses filled only with tea, or with a very small amount of hot water from the kettle. For others, tea and hot water should be combined in varying proportions.

Bibliography

Eren, Neşet, *The Art of Turkish Cooking; or, Delectable Delights of Topkapi*, New York, 1961.

Koşay, H.Z., and A. Ülkücan, *Anadolu Yemekleri ve Türk Mutfağı*, Ankara, 1961.

Makhmudov, K., *Uzbekskie Blyuda*, Tashkent, 1963.

Oral, Zeki, "Selçuk Devri Yemekleri ve Ekmekleri," *Türk Etnoğrafya Dergisi*, I: 2/3 (1956-1957).

Rodinson, Maxime, "Recherches sur les documents arabes relatifs à la cuisine," *Revue des Etudes Islamiques*, 1949.

Turabi Efendi, *A Turkish Cookery Book*, London, 1864.

Necip Usta, *Türk Mutfak Sanatı*, Istanbul, 1971.

Necip Usta, *Türk Tatli Sanatı*, Istanbul, 1971.

Yêgen, Ekrem Muhittin, *Yemek Öğretimi*, 13th edition, Istanbul, 1979.

Yeğen, Ekrem Muhittin, *Tatlı-Pasta Öğretimi*, 11th edition, Istanbul, n.d. (two standard reference works by the acknowledged master of Turkish cuisine)

Zübeyr, Hamit, "Mevlevilikte Mutfak Terbiyesi," *Türk Yurdu*, V:28 (March, 1927).

Index